1988

U.S. POLICY TOWARD ★ THE ★ SOVIET UNION

U.S. POLICY TOWARD ★ THE ★ SOVIET UNION

A LONG TERM WESTERN PERSPECTIVE 1987-2000

THE ATLANTIC COUNCIL'S WORKING GROUP ON U.S.-SOVIET RELATIONS

EDITED BY
ANDREW J. GOODPASTER
WALTER J. STOESSEL, JR.
ROBERT KENNEDY

UNIVERSITY
PRESS OF
AMERICA

Lanham • New York • London

Copyright © 1988 by

University Press of America,® Inc.

4720 Boston Way
Lanham, MD 20706

3 Henrietta Street
London WC2E 8LU England

All rights reserved

Printed in the United States of America

British Cataloging in Publication Information Available

Co-published by arrangement with the Atlantic Council
of the United States

Library of Congress Cataloging-in-Publication Data

Atlantic Council of the United States.
U.S. policy towards the Soviet Union : a long-term western
perspective, 1987–2000 / edited by Andrew J. Goodpaster,
Walter J. Stoessel, Jr. and Robert Kennedy.   p. cm.
Prepared by the Atlantic Council's Working Group on U.S.-Soviet Policy.
"Co-published by arrangement with the Atlantic Council of the
United States"—Verso t.p.
Includes bibliographies.
1. United States—Foreign relations—Soviet Union. 2. Soviet Union—
Foreign relations—United States. 3. United States—Military relations—
Soviet Union. 4. Soviet Union—Military relations—United States.
5. United States—Foreign relations—1981–   . 6. Soviet Union—Foreign
relations—1975–   . I. Goodpaster, Andrew Jackson, 1915–   .
II. Stoessel, Walter J. III. Kennedy, Robert, 1939–   . IV. Title.
E183.8.S65A87   1988   327.73047—dc19   87–30431 CIP
ISBN 0–8191–6693–6 (alk. paper).
ISBN 0–8191–6694–4 (pbk. : alk. paper).

All University Press of America books are produced on acid-free
paper which exceeds the minimum standards set by the National
Historical Publications and Records Commission.

TABLE OF CONTENTS

FOREWORD

This book reaffirms the commitment of the Atlantic Council's Working Group on U.S.-Soviet Policy to the development of improved relations with the Soviet Union within a peaceful framework. At the same time it emphasizes continued resolve to resist attempts by the USSR (or any other nation) to extend its influence through military means or intimidation.

The world has changed profoundly in the last few decades. Old colonial empires have crumbled. Advances in communications and transportation have reduced the size of the planet. Technology has advanced at a speed that frequently outpaces our ability to ensure that advances serve our aims rather than compound our problems. We have grown to recognize the fragility of our environment and are beginning to realize the limitations on our resources.

As the world has become more complex, more diverse, and more dynamic, it has also become potentially more dangerous. Advances in military firepower have greatly increased the lethality of the armed forces of even small nations. A further proliferation of nuclear weapons would add an even more ominous dimension to interstate relations. Of most concern, however, has been the massive destructive potential of the nuclear arsenals of the Soviet Union and the United States. In today's world, the avoidance of miscalculation which might lead to war, conventional or nuclear, as well as the need to address the many other serious problems we now confront, underscores the need for a new and strengthened framework for U.S.-Soviet relations.

New leadership in the Soviet Union may offer new opportunities in this regard. However, we cannot afford to be overly optimistic. The complexities involved in resolving the conflictual elements in U.S.-Soviet relations should never be underestimated. Serious risks are inescapably involved. Even under the most favorable conditions, future U.S.-Soviet relations seem certain to be characterized by simultaneous conflictual and cooperative dimensions. No escape from this complex pattern of interaction is evident.

Nevertheless, given the dangers we now confront and the fragility of the world in which we live, it is imperative that the United States make every effort to develop a more stable and constructive relationship with the Soviet Union and extend every opportunity to the Soviet Union to meet us halfway. We may not succeed—or more likely, may succeed only in part—but we must try.

Although the Soviet system is one which fails to meet many of its own people's aspirations and is a chronic source of international disturbance, the Soviet Union is nevertheless an immense fact of life—a military power of great strength, the world's third largest economic entity, and the source of considerable influence in several regions of the world. It is unlikely to collapse or to disappear through internal revolution. For the United States and the West as a whole, therefore, the challenge is to identify and cultivate areas of actual and potential shared interest—starting with crisis stabilization and the avoidance of war—without jeopardizing our basic interests and value systems. This would be neither Cold War nor convergence, but a positive type of active and sustained engagement.

The future course of U.S-Soviet relations will depend greatly on Moscow's willingness and ability to convert words to deeds. One task of U.S. policy is to encourage the Soviet Union to do so.

The Working Group believes that the policy recommendations outlined in this book provide the necessary foundation for such a positive, sustained engagement toward improved U.S.-Soviet relations over the long term. The recommendations are the product of extensive consultations in Washington and in Western Europe with a wide variety of statesmen, parliamentarians, and scholars as well as discussions in Moscow and Washington with senior Soviet representatives.

This book focuses on *long-term* U.S.-Soviet relations and therefore does not dwell on short-term issues and controversies. There is good reason to do this. It is a truism that the political dynamics of contemporary democracies make it difficult if not impossible to pay due attention to long-term policy planning. In addition to this systemic difficulty, which results from the political necessity to take positions and respond to short-term developments and crises, the bipartisanship that long characterized U.S. foreign policy has eroded. These factors have led the Atlantic Council to focus consideration on long-term policy interests and long-term policy formulation, and to do so from a rigorously bipartisan perspective.

As in all studies of the Atlantic Council, the Policy Paper (Chapter 1) reflects the narrowing of differences, at times amounting to a consensus, that emerged from extended discussions and correspondence among well-informed Americans. Chapters 2 through 8 are papers commissioned by the Working Group from among its members and constitute important elements of the analyses upon which the consensus was formed. Our work also profited from consultations with European colleagues in visits to the North Atlantic Assembly, and from discussions with the Soviet Institute for the Study of the USA and Canada, the Institute of World Economy and International Relations, the Central Committee of the Communist Party, the Ministry of Foreign Affairs, and the Ministry of Defense held both in Moscow and Washington.

The inclusion of individuals possessing varied expertise and convictions in a Working Group such as this on the one hand reduced the prospect for unanimity while on the other increased the likelihood that differing views would be appropriately aired and weighed. The conclusions and recommendations presented in the Policy Paper reflect the results of such a process, and correspondingly no individual member of this Working Group can be assumed to agree with every word. The individual authors of Chapters 2 through 8 are alone responsible for their respective papers.

It will no doubt be noted that the discussion of arms control measures, which hold a special place of importance in U.S.- Soviet relations, is relatively limited in this book. The reason is that long-term strategic stability and arms control are the focus of a parallel Atlantic Council bipartisan Working Group co-chaired by Brent Scowcroft and R. James Woolsey, with Thomas Etzold as rapporteur. That companion book has also been published by University Press of America.

On behalf of the Atlantic Council and particularly of this Working Group, I want to thank publicly the organizations that have provided the financial support enabling us to undertake and to complete this valuable work: the Andrew W. Mellon Foundation, the W. Alton Jones Foundation, PepsiCo, the William and Mary Greve Foundation, Archer Daniels Midland, the Eisenhower World Affairs Institute, Monsanto International, Northrop Corporation, and the Occidental Petroleum Corporation.

It was my honor to co-chair this Atlantic Council Working Group with Walter J. Stoessel, Jr. Ambassador Stoessel died of leukemia on December 9, 1986. His passing has been a source of great sadness to all of us who knew him and worked with him, and a great loss for the nation.

A last word of thanks is due to the members of the Working Group, who out of personal interest in U.S. policy often devoted considerable time and attention *pro bono publico*. It is an excellent and welcome example of the American volunteer tradition of sharing thought, experience, and wisdom—a tradition from which the Atlantic Council and the nation have drawn great benefit.

ANDREW J. GOODPASTER
Chairman
Atlantic Council of the United States

MEMBERS OF THE
WORKING GROUP†

CO-CHAIRMEN:

Andrew J. Goodpaster*, Chairman, Atlantic Council; former Supreme Allied Commander, Europe.

Walter J. Stoessel, Jr. **, former Ambassador to the USSR and Deputy Secretary of State; Chairman, Presidential Commission on Chemical Warfare.

RAPPORTEUR:

Robert Kennedy, Civilian Deputy Commandant, NATO Defense College; co-rapporteur, Atlantic Council's Working Group on "Western Interests and U.S. Policy Options in the Caribbean Basin".

PROJECT DIRECTOR:

Joseph W. Harned, Executive Vice President, Atlantic Council.

MEMBERS:

Madeleine K. Albright, Professor of International Affairs, Georgetown University; former Staff Member, National Security Council.

Willis C. Armstrong, Consultant; former Assistant Secretary of State.

James H. Billington, Director, Woodrow Wilson Center, The Smithsonian Institution.

George S. Blanchard, former Commander-in-Chief, U.S. Army Europe, and Commander, Central Army Group.

Barry M. Blechman, President, Defense Forecasting Inc.; former Assistant Director, U.S. Arms Control and Disarmament Agency.

Robert R. Bowie, Professor of Government, Harvard University; former Director, Policy Planning Staff, Department of State.

Robert Byrnes, Distinguished Professor of History, Indiana University.

Kenneth W. Dam, Vice President, IBM Corporation; former Deputy Secretary of State.

Robert H. Donaldson, President, Fairleigh Dickinson University.

Russell E. Dougherty, Attorney; former Commander-in-Chief, SAC, and Chief of Staff, NATO Allied Command Europe.

Herbert J. Ellison, Secretary, George F. Kennan Institute for Advanced Russian Studies, Woodrow Wilson Center; former Professor of Slavic Studies, University of Washington.

Paul S. Ello, Vice President, International Security Programs, BDM Corporation.

Robert F. Ellsworth, President, R. F. Ellsworth & Co.; former Deputy Secretary of Defense, and Ambassador to NATO.

---

†Affiliations listed are those current at the time of each member's participation in this project.
*Names of Directors of the Atlantic Council are in italics.
**Served until his untimely death in December 1986.

Murray Feshbach*, Former Chief, Soviet Section, Foreign Demographic Analysis Division, U.S. Department of Commerce.

Raymond Garthoff, Fellow, Brookings Institution; former Ambassador to Bulgaria.

Harry Gelman, RAND Corporation.

Lincoln Gordon, Guest Scholar, Brookings Institution; former Assistant Secretary of State.

William Griffith**, Ford Professor of Political Science, MIT; Adjunct Professor of Diplomatic History, Tufts University's Fletcher School of Law and Diplomacy; Chief Roving Editor of *The Readers' Digest.*

John Hardt, Associate Director for Senior Specialists, Congressional Research Service, Library of Congress.

Douglas Hart, Analyst, Pacific-Sierra Research Corporation.

Martin J. Hillenbrand, Dean Rusk Professor of International Relations, and Director, Center for Global Policy Studies, University of Georgia; former Director General, Atlantic Institute for International Affairs, and Ambassador to Germany.

Guocang Huan, Visiting Senior Fellow to the Atlantic Council from the People's Republic of China.

Donald M. Kendall, Chairman, PepsiCo. Founder, Commitee on East-West Accord.

John M. Leddy, former Assistant Secretary of State and Treasury.

Winston Lord†, former President, Council on Foreign Relations.

Stanley J. Marcuss, Partner, Milbank Tweed Hadley & McCloy.

Bernard J. O'Keefe, Chairman, EG & G, Inc.

Michael A. Petrilli, Manager, Information Analysis, Europe-Africa, Monsanto International.

Joel Pritchard, Director of Government Relations, Bogle & Gates; former United States Congressman.

Olin C. Robison, President, Middlebury College.

Brent Scowcroft, Vice Chairman, Kissinger Associates; Chairman, President's Commission on Strategic Forces; former Assistant for National Security Affairs to the President.

William T. Shinn, Jr., former Consul General, Leningrad; former Director of Soviet Affairs and Deputy Director of NATO Affairs, Department of State.

Dimitri Simes, Senior Associate, Carnegie Endowment for International Peace; former Professor of Soviet and East European Studies, Johns Hopkins University.

Stanley R. Sloan, Foreign Affairs and National Defense Division, Congressional Research Service.

Helmut Sonnenfeldt, Guest Scholar, Brookings Institution; former Counselor of the Department of State.

---

*Served until his appointment as Sovietologist-in-Residence, Office of the Secretary General, NATO.

**Served until his appointment as Senior Advisor to the U.S. Ambassador to the Federal Republic of Germany.

†Served until his appointment as Ambassador to the People's Republic of China (June 1985).

Chapter I

THE POLICY PAPER

U.S. POLICY TOWARD THE SOVIET UNION: A LONG-TERM WESTERN PERSPECTIVE, 1987–2000

Report Of The Atlantic Council's Working Group On U.S.-Soviet Policy

INTRODUCTION

No foreign policy issues have commanded more attention in the post-war period than those arising from our relationship with the Soviet Union. Since the Bolsheviks came to power on a platform which called for class struggle and revolution on a global scale, our relationship has been predisposed to friction. De Tocqueville correctly perceived the basic differences between us and the Russians. Mackinder predicted that geopolitics would put Russia and America on a collision course.

In the wake of World War II, the increasingly omnipresent political and military dispositions of these two powers, their growing nuclear arsenals, and the attendant dramatic increase in destructive potential added to concerns over the future course of Soviet-American relations. Today, the avoidance of miscalculation which might lead to unimaginable catastrophes holds the attention of policy-makers worldwide and underscores the need to search for policies that will reduce the risk of crises and conflict while preserving U.S. interests and those of its allies in promoting freedom, human dignity, and progress.

The need to expand areas of cooperation and to institutionalize mechanisms of conflict avoidance and conflict resolution and thus alter the basic pattern of U.S.-Soviet post-war relations is also driven by powerful world trends. The world has changed profoundly since the late 1940s and early 1950s. While the explosion of the world's first atomic device at Trinity Site on July 16, 1945, ushered in the atomic

1

age with all its uncertainties and potential dangers, it was only the first of a remarkable series of technological changes that have had a major impact on interstate relations. Post-war advances in communications and transportation have compresssed both time and distance. Events in one country, for the most part, are now instantly portrayed around the world. The war in Vietnam was presented nightly on television in the United States and elsewhere. Events in El Salvador, or Nicaragua, or Guatemala are instantly open for examination in Europe and in many other countries. Daily carnage in Beirut and in Afghanistan, terrorist bombings in Rome, Paris, and Vienna, the fall of a government in Manila, human suffering and starvation around the globe are subject to the immediate scrutiny of those world publics whose press freedoms are not constrained. As a result, diplomacy has changed, publics are energized. Even peasants in remote villages have contact with the modern world through the transistor radio. Perceptions and expectations are inevitably altered.

As the world has become smaller, it has also become more complex, diverse, and dynamic. The inevitable post-war breakup of old colonial empires, the dramatic increase in the world's population, the huge economic gap between the industrialized and most of the non-industrial countries, continued concern over the availability of renewable and non-renewable resources, major advances in the firepower and lethality of the armed forces of even the most impoverished nations, the growth of international terrorism, concerns over the future proliferation of nuclear weapons, and heightened awareness of the fragility of the environment and the dependence of all nations on its condition are viewed against a backdrop of an explosion of human potential and rising expectations which are now imposing immense demands on governments around the world.

Such factors make for an interdependence among nations unparalleled in history and signal the need for intense cooperative efforts. They also have given impulse to resurgent nationalism and to a rising tide of religious fundamentalism driven, in part, by a lingering resentment of some over the continuing primacy of Western institutions in international politics and the inability of states to overcome their preoccupation with East-West relations in order to address the range of North-South issues. As a result, the international environment of the next several decades is likely to be characterized by a further diffusion of power and the continued devolution of the bipolar structure. The world will be increasingly polycentric, nationalistic, and spontaneous.

The sustained achievement of U.S. security goals will become more difficult in this increasingly fragmented and fluid environment. North-South and intra-alliance relations will take on added significance for the United States and are likely to demand a degree of attention heretofore reserved primarily for superpower relations. In such an environment, the relevance and influence of the great powers will depend increasingly on their willingness and ability to moderate their adversarial relationship and to commit more of their mutual energies to a solution of the many problems which now or soon will confront mankind.

Nevertheless, the difficulty of encouraging the Soviet Union to effective cooperative efforts to reduce tensions and the risk of conflict and to meet the social and economic challenges of the contemporary world should not be underestimated. Profound differences of interest, policies, and standards of conduct separate the United States and the Soviet Union. These differences are unlikely to be resolved in the foreseeable future. On the other hand, the imperative of avoiding nuclear war underscores the need for the United States to press the Soviet Union in the mutual exploration of all avenues in an attempt to limit and, if possible, diminish the conflictual pattern that has tended to dominate their post-war relations.

THE SOVIET CHALLENGE

At the 27th Communist Party Congress in February 1986, General Secretary Gorbachev, after offering standard invectives against capitalism, Western and U.S. imperialism, and discussing the changing correlation of forces, indicated that Soviet leaders are prepared to do everything they can "to improve radically the international situation". He acknowledged that the military balance is "inordinately high" and that man now has for the first time in history the physical capacity for destroying all life on earth. He emphasized the importance of arms control and comprehensive verification measures and called for a considerable reduction in the intensity of military confrontation and a comprehensive system of "international security". He also spoke of such factors as "the dignity of the individual", "the political, social, and personal rights of man", "dialogue", "cooperation", "the development of contacts between peoples and organizations", and "the dissemination of ideas". He rejected terrorism and emphasized the futility and inadmissibility of "pushing revolutions from outside" especially by military means. Despite all of these formulations, however, it is clear that a gulf remains between Soviet words and actions—a gulf that is not new. The rigid and closed nature of Soviet society and its continued militant outward manifestations suggest that if Gorbachev is to translate words into deeds much will need to be done. So far this decade, the record of Soviet actions has been less than encouraging.

The continuing buildup of Soviet strategic and theater nuclear forces and major improvements in conventional forces remain serious causes for concern. The apparent Soviet quest for complete security inevitably leads to instability and insecurity. Such trends, if continued, will ultimately undermine the credibility of Gorbachev's commitment to compete "in a setting of lasting peace".

Another disturbing factor has been Moscow's continued interference in the affairs of the nominally independent states of Eastern Europe. Despite pledges concerning human rights and national independence in Europe made by the Soviet Union when it signed the Final Act of the Conference on Security and Cooperation in Europe in 1975, Moscow clearly remains unwilling to countenance meaningful national independence or individual liberty in Eastern Europe.

Furthermore, the USSR has continued to play a highly unconstructive role in many of the unstable areas in the Third World. In Afghanistan, 120,000 Soviet soldiers continue to wage a brutal war in support of an imposed regime. Elsewhere in Africa, Asia, and Latin America the Soviet Union contributes to unrest, instability, and conflict through the sale of arms, advisers, and military force. For example, in Ethiopia and Angola, Soviet advisers are involved in military planning and support operations along with thousands of Cuban combat troops. In Cambodia, the Soviet Union is backing 140,000 Vietnamese soldiers waging a war of occupation. In Nicaragua, Soviet bloc and Cuban personnel are actively supporting the maintenance of an increasingly repressive regime.

Finally, Moscow continues its apparent violations of a variety of international acts and agreements. Moscow's human rights record, its failure to comply with the provisions of the UN Declaration of Human Rights and with the more recent Helsinki Final Act and, of course, self-serving Soviet interpretations as well as significant outright violations of such arms control commitments as the ABM and SALT Treaties and the Biological and Toxin Weapons Convention and Geneva Protocol, raise serious questions concerning the Soviet commitment to peace and cooperation.

FACTORS INFLUENCING SOVIET FOREIGN POLICY

The closed nature of Soviet society sharply limits the ability of outsiders to discern with any high degree of certainty the factors that influence Soviet objectives, means, and responses to specific international stimuli. Indeed, all that one can say with a high degree of confidence is that a broad range of variables influence specific policy decisions. Nevertheless, many observers point to several major factors which have had and continue to have an important influence on the formulation of foreign policy in the Soviet Union.

First, **geography** has strongly shaped the world view and accompanying political system of the Soviet Union. The absence of natural barriers has been an important element in the political history of the Russian empire. While geography later favored the political expansion of the Russian State, which now spans eleven time zones across the Eurasian continent, at an earlier time, the absence of natural barriers greatly facilitated the invasion of Russian territory. Over the centuries came invasions from all directions by Cumans, Mongols, Crimean

Tatars, Poles, Lithuanians, Teutonic Knights, French, Germans, and others, including intervention by Western powers during the Russian Civil War. The pillage, the plunder, the enslavement of peoples, the uprooting and successive scattering of developing civilization are reflected in a deep-seated urge to control the vast expanses of its own empire and to dominate events, peoples, and countries on the periphery, and have led to reliance upon a massive military and a highly centralized bureaucracy to do both.

Second, inseparable from its geography, Russian **historical experiences** have helped fashion a psychology which, in some important respects, differs considerably from that of Americans or Western Europeans. Fear of invasion has led to an obsession with security. The quest with security has given rise to a tolerance of, even a preference for, absolutism and the subordination of the individual to the well-being of the state. To protect the existence of the state and to enforce its authority, a supreme instrument of coercion has usually emerged—the secret chancellery of the monarch, or, in Soviet times, the MVD or KGB.

Largely from a very different developmental experience comes a sense of cultural uniqueness and even superiority—repeatedly manifested in the Messianic and proselytizing outlook of the "Third Rome," in the Slavophiles who rejected the need to adopt Western cultural ideas, and in the expansionism of communist ideology.

Third, **ideology:** Long before Karl Marx expounded his theories for reform, the Russian state under Peter the Great had become the largest landowner, factory owner, employer of labor, trader, and owner of capital in Russia. Long before Lenin offered the notion of the "vanguard of the proletariat"—a highly disciplined, centralized party which would serve as mentor, leader, conscience, and guide—the Russians had become accustomed to the principle of unquestioning submission to the leader of the state. Indeed, the tsar was known as the "little father" and thought to be the very incarnation of truth and justice. Thus, while it can well be argued that ideology is largely irrelevant as a specific guide for the majority of Soviet citizens, including party members, ideology in the Soviet Union today represents an underlying set of values which, in some cases, predate Marxism-Leninism and which help shape the frame of reference within which issues are evaluated and decisions made. Nevertheless, ideology is neither the only nor necessarily the dominant factor affecting the formulation of Soviet foreign policy. As within any bureaucratic structure, a myriad of factors influence decisions, not the least of which are institutional and bureaucratic pressures and perceptions of short and long-term national interests.

Fourth, the **heterogeneity** of the Soviet empire inevitably plays a role in Soviet foreign policy formulation. The Great Russians, the dominant ethnic group, comprise approximately 50 percent of the total population. The existence, however, of over 100 different nationalities with dozens of religious creeds, many of which would not remain by their own volition as members of the empire, adds to the historic Russian sense of insecurity as well as to the constant concern that rebellion or dissidence starting at the periphery could ultimately threaten the very existence of the state. It also produces the suspicion that external forces might, if given a chance, seek to create or exploit rebellion and dissidence. As a result, the Soviet Union has undertaken, at great cost, extensive efforts to insulate from outside influences the many diverse groups which comprise the USSR.

A fifth factor is **demographics**. Shifting patterns of population growth threaten to challenge the dominance of the Great Russians and their fellow Slavs while imposing upon them difficult economic and political decisions. While the Slavs comprised approximately three quarters of the population in 1959, if current trends continue they will represent only about 60-65 percent of the population by the year 2000.[1] Moreover, the general shifting of the center of population from the West toward Central Asia is likely to have profound effects, not the least of which may well be increasing demands from the Asian republics for the reorientation of investment and redistribution of wealth.

Sixth, the Soviet **economy** is encountering serious difficulties. A period of growth from the late 1940s until the early 1980s helped double the post-war standard of living and transform the Soviet Union into a leading military power of global importance. Since then, there has been a substantial decline in the rate of growth in the Soviet economy.[2] Under Brezhnev, western specialists predicted continued retardation with 2 percent per annum growth in Gross National Product (GNP) the maximum trend. Gorbachev's aim to double growth rates in the 1986-2000 period is viewed as ambitious, but increased growth is widely accepted as attainable.[3] The problem is not with potential. Rather, it is with the efficiency necessary to exploit the potential. Overly-centralized planning and management, regional shortages of skilled and unskilled labor, low labor productivity due to alcoholism, corruption and sloth, the absence of incentives, unrealistic pricing mechanisms, and persistent agricultural difficulties all point to inadequacies which cannot fail to exert a strong influence on the behavior of the Soviet Union at home and abroad in the decades ahead. Additionally, falling oil prices have denied the USSR hard currency needed for continued access to and acquisition of sorely needed Western technology. Nevertheless, a two trillion dollar GNP, abundant natural resources, and a 145-million-person work force make the Soviet economy one of tremendous potential impact on world affairs.

Seventh, while the Soviet collegial **leadership** has managed a smooth transition from Brezhnev to Andropov to Chernenko to Gorbachev, the latter will require time to end the paralysis apparent during the last years of Brezhnev's rule. Clearly it would be a serious mistake to underestimate the magnitude of the problems he must confront, and the impact that political intrigue and bureaucratic and in-stitutional resistance and maneuvering will have on foreign policy formulation.[4]

And finally, despite all these predispositions—the result of historic, cultural, and ideological factors, the Soviet Union (and Russia before it) has often been markedly pragmatic in foreign policy. For example, Russia's participation in the alliance against Napoleon, as well as the Soviet Union's non-aggression pact with Nazi Germany and its subse-quent World War II alliance with the Western allies, clearly demonstrate its willingness to subordinate ideological principles and traditional animosities to the pursuit of objectives deemed critical to state survival and well-being. Moreover, even where survival interests are not at stake, Soviet policy has had a remarkably practical side. For example, Soviet policy in Africa toward Morocco versus Algeria and the Polisario guerrillas, and at an earlier time between Somalia and Ethiopia, as well as on the African frontiers issue, suggest that pragmatism and Realpolitik frequently win out over ideological purity. Thus, the genuine Soviet desire to avoid a nuclear holocaust as well as other practical considerations provide a basis for guarded optimism that a substantial area of common ground with the West can be found and that mutually beneficial initiatives can be successfully pursued.

Indeed, the myriad economic problems described above, especially critical at a time when the Soviet Union may be called upon to effect an internal redistribution of wealth while simultaneously undertaking massive industrial and military modernization programs, offer incen-tives for Soviet leadership to promote trade and economic cooperation with the West. Also, the need to deal with their economic shortcom-ings may encourage the partial abandonment of ideologically-mandated centralization of the economic forces of that society. Reminiscent of the past efforts to increase private incentives and decentralize the economy in order to overcome the stifling strictures of the state plan-ning bureaucracy, the economic reforms of General Secretary Gorba-chev may well embrace pragmatic improvements designed to revitalize the economy. At present, it is too early to make any predictions.

However, while bureaucratic centralization at the highest level is one of Gorbachev's principal objectives, he appears to favor decentraliza-tion below the ministerial level. Furthermore, the Soviet Union's in-ability to sustain the economies of its Eastern European allies, many of which are similarly in trouble due to the excesses of centralization, may lead the Soviets to extend their countenance of greater economic decentralization by certain allies—Hungary and East Germany in par-ticular. Whether the imperatives of economic reform will result in more cordial relationships with the West, sustained over time, certainly re-mains to be seen. Nevertheless, Soviet interest in domestic economic revitalization does offer some possibility for the development of mutually beneficial relations in the economic dimension and an op-portunity the West should explore.

Likewise, the need to address such long-term environmental problems as the pollution of the world's atmosphere, oceans, rivers, and streams, as well as the need to ensure the safety of nuclear power plants, reduce terrorism, halt the flow of narcotics, and improve world health and the human condition, offer multiple avenues to mutually beneficial cooperative relations based on pragmatic assessments of national interest.

The factors mentioned above underscore two critical theses for U.S.-Soviet relations. The first is that despite Soviet xenophobia and the historical tensions that have characterized U.S.-Soviet relations, there has been and can be at least a limited cooperative interactive dimension, predicated upon constant and emerging shared interests. Furthermore, the domestic and foreign policies of the USSR are not formed in a vacuum. Soviet leaders have adjusted and will continue to adjust policy to accommodate changing domestic and international realities, thereby providing opportunities for the United States to influence Soviet behavior.

U.S.-SOVIET RELATIONS:
A FRAMEWORK FOR PROGRESS

As we look toward the 21st century and ask ourselves how the United States should deal with the Soviet Union, we must recognize the simultaneous existence of conflictual and cooperative dimensions in superpower interactions. Substantial differences of philosophy, interests, and standards of conduct are capable of propelling the superpowers to mutual annihilation. The risk of conflict is made even more palpable by a balance of destructive capabilities which, if unmanaged or managed injudiciously, could place a premium on shooting first and asking questions later. The key to dealing with such a risk is to ensure that the Soviets recognize that superpower relations must be on a *quid pro quo* basis. The West does not seek unilateral advantage by military means and will not concede such an advantage to the USSR. In other words, no unilateral advantages in areas of crucial national interests that could undermine the deterrent balance will be countenanced. In short, the United States must pursue policies that elicit the Soviets' pragmatic bent.

First, the United States must continue to seek an active and productive dialogue with the Soviet Union. Specifically, this dialogue should entail on our part an explicit delineation, without rhetorical excess or hyperbole, of critical U.S. interests such as continued commitment to defense obligations in general and to the Western alliance in particular, and our firm resolve to resist any Soviet attempts to extend its influence by military means. The dialogue must also emphasize our determination

- to reduce the risk of war by enhancing our ability to maintain a stable environment during crises;

* to reverse the arms race by reducing armaments through sound and verifiable agreements, and ultimately to ease the burdens of military spending;
* to improve bilateral relations on the bases of reciprocity and mutual interest;
* to manage and resolve regional conflicts based on the principles of non-intervention and the self-determination of peoples;
* to seek improvements in human rights and to convince the Soviets of the advantages to them of joining us in this effort;
* to improve close coordination and joint action with our allies to accomplish the above objectives.

Implicit in the communication of U.S. interests is the recognition that the Soviet Union also has critical interests which will be respected providing they are pursued peacefully and are not in violation of international covenants.

Second, the effectiveness of dialogue will depend upon realism, strength, and flexibility. Realism dictates that a foreign policy based only on declaratory platitudes is hollow and ultimately frustrating and dangerous. The maintenance of peace and freedom depends upon a sustained Soviet perception that this country has the necessary resolve, as manifested in a full range of credible military capabilities that can be exercised in conjunction with diplomatic instruments, to preserve the peace and maintain its freedom and that of its allies and friends.

Nevertheless, it must be made clear to the Soviet leadership that the United States is flexible in its approach to superpower relations and that it recognizes that the complexity of many outstanding problems will require a long-term consistent commitment to their amelioration, if not resolution. A readiness to negotiate with Soviet leaders on the many issues that affect Washington and Moscow is a fundamental requisite of improved relations. This willingness to negotiate with the Soviet Union must be an unalterable aspect of U.S. foreign policy.

Moreover, it must be made clear to the Soviet Union that this commitment to strength and dialogue is not a call for renewed U.S. military superiority. Rather, the Working Group believes that parity is an essential element in superpower relations and that effective dialogue in the search for shared political, economic, and security interests can only be achieved if both sides approach that dialogue from positions of adequate strength, confident in their capabilities and in their position within the international order. Furthermore, the Working Group believes that the search for shared interests will be better advanced by consistency and regularity in the negotiating process. Such consistency will do much to stabilize the pattern of superpower relations as well as reduce the probability of misperceptions of U.S. intentions abroad, and the development of unrealistic expectations at home.

Finally, a constructive relationship with the Soviet Union cannot be built independent of our allies and friends. The United States must maintain a continuous dialogue with them in order to understand their

interests and to convey our own. The mutuality of U.S. and allied interests is the principal thread of the fabric of East-West relations.
However, owing to differences in geography, historical experience,
and domestic political realities, certain divergencies do exist between
the United States and its allies. Indeed, the rifts between the United
States and some significant elements in Western Europe have now
begun to approach unhealthy proportions. Through continuous communication, coordination, and compromise, the United States together
with its Western allies must seek to narrow their differences and to
develop policies that maintain Alliance solidarity, while exploiting a
wide range of approaches to strengthen peace and advance social and
economic development in the decades ahead.

THE FUTURE OF U.S.-USSR RELATIONS

There is much to suggest that U.S. foreign policy can and should
change only at the margins. Indeed, some argue that the rivalry between the United States and the Soviet Union is close to immutable
and that our task is not to end it, but merely to keep it under control.
Nevertheless, given the gruesome potential for conflict in the nuclear
age as well as imperatives that mandate that we seek Soviet collaboration in addressing the many social, economic, and ecological problems
now confronting the planet, the Working Group believes that the time
may be propitious for renewed emphasis on improving U.S.-Soviet
relations.

The Soviet Union itself is currently confronted with a series of
political, economic, and military dilemmas that include growing
restiveness among its East European allies; growing recognition of the
inappropriateness of the Soviet model for Third World development;
declining hard currency earnings due to the precipitous drop in oil
prices; stagnant industrial productivity due mostly to systemic problems of centralized management but aggravated by corruption, an increasingly obsolete physical plant which is in dire need of technological
modernization, and an excessive orientation toward the military end
of the industrial spectrum; demographic trends that portend calls for
a redistribution of wealth within the USSR; failure to resolve regional
border and political differences with the People's Republic of China
and Japan; revitalized U.S. and NATO military capabilities; and above
all the need to avoid nuclear war. At the same time the mantle of leadership is being passed to a new generation of leaders in the Soviet Union.
This leadership is seen by some as increasingly rational, technocratic,
and reformist. Pragmatic approaches to reform may well come to be
viewed by the Soviet hierarchy as increasingly attractive in light of the
sustained inability of marginal adjustments, undertaken within the strictures of ideological rigidity, to resolve the monumental problems confronting that country.

This is by no means to say that the conflictual dimension of U.S.-

Soviet relations is likely to disappear. Rather, it is the combination of cooperation and conflict on a multitude of issues that will determine the tenor of superpower relations. At one extreme, an effort to deal chauvinistically with the trends noted above could emphasize military force as the preferred foreign policy instrument, resulting in a conflictual relationship reminiscent of the Cold War years and, more recently, the early 1980s. At the other extreme, both nations could recognize their diminished abilities to control unilaterally the outcome of global developments as well as the unacceptable price of unrestrained conflict, thereby paving the way for mutually beneficial relations keyed to areas of mutual advantage. The actual state of U.S.-Soviet relations however, is more likely to rest somewhere between these extremes. In fact a certain amount of tension in relations may serve the useful purpose of constraining behavior, sharpening perspectives, and encouraging dialogue.

How then should the United States deal with the Soviet Union, which is generally both assertive and insecure in its dealings with the rest of the world? How do we build a constructive relationship with a nuclear power with numerous interests and objectives that differ greatly from our own? How do we encourage dialogue and discourage coercion or aggressive behavior? How do we forge a relationship that will allow our energies to be dedicated increasingly to peaceful endeavors? Clearly, many dimensions are involved—extending from military competition to arms control to trade and cultural contacts.

Military Competition

No other dimension of U.S.-Soviet interaction has been as prominent as has the military. The USSR has been steadily improving the size, quality, and operational capabilities of its armed forces for over two decades. After achieving a rough parity with the United States in the 1970s, the Soviet Union has fielded new generations of strategic weapons which threaten the survivability and thus the deterrent value of a sizeable fraction of the U.S. strategic arsenal and its supporting command, control, and communications (C^3) capabilities. With the addition of SS-20 intermediate range missiles, the Backfire bomber, new shorter range missiles, and nuclear self-propelled artillery, the USSR has improved significantly its theater nuclear capabilities. The Soviet Union also has modernized and enhanced its conventional and maritime forces, streamlined its logistics train, and thus greatly improved its ability to project military power. To maintain a balanced and stable military relationship in light of growing Soviet military capabilities, the United States has begun modernizing its strategic missile and bomber forces[5] as well as its theater nuclear and conventional capabilities.

In the absence of verifiable arms control agreements, realism in U.S.-Soviet relations as well as the search for a more stable security environment make military force modernization essential. As the United States looks to the 1990s and beyond, three objectives must dominate military force planning: U.S. forces must continue to serve as a credible deterrent to Soviet aggression and Soviet blackmail against the United States and its allies; the forces chosen must contribute to stability during crisis; and however incredible or unthinkable it may be, should deterrence fail, U.S. forces must be structured so that they add to the possibility of terminating conflict short of Armageddon. To accomplish these tasks the United States must reduce the vulnerabilities of its strategic retaliatory arsenal and its supporting C^3; maintain a capacity for limited nuclear options; maintain modern, fully sustainable conventional air, land, and maritime forces; and engage the Soviet Union in the vigorous pursuit of stability through arms control across the spectrum of military capabilities.

In this context, America's strategic arsenal must remain capable of retaliating decisively against the range of assets valued by an adversary after absorbing a Soviet preemptive first strike. This will remain the key to strategic deterrence and stability into the foreseeable future. The current diversity of strategic forces (land, sea, and air) serves several purposes. Diversity provides a hedge against a technical surprise that might render one or even two legs vulnerable to preemptive attack. Force diversity also poses attack timing problems, which make it difficult for the Soviets to coordinate simultaneous strikes on all three legs of the Triad. Thus, while one leg may be technically vulnerable, its elimination from the force mix would heighten the vulnerability of the remaining legs. Diversity also provides a hedge against tactical surprise—bombers can be placed on airborne alert where they are virtually invulnerable to a preemptive attack; nuclear submarines can stay submerged and hidden for months; and the alert status of Intercontinental Ballistic Missiles (ICBMs) allows a high percentage of them to be launched quickly if attacked. Finally, force diversity dilutes the ability of an attacker to defend itself successfully against retaliatory strikes. What then should be done to reduce vulnerabilities?

First, modernization of the land-based component must continue. This need be undertaken neither at panic speed nor in disregard of long-term arms control objectives. Nor should the United States sacrifice the modernization of those other military capabilities likely to be needed to provide stability and protect U.S. interests in a world plagued by numerous conventional and unconventional conflicts. However, planning for the eventual replacement of the Minuteman missile force should begin now. As terminal guidance technologies permit missile accuracies to approach zero CEP (Circular Error Probable), the likelihood of success of a preemptive attack on the Minuteman force would become very high, if it were attempted. Under such circumstances, mobility offers the most promising prospect for reducing the vulnerability of the U.S. strategic ICBM force.

Mobility was one of the desired features of the MX program as originally conceived. But the size of the MX missile makes real mobility a difficult task. As a result, and in light of the Scowcroft Commission's realistic assessment of Soviet hard-target kill capabilities, a decision to deploy the MX in existing, hardened Minuteman silos was made. As a future replacement for the Minuteman missile force, the United States should field a small, mobile, single-warhead ICBM. The Working Group recognizes that the concept of a truly mobile missile has yet to be accepted by the public and may pose political difficulties. But such a missile would not only be likely to reduce vulnerability through its very mobility, but also be a useful move away from the MIRV (Multiple Independently-targetable Reentry Vehicle) which has been a principal culprit in the creation of strategic force vulnerabilities. It is inherently more costly, however, to build additional missiles than additional warheads. Thus, whether future replacements for U.S. strategic missiles have single warheads may well depend on whether the Soviets can be convinced of the inherent stability of beginning now to replace all or most of their MIRVed systems with single-warhead systems, whether they are willing to spend the money for what would be a major alteration of their strategic force arsenal, and whether adequate arms control verification procedures can be negotiated to preclude cheating.

Second, the United States should continue to modernize its SLBM (Submarine Launched Ballistic Missile) force. The ballistic missile submarine force when at sea is the most survivable leg of the Triad and is likely to remain so in the foreseeable future. The new *Ohio*-class Trident submarines are significantly quieter than America's older Poseidon SSBNs, making their location by the Soviets highly unlikely. With the planned addition of the longer-range Trident II (D-5) missile, U.S. strategic submarines will be capable of retaliating from greater distances than was previously the case with the Polaris or Poseidon fleet or with the Trident I (C-4) missile. This will permit the U.S. SSBN fleet to use the protection of a vaster expanse of the world's seas to increase its survivability or to improve our ability to cover the Soviet target base. The planned deployment of the D-5 missile, however, has not been without criticism. The principal criticism has been that the planned accuracy of the D-5 missile will permit it to destroy hardened Soviet targets. Such a capability is seen by some as dangerously destabilizing.

Strategic instability, however, is more a function of the overall vulnerability of a country's strategic forces than of the accuracy of a nation's missiles. While the Soviet Union may be concerned over the improved accuracy and resulting hard target kill potential of U.S. SLBMs, U.S. missile firing submarines are virtually invulnerable when at sea. Therefore, there is very little incentive for a destabilizing preemptive strike on these forces by the Soviets. Perhaps, the real concern is less the near-term implications for crisis stabilization and more the potentially destabilizing arms race at sea which might ensue as the USSR searches for ways of locating U.S. SSBNs, as well as the long-term implications should the seas become less opaque.

Two factors should guide future developments in the U.S. sea-based force if such instabilities are to be avoided: the invulnerability of SSBNs must be preserved, and as a hedge against potential failure in this regard, the United States must avoid putting too many eggs in a single basket. Today, a high percentage of U.S. striking power resides in slightly more than 30 SSBNs. This percentage will increase as *Ohio*-class submarines with 24 missiles replace Poseidon submarines with 16. Thus, while it is probable that for the foreseeable future *Ohio*-class SSBNs will remain invulnerable to preemptive attack while at sea, it is important that we continue to guard against future vulnerabilities and the instabilities they may beget. In this regard, the United States should look to a future nuclear submarine fleet that includes smaller boats that could be less costly but more numerous. To increase stability, the Soviet Union should be encouraged to do the same. The United States should also engage the Soviet Union in discussions to identify ways to preserve, and perhaps enhance, the invulnerability of SLBM forces.

Third, the United States should modernize its strategic bomber forces. Bombers are the most flexible and stabilizing element of the Triad. They can be used to demonstrate U.S. interest, concern, and determination during severe crisis situations. They can be placed on ground and airborne alert as well as launched on warning and recalled. Their long flight times preclude their use in first-strike counterforce attacks. Furthermore, since airborne bombers are virtually invulnerable to a preemptive first-strike and since a large percentage of America's megatonnage is carried by bombers, an airborne alert called during a critical confrontation with the USSR might deter direct hostilities between the United States and the Soviet Union. However, bomber forces must penetrate increasingly sophisticated air defenses and are vulnerable to surprise attacks while on their airfields.

Fourth, the United States must place great emphasis on insuring the survivability of its strategic C^3 nets. Perhaps the most vulnerable components of our strategic retaliatory forces are the communication links that make timely retaliation possible. Soviet doctrine and nuclear warfare exercise scenarios, their emphasis on communications disruption through the use of electronic warfare, and their preoccupation with the survivability of their own command and control links suggest that the Soviet Union would devote a significant portion of attacking forces to the severing of links between the President and U.S. nuclear forces in an effort to delay or disrupt a U.S. strategic retaliatory response.[6]

Finally, President Reagan in his address of March 1983 on military spending presented his vision of a future in which American defenses could "intercept and destroy strategic ballistic missiles before they reached our own soil or that of our Allies." Thus was launched the Strategic Defense Initiative (SDI). Critics of the initiative caution that SDI opens another chapter on the now well-worn path of strategic competition, a chapter which will lead to increased instability at the strategic level at increased cost. They also have argued that the initiative is unnecessary since one of its principal near-term objectives— strengthening deterrence through undermining Soviet attack confidence—can be achieved at lower political and economic costs by making U.S. forces more mobile and thus more survivable against strategic preemption. Finally, they maintain that a push for SDI is likely to raise a variety of potentially divisive concerns among our allies.

Proponents argue that since the dynamic relationship between offense and defense has never insured the permanent ascendancy of one over the other, SDI is a prudent hedge against long-known Soviet efforts in this area. They also contend that new strategic defenses that might evolve from the current research effort may be capable of restoring stability, perceptions of which have been undermined by the Soviet Union's increasing capability, under certain scenarios, to mount a damage-limiting first strike against the United States. Furthermore, it is argued that since the horror of war has by no means completely prevented its occurrence, SDI offers, as a minimum, the prospect of partially protecting the population and of limiting damage to the United States, and perhaps its allies, while providing the time necessary to control escalation or to terminate hostilities should deterrence fail.

The strong support that exists for each of these two conflicting positions underscores the proposition that in the nuclear age both the United States and the Soviet Union are highly dependent on each other for their future security. Thus, the Working Group supports the findings of the Scowcroft Commission and believes that given Soviet efforts in this area, a vigorous research program on anti-ballistic missile technologies is needed, as a minimum to avoid technical surprise. The judgment on whether to proceed beyond research, however, remains dependent on whether the research indicates that the objectives set by the President for SDI can be obtained, as well as on the progress of arms negotiations with the Soviet Union. If strategic defense proves technically feasible, the essential questions are whether deploying strategic defensive systems will increase stability at the strategic level and, if so, to what degree and at what cost. In this regard, it is imperative that the United States seek to engage the Soviet Union in an attempt to determine together whether strategic defense is feasible; if feasible, whether it is desirable; and what mix of defensive and offensive systems would best support continued deterrence and encourage caution in crisis.

While modernizing its strategic forces to reduce their vulnerability to preemptive attack, the United States and its Western allies must maintain survivable theater nuclear deterrent forces. Likewise, the West must maintain substantial, well-modernized, and fully sustainable conventional forces—including naval forces, capable of deterring, in conjunction with its nuclear forces, Soviet conventional aggression or intimidation.

Arms Control

While the increasing costliness of U.S. and Soviet defense expenditures emphasizes the need to reexamine defense expenditures,[7] the importance of ensuring that future defense postures are consonant with the requirements of strategic and theater stability will remain paramount. In this context, arms control will remain central to the process of improving U.S.-Soviet relations. Nevertheless, as the meeting at Reykjavik once again has emphasized, arms control is one of the most complex undertakings of modern times. The extreme risks of modern warfare coupled with differing perceptions of threat and potential vulnerabilities, differing approaches to deterrence, differing interests and needs of allies, dissimilar strategies, doctrines, force structures, weapons systems characteristics and capabilities, different rates of technological advance, the complexities of verification, differing historical, geographical, and political–bureaucratic factors, and the inability to know with any certainty the potential adversary's actual objectives and intentions enormously complicate efforts to achieve balance and stability through negotiations. Indeed, in light of such complexities, easy solutions to the twin problems of achieving balance and stability are not likely be be forthcoming. Success in arms control will require time and patience.

On the other hand, the arsenals of the superpowers have reached levels at which genuine security increasingly will depend not just on military hardware, but on arms control. It may be theoretically feasible to plan and build strategic or theater forces, both offensive and defensive, in the absence of arms control. In practice, however, such efforts are likely to result in increasing levels of insecurity at increased costs—the result of the unpredictability of each side's acquisitions and the other side's need for worst-case planning as a prudent hedge. Thus, future strategic and theater programs designed by one side to increase stability are likely to require the cooperation of the other side if stability is to be assured.

While much useful progress on arms accords has been made over the past twenty-five years, the tasks ahead remain increasingly formidable. Rapidly advancing technologies are multiplying the complexities of armaments and countermeasures. In the past, arms control efforts frequently have given the appearance of codifying armaments planned by both sides, while preserving the freedom to exploit potential future advances in weapons capabilities through technological innovation. The problem has been that we are never quite certain where technological advance will lead us and whether that advance will strengthen or weaken stability.

To break such a cycle, the Working Group believes we must begin to take a much longer-term view of arms control. While continuing our efforts to improve deterrence and stability with the forces at hand today, we must look beyond current force structures if we wish to overcome bureaucratic and institutional inertia and thus make the progress demanded by an increasingly dangerous environment. We must continue to ask ourselves the timeworn question: how much is enough? Equally if not more important, we must ask ourselves how little is too little? If we are to get agreement on the paths to take in arms control negotiations, we must know where we wish to go and have charted a course which offers a reasonable chance of getting us there. We must also ask: are we to be captive of technology? Or, can technology be made to serve strategy? Must we insure that arms control negotiations do not interfere with defense programs? Or can the superpowers make both arms control and defense programs serve the ends of strategies fashioned to improve deterrence and stability?

As the Atlantic Council Working Group on strategic stability and arms control chaired by Brent Scrowcroft and R. James Woolsey has noted, it is becoming evident that the concept of stability must encompass more than the absence of war, whether or not nuclear weapons are employed.[8] To this end, increasing the flow of communications, reducing the fear of being rendered militarily inferior or ineffective as a result of technological or military surprise, and the avoidance of overreaction to marginal changes in force structures or force dispositions all play an important part in managing relations and avoiding conflict during periods of tension or crisis.

If we are to be successful in addressing such issues, we should engage the Soviet Union in talks designed to outline the strategic environment desired by the end of the second decade of the next century and beyond. Specifically, we should examine with the Soviets concepts of deterrence and crisis stability, delineate those weapon system characteristics considered to be potentially destabilizing in the future, and define in broad terms the preferred future strategic and theater force structures. It may be argued by some that technology cannot be controlled, but only managed. This may be true to a degree. However, even the managing of technology requires a degree of advance planning not always characteristic of past approaches to force modernization.

While engaging the Soviet Union in such long-term efforts, the United States should, of course, continue to pursue arms control agreements that bring about real reductions in the level of conventional and nuclear forces and in the destructive power available. It should also continue to seek reductions or the elimination of those weapons systems with characteristics that pose the greatest threat to stability, be it at the theater or strategic, conventional or nuclear levels. In this regard, the following bilateral arms control approaches merit further consideration: (1) a reduction in land-based MIRVed strategic systems and their replacement with single warhead systems; (2) a move away from fixed site land-based systems and the prompt development of mobile systems; (3) an increase in the proportion of strategic warheads at sea; (4) an overall sizeable reduction in time urgent hard-target kill capability; (5) a ban on terminal-homing ICBM and SLBM warheads; (6) a ban on depressed trajectory SLBMs; (7) a reduction of non-strategic nuclear–tipped missiles deployed by the superpowers in Europe; and (8) a comprehensive ban on chemical weapons. All reductions, however, should be based on the principles of equality or balance of remaining forces and verifiability.

Equally important is the need to create an environment of increased trust and confidence, at least in certain key areas. Thus, the United States should continue to support those confidence building measures that offer the greatest promise of increasing warning time prior to a conflict. With confidence in increased warning time both the United States and the Soviet Union would have more time to consult during a crisis and thus might be less likely to be impelled to conflict.

Of grave concern to the United States is what appears to be Soviet disregard for some provisions of certain arms control agreements. Such apparent disregard not only emphasizes the need for effective verification measures; it also, unless dispelled, endangers the entire arms control process and places obstacles in the path of a general amelioration of the environment of superpower relations. The Working Group recommends that questions as to compliance be handled whenever possible within the Standing Consultative Commission (SCC) which can operate away from the glare of publicity.

Trade

In the past, U.S.-Soviet trade relations have varied considerably. Following the Revolution of 1917, the USSR purchased American capital goods and current technology, paying with scarce foreign currency. American businessmen were active in commercial dealings with the Soviet Union well before we established diplomatic relations in 1933. An American engineer designed the first of the gigantic hydroelectric dams on the Dnieper. American automotive specialists helped the USSR get started on constructing an auto assembly line. American entrepreneurs have always had a special yen to do business with the Soviets, who, all else being equal, have favored the United States over other foreign suppliers.

The world depression of the 1930s, while fostering greater mutual interest in trade, saw a curtailment of U.S.-Soviet trade. After the establishment of diplomatic relations in 1933, the United States and the Soviet Union signed an annually renewable trade agreement based on the Reciprocal Trade Act of 1934. Most Favored Nation (MFN) status—that is, standard, non-discriminatory trade status—was provisionally accorded the Soviet Union. Although U.S.-Soviet trade was insignificant during the remainder of the 1930s, the United States began shipping a wide range of military and civil goods under lend-lease following the German attack on the USSR in 1941. Most of the goods were consumed during the conflict, but the United States maintained its claim for the value of civilian goods on hand in the USSR at the close of the war.

During the "Cold War", the United States first imposed export controls on trade with the USSR and then terminated the bilateral agreement when Congress ended Soviet MFN status. Since then U.S.-Soviet trade has had its ups and downs. In recent years, the result of poor harvests and inadequate storage facilities and transportation nets, Soviet demand for grain has become a major factor in U.S.-USSR trade relations. Nevertheless, discussions that focus on U.S.-Soviet trade arrangements have aroused strong emotions in the United States. In 1972 a "triangular" trade and finance arrangement was negotiated in which the lend-lease debt would be settled, the Executive Branch would seek MFN status from Congress for the USSR, and Export–Import Bank credits would be extended. In 1974-1975 the Jackson-Vanik and, especially, Stevenson Amendments to trade legislation scuttled the arrangement by linking it to the Jewish emigration question. The amendments had a debatable impact on Soviet policy toward Jewish emigration. Moscow seemed determined to demonstrate that its policy could not be shaped by such overt outside influence and, hence, deliberately reduced the level of emigration.

Today there is no trade agreement between the United States and the USSR. Nevertheless, there is good reason to believe that, in light of Soviet economic conditions, an expansion of U.S.-Soviet trade would be welcomed by the Soviets as well as by U.S. businessmen.[9] Two major security–political concerns, however, confront American decision-makers. Both grow out of an apprehension over the continued Soviet military buildup. First, the United States is reluctant to provide the Soviet Union with technology which has significant military potential or utility. U.S. attempts to curtail the flow of technology, especially technology with potential military applicability, have frequently been at odds with the interpretation of European allies as well as U.S. businessmen as to what constitutes goods of potential military utility. It was to resolve differences of this kind that the Coordinating Committee (COCOM) was founded in 1950. Separate and more informal arrangements were later made with Sweden, Switzerland, and Japan. Under COCOM, military arms are not sold to the USSR or its allies. COCOM has also been successful in curtailing sales of technologies closely identified with the production of military hardware.

There is, however, a limit to what can be achieved through such a cooperative arrangement. Where products have a direct civilian application and only tangentially affect military systems, so-called "dual-use" technologies, agreement on limiting sales has been more difficult. In the recent past, to enforce its attempt to limit the transfer of technology (such as in the Soviet pipeline case), the United States has forbidden the sale of goods produced in other countries by subsidiaries or licensees of American companies. The United States has also initiated procedures to prevent the transshipment to our adversaries of goods sold to our allies. Because Western European governments frequently characterize such actions as an assertion of extra-territorial jurisdiction, the result on occasion has been a deterioration in U.S. relations with its allies with the risk of countervailing action in the affected countries. While working through COCOM may be difficult at times, the Working Group believes that the COCOM process continues to offer the best prospect for reaching enforceable agreements on constraining the flow of military technology from the West to the Soviet Union. Recent improvements in the efficiency, timeliness, and technical analytical work of COCOM determinations support this judgment.

The United States, however, should resist temptations to use COCOM for other foreign policy purposes. COCOM is an inappropriate tool for such purposes. Moreover, while dialogue is essential to the COCOM process, the United States should avoid heavy–handed efforts to coerce allies to agree to its positions and, whenever possible, should avoid unilateral action. Such actions are likely to be costly to the system of Alliance cooperation and may well contribute to a breakdown in the very unity upon which an effective long-term U.S. policy toward the Soviet Union must be built.

A second concern which policy-makers confront is the fear that increasing trade between the United States and USSR will assist the Soviet Union in overcoming its economic difficulties. Soviet leaders would then be in a position to devote increased efforts to a further expansion of their military capability. Mindful of the fact that U.S.-Soviet trade represents a minimal fraction of the Soviet GNP and that much of what the United States sells to the Soviet Union is available from other sources, it seems clear that such concerns should not be weighted too heavily. Moreover, even if U.S.-Soviet trade were larger and potential Soviet economic gains from expansion of trade with the United States were greater, it is not at all clear that Soviet economic weakness would be in our best interest. In the past, Soviet economic weakness has coincided with periods of xenophobia and domestic repression.

Thus, trade per se need not be avoided. Working in conjunction with our allies, we should rather avoid subsidizing West-Soviet trade. Such trade as is conducted should be undertaken on a normal commercial basis. Recently, Gorbachev has reaffirmed his willingness to seek those changes within the Soviet system and to the Soviet Constitution that would be necessary to permit joint ownership ventures and direct U.S. private investment in the Soviet economy. He has also suggested twenty-two projects for consideration for joint venture/investment. It is, of course, not realistic to expect American businessmen to subsume U.S. national interests in their decision-making. Nevertheless, Gorbachev's offer must be assessed in terms of the national interest. There is little doubt that such an offer is likely to entail potential risks, for example, in the area of direct and indirect technology transfer. However, the Working Group believes this offer should be carefully explored as part of a general attempt to normalize U.S.-Soviet economic relations.

Perhaps the area of greatest controversy is the question of economic sanctions. The political impulse to "do something" when confronted with Soviet actions that are repulsive is powerful and even perhaps required in democratic countries. Economic sanctions often appear to be the only practicable and immediate choice to express disapproval in the age of nuclear weaponry. The problem, however, is that economic sanctions are most unlikely to be successful in getting the targeted country to alter its decisions except under highly specialized circumstances that are not generally applicable to the U.S.-Soviet relationship. Furthermore, although offering some initial psychological satisfaction, sanctions entail an economic cost to the country that imposes them. Nevertheless, in an environment where policy instruments are severely constrained, the use of economic sanctions may be warranted on certain occasions. Each situation must be judged on its own merits taking into account such factors as the nature of the outrage, the degree of Western consensus, and whether alternative suppliers will also support the sanctions. In sum, sanctions must be undertaken in clear recognition of domestic costs and the very low probability that the sanctions will have any appreciable effect on altering decisions already taken by Soviet leadership. For this reason, sanctions that are undertaken must not be open-ended or indefinite and should be proportional to the offense committed. A time-frame should be identified to allow the levying state to return to a more normal relationship without loss of face.

Professional Contacts, Cultural Interactions and Information Flow

As President Reagan has said, "enduring peace requires openness, honest communications, and opportunities for our peoples to get to know one another directly."[10] Greater professional, cultural, and educational interchange and an improvement in the quantity and quality of communications between our two societies can play a role, albeit limited, in improving relations.

An increase of government-to-government contacts at all levels might serve to reduce the causes of mutual distrust. It might also open avenues for pre-crisis resolution of issues likely to be explosive. Moreover, the establishment of dialogue at various levels among U.S. and Soviet military personnel (e.g. Joint Chiefs of Staff, Service Chiefs, and field commanders) might serve to lessen tendencies toward worst-case planning, as well as reduce the frictions which could result in escalatory political and military situations. The precedent for such dialogue already exists. At the level of field commanders, a dialogue began with General Eisenhower and has continued sporadically in the European theater ever since.

Furthermore, greater cultural and intellectual interchange between our societies may serve to discourage the sense of uniqueness and ethnocentrism characteristic of both superpowers which frequently has impeded more pragmatic and objective relations. Specifically,

Americans might become disabused of the notions that the Soviets want to and can be like us, that the correctness of U.S. views is self-evident, and that U.S.-Soviet disagreements are due solely to the latter's unreasonable obstructionism. On the other hand, it is possible that greater Soviet exposure to Americans could provide a basis for more informed and balanced views of the United States and help to counteract the distortions imposed by Soviet official news control. On the positive side, a firmer basis for cooperation and mutual trust can be built on increased contact across the spectrum of interests. In the area of science and technology, cooperative endeavors could be undertaken in such fields as catalytic chemistry, nuclear fusion energy, biotechnology, agriculture, and food packaging. As proposed by the President, we could launch new joint space ventures and establish joint medical research programs, all based on criteria of mutual benefit. We could increase exchanges of citizens from educational, fraternal, and cultural groups. We could increase scholarship programs; improve language studies; conduct courses in history, culture, and other subjects; establish libraries and cultural centers; and increase athletic competition. Perhaps through such programs we can begin to see what is best in each other's societies and thus reduce the tendency to focus on the worst.

Especially important, but perhaps more difficult, is the need to improve the general flow of information between the United States and the Soviet Union and between West and East. Restrictions on travel and communications of all kinds as well as the deliberate use of disinformation can only undermine attempts to improve relations. The Soviet Union has clearly registered its concern to every available Westerner over the rhetoric that has accompanied statements concerning U.S.-Soviet affairs in recent years. However, no mention has been made of the anti-American diatribes that have consistently characterized almost every aspect of Soviet reporting on the United States. Future Soviet-American relations cannot be built satisfactorily on such a one-sided foundation. Rhetorical excess, vitriolic reporting, and deliberate disinformation can only serve as promoters of distrust, reinforcing notions held in each capital that the other's ultimate goal is the elimination of its principal adversary.

Eastern Europe

Eastern Europe is a region of continuing importance to the United States and the West. It is the focus of an immense military standoff and a restive and uneasy component of the Soviet external empire. Indeed, the key to long-term stability in Europe may well be in Eastern Europe.

The post-war policy of the United States toward Eastern Europe has been shaped by three basic factors: (1) the region's critical position in the context of West European security and the global superpower confrontation; (2) the influence of organized ethnic groups, representing immigrants and their descendants from Eastern Europe; and (3) the idealistic pursuit of the universal desiderata of national self-determination and respect for human rights. Economic interests in trade and investment have had a marginal impact on overall U.S. policy toward Eastern Europe. Within this context, the general thrust of U.S. policy has been to seek an ultimate relaxation of the Soviet imperial system, including the long-term aspiration of eliminating the division of Europe.

At the outset, however, the Working Group recognized that the maintenance of close political, economic, and military relations between the Soviet Union and Eastern Europe remains one of Moscow's foremost objectives. Nevertheless, in response to pressures from within their own societies, some East European regimes, in search of legitimacy, have displayed a long-term trend toward increasing "domesticism"—the pursuit of separate national interests in lieu of "community" interests where national and "community" interests diverge. Soviet responses to such evolutionary developments in Eastern Europe have been plagued by the difficulty of securing both "cohesion" and "viability". Maintaining cohesion is not simply a matter of physical security for the Soviet State, as important as Moscow considers this to be. For political and ideological reasons as well, the cohesiveness of the "socialist community" is an important element in the Soviet goals of legitimizing Communist rule in the USSR and affirming the appeal of "Marxism-Leninism" beyond Soviet borders. On the other hand, the Soviets recognize that the search for stability within Eastern Europe, the concomitant need to avoid undermining the national legitimacy of Communist regimes there, and the desire for economically viable allies which contribute to, not drain, the Soviet economy have resulted in a need for a degree of tolerance of national views, concerns, and approaches.

Thus, while the Soviet Union is obviously concerned about trends in a number of East European countries, Soviet leaders are sophisticated enough to know that it is not the United States that provides the primary impetus for change.

It was inevitable that, given historical patterns of relations in Europe, distinctive national characteristics and yearnings for a greater measure of autonomy would emerge even under Communist regimes.

Within this context, it has appeared to the Working Group that possible pathways toward an ultimate relaxation of Soviet control in Eastern Europe essentially are confined to a spectrum from (a) accommodation to Soviet control through (b) transformation of Soviet control to (c) dissolution of Soviet control. Of these, accommodation has been consistently rejected as offensive to American and Western public opinion, unacceptably close to appeasement, and unworkable because internal forces for change in Eastern Europe rule out static forms of stability. Dissolution by force has been viewed as impossible without risking a possible Third World War and has not received serious consideration. Dissolution through Western encouragement of ferment and revolution within Eastern Europe is a high risk venture which could easily result in the imposition of even greater Soviet control. Especially important, such a policy would almost certainly create fissures within the Atlantic Alliance. It would run counter to the policies of a number of Western European states who, since the sixties, have sought increased stability in and improved relations with Eastern Europe and who would have to face the consequences of instability at their front door. Moreover, such an approach, in the absence of a dissolution of the Soviet state, would clearly be counterproductive to the long-term improvement in U.S.-Soviet relations. However, continued transformation—a gradual change in the Soviet imperial relationship with Eastern Europe—holds some promise as a potentially effective and realistic operational goal.[11] The situation in Eastern Europe is fluid, not frozen. Eastern Europe has room for maneuver between the extremes of total accommodation to Soviet hegemony and confrontation. There has been and can be evolutionary change.

While the most powerful forces influencing change are and will remain internal to Eastern Europe, the evolutionary process can be aided by contact and dialogue with the West at the governmental level and with the people. Concerning the latter, an important part of Western influence in Eastern Europe comes from examples of political freedom and economic success provided through Western radio and TV broadcasting, cultural exchanges, travel, business contacts, and non-state relations. Such contacts should be continued and their expansion encouraged. Concerning dialogue with East European regimes, East European governments are likely to remain interested in pragmatic relations with the West. They seek trade, credits, and investment. They are searching for new means to enter Western markets, both to repay debts and to reinvigorate their imports of Western goods.

The East European dilemma is that the USSR needs high quality machinery, consumer goods, and an increased output of "hard goods" from East Europe. To meet Soviet needs, Eastern Europe must modernize its industries and expand its economic exchanges with the West. Furthermore, economic growth and a consequent improvement in living standards is essential to political stability. While Moscow wants modernization and political stability, it is not enthusiastic about reforms that will potentially reduce party control and systemic orthodoxy.

The critical question as future years unfold will be how far and at what rate the Soviet Union is prepared to let the Eastern Europeans go. While there can be no definitive answer to this key question, U.S. and especially Western European policy can play a role, albeit limited, in that decision. Soviet leaders will remain involved in an active debate on how far to tolerate, even encourage, experimentation with economic systems and cultivation of relations with the West. The task of U.S. and Western policies is to encourage Soviet tolerance while expanding dialogue and contact in Eastern Europe. Given the predispositions of the Soviets, the former will clearly be more difficult than the latter. By encouraging the Soviets to recognize that there is an inherent element of instability in the antagonism of the peoples of Eastern Europe to their regimes as a result of Soviet control; by emphasizing the need to normalize relations among the states of Europe and ultimately the desirability of establishing closer ties between East and West Europe without threatening Soviet perceptions of their own basic security interests; by underscoring the cooperative rather than the conflictual side of East-West relations in Europe; by emphasizing the non-zero-sum nature of U.S. and Soviet relations with the East European states; and by seeking ways to reassure the Soviet Union of its essential security needs through negotiated agreements, the West may help to encourage Soviet leaders to accept and indeed facilitate a gradual transformation in Eastern Europe.

There can be no purely U.S. policy toward Eastern Europe and the Soviet Union. Some of our West European allies and friends, notably Germany and Italy, as well as Austria, have more extensive ties and closer contacts with Eastern Europe than do we. U.S. policy toward Eastern Europe also must take into account the enormous variations that exist among the nations of Eastern Europe. Frictions are inevitable in Eastern Europe. The absence of normalization in Poland, the dubious economic conditions in Romania and Czechoslovakia, the uncertainty of leadership successions in most of Eastern Europe and lower levels of Soviet economic support all point to future crises in the region. While there is no lack of formal machinery which might be employed to coordinate Western policies toward Eastern Europe, there remains a need to encourage a refinement in the Western consultative and policy coordinating processes in hopes of achieving a flexible harmonization of policies.

In all of this, however, the United States must make it clear that in dealings with the Soviet Union the West is not prepared to sacrifice its East European interests nor the interests of the East Europeans themselves in favor of a "condominium" arrangement which would abandon Eastern Europe to the permanent and exclusive sphere of Soviet influence. It also must continue to underscore its belief that long-term stability in Europe—as elsewhere—can only be assured in an environment of national self-determination, respect for human rights, and the opening up of societies.

The People's Republic of China

American policy since the Nixon Administration, openly or tacitly, has seen improved relations with China as an influence for restraint by the Soviet Union. It is, of course, a mistake to understand U.S.-PRC relations only in the context of the triangular relationship with the Soviet Union. Indeed, the improvement in Chinese-American relations during the past fifteen years has been a development of historical importance in its own right.

More recently, the initial euphoria over improving U.S.-PRC relations has given way to the daily toil of managing a relationship which
involves not only short, medium and long-term Chinese and U.S.
strategic interests, but also a complex web of political, economic, and
security relations with allies and friends throughout Asia and elsewhere.
With a view to the future, the United States should continue to explore and develop every opportunity for cooperation with the PRC
as China manages its emergence as a more dynamic international
power.

In recent years, profound changes have taken place in China which
suggest reasons for optimism. Some observers note that political
reforms have led to what appears to be a degree of intraparty
democracy. Moreover, they contend that the decision-making process
has been made less personalized and more consultative. Mass political
terror has ended. A degree of personal freedom, though not political
freedom, has been allowed. Formal and informal channels have been
made available to different groups, however, which allow them to express their interests and pressure policy-makers indirectly[12].
Economic reforms have gone even farther. The central planning system
has been modified somewhat to permit greater local flexibility and initiatives. Realistic pricing methods are being debated as a means of encouraging market mechanisms. There has been a decollectivization of
the agricultural commune system. Private sector development has been
encouraged. Through an "open door" policy China's ties to industrial
market economies and international economic institutions are developing rapidly. Nevertheless, despite reform successes in the agricultural
sector, inflation, balance of payments difficulties, challenges to traditional Chinese values, and a variety of other factors have led to a strong
counter-attack on the "open-door" policy by conservatives. Where
the current course of political and economic reforms will ultimately
take the PRC is, of course, unknown. Leadership succession still remains uncertain as does the question of whether reforms will achieve
a sufficient degree of institutionalization and legitimacy to resist future
counter action by "conservatives".

In foreign affairs, since 1982 when the PRC formalized its "independent foreign policy", Sino-Soviet relations have gradually improved.
Both Beijing and Moscow continue to repeat their willingness to normalize relations further. Gorbachev reaffirmed his satisfaction about
that improvement at the 27th Party Congress. Border tensions have
been reduced. Both governments are less critical of each other's foreign
policy, and trade, though still relatively modest, doubled between 1982
and 1984. A long-term trade agreement has been signed. Cultural ties
have been expanded.[13]

Despite these improvements, however, the strategic relations between Beijing and Moscow have not changed fundamentally. China's
preconditions for normalization of relations have neither been met nor
altered. There has been no breakthrough in border negotiations or out-

standing Chinese territorial claims. Especially, there has been no reduction in Soviet support for Hanoi's occupation of Kampuchea, nor has there been a Soviet withdrawal from Afghanistan. Rather, Moscow has enlarged its Pacific fleet, strengthened its air power and deployed large numbers of SS-20 missiles in the Far East, and increased its aid to Hanoi and its military presence in Vietnam. Thus, for Beijing, the Soviet Union remains the primary threat to its security.

Consequently, the United States and China share certain geopolitical objectives which suggest cooperative efforts in various forms. Both view Moscow as the principal threat. Both are concerned about Moscow's increasing military power in the Far East. Both are pursuing similar objectives in Afghanistan and Indochina. Both seek to curb Soviet expansionism. Despite this confluence of interest, however, there are good reasons why Washington's approach on security issues should be kept low key. Ultimately, attempts to inflame animosities between China and the Soviet Union are likely to be counterproductive to U.S. relations with both. Rather, the United States should continue the present trend of U.S.-PRC relations by expanding economic and cultural ties, encouraging China to play a constructive role in enhancing stability in Asia, and offering continuing, quiet assistance and support for Chinese efforts to reduce Soviet military and political pressure. Such an approach by the United States, taken in conjunction with European and Asian allies, could strengthen relations with the PRC while perhaps encouraging the Soviet Union to more moderate action in Asia.

The Third World

Perhaps no other area of Soviet-American interaction will be more difficult to deal with than the Third World. The temptation to seek local advantage at the expense of advances in great power cooperation may continue to plague the new generation of Soviet leaders as it has preceding ones. The lessons of their failures in Indonesia and Egypt will continue to pale in light of lingering ideological dogma which draws Soviet leadership toward support for "national liberation" movements. However, at the recent Party Congress, while Gorbachev reaffirmed the solidarity of the Soviet Union with the forces of national and social liberation, the endorsement was notably less strident and enthusiastic than in the past. Nevertheless, in the Third World opportunities for potential U.S.-Soviet cooperation seem likely to remain limited. On the other hand, as an Atlantic Council Working Group suggested in an earlier report, the animation and agitation, the turbulence and terror, the rising expectations and rising resentments in developing countries will continue to have an impact on U.S.-Soviet relations and on our Atlantic and Pacific alliances.[14]

The so-called "Third World" is a politically, economically, militarily, culturally, and geographically diverse grouping of nations that includes the majority of peoples, lands, and ocean islands and sits astride most of the world's maritime choke points. As a result, no single set of variables can describe the current conditions in Third World countries or the cures for the many problems which these countries confront. What is clear, however, is that most countries in the Third World are undergoing dynamic change. With the break-up of old colonial empires and the increasing diffusion of political, economic, and military power, the Soviet Union has chosen to exploit this unsettled atmosphere. It has been busy building an infrastructure of people from Third World countries who are being educated and indoctrinated in the Soviet Union and returned to their homelands. Should the right political situation arise, the Soviets hope such an infrastructure of trained cadres will propel them to greater influence in the countries affected.

Here as in other areas, we can reduce the risk of dangerous miscalculation by encouraging, where possible, Soviet pragmatism and restraint. Despite the expenditure of massive resources, it must be clear even in the Kremlin that the USSR has relatively little to show for its three decades of effort in the Third World. In this regard, it could be argued that Soviet policy in the Middle East has shown, perhaps, a glimmer of pragmatism. In that area, the Kremlin has played a relatively careful and circumspect role during recent years. Moscow, of course, would like a larger voice in the Middle East and the Soviets have given a considerable amount of arms aid to Syria and Iraq. However, few who know the region would describe those countries as totally subservient to Soviet policy. Nor have close American ties with Israel permitted the USSR to play as politically expansive a role in Arab countries as might have been expected. Perhaps Moscow has been as much confounded as Washington by the turbulence and unpredictability of events in that troubled part of the world.[15]

In Central America and the Caribbean the Soviet Union's role has been mixed. Until the successes of the Sandinistas in Nicaragua, Moscow refused to endorse Fidel Castro's notion of open revolution, preferring instead what it believed to be the more pragmatic approach of working with local communist party organizations to improve their position from within existing political structures. While Moscow recently has been more active in encouraging and arming guerrilla forces throughout the region, the Soviets generally have done so through third parties—as revealed in the papers captured in Grenada. Nevertheless, Moscow would like to encourage what it perceives to be continuing antagonism toward the United States by certain groups within the region. Moscow, also is likely to continue its active, vigorous support for the Sandinista regime in Nicaragua. The Kremlin, however, is unlikely to delude itself—especially in the wake of Grenada—that the United States will remain indifferent to developments judged to be critical to its security. Unfortunately, it may be difficult to find significant common areas of interest for active great power cooperation anywhere in Latin America other than the prevention of nuclear proliferation and the possibility of direct confrontation.

The Soviet Union also can be expected to continue to exploit opportunities as they arise in Africa. It has shown itself willing to deliver arms at marketable prices and has invested in the region with its own forces and advisers and those of surrogate Cuba. Perhaps it was only natural for ambitious leaders emerging in the poor, post-colonial countries of Africa, many of which were inadequately prepared for independence, to find in some form of Marxism adapted to African conditions a congenial ideology to justify the essentially dictatorial practices they imposed. Western educated elites exposed to left-wing doctrines in Western Europe or the Soviet Union frequently returned to Africa with strong antipathies toward international capitalism and the multinational corporations and banks which were its institutional embodiment. It was relatively easy for these elites, many of whom harbored resentment toward their former colonial masters, to lean towards the Soviet Union during the post-colonial period, and Moscow was quick to exploit the ensuing instabilities.[16] Since then, the Soviet Union has remained active in Africa, from the northern tier with its open support for Libya's Gadhafi, through its substantial intervention on the Horn, to southern Africa where the USSR has attempted to exploit the woes of blacks and whites alike in an effort to gain propaganda advantage as a "supporter" of Black Africa. While on the whole Moscow's activities in Africa have failed to achieve their objectives, new Soviet leaders probably will continue to respond to opportunities for exploitation. In this region, as well as in Asia, ties between America's European allies and elites in their former colonies may mitigate Soviet influence. Thus, the United States can and should rely on closely coordinated policies with its European allies to counter Soviet influence in this part of the world. American policy should continue to emphasize non-intervention in the internal affairs of African nations and the removal of foreign forces. Economic and social progress in the region can only be achieved if Africans are allowed to deal with their internal difficulties free from the interference of outside military forces. Such forces represent a new colonialism and inhibit further progress by the nations of the region.

In Asia and the Pacific region, Korea, Thailand, Kampuchea, Afghanistan, Pakistan and Iran are among the potential areas of clash between Washington and Moscow. Nor should the Philippines be dismissed as a potential area of Soviet intrigue. During the past decade, the Asia-Pacific region has experienced an exceptionally broad range of important changes. Economically, it is the world region with the highest growth rate. Intra-regional economic activities have expanded rapidly. The region also continues to become ever more competitive in the international market and its share of world trade continues to increase. Indeed, the region has surpassed Europe in the list of principal U.S. trading partners.

From a political and security perspective, the region presents a more complicated picture. The U.S.-Soviet military power balance in the region has shifted to one which is increasingly less favorable to the United States and, in the absence of countering capabilities, will in all probability continue to do so. As noted earlier, the Soviet military buildup in Asia over the past decade has been significant, as has its improvement of transportation, communications and supply facilities. Indeed, it is no longer an exaggeration to say that the USSR now has in place the capability for fighting a two-front war.[17] Moscow, clearly, is now in a strong strategic position in the region and might be tempted to exploit that position.

In Northeast Asia, Moscow appears to be interested in playing a greater role on the Korean peninsula just when South Korea is experiencing domestic difficulties and North Korea faces an important political transition. Furthermore, while the Kremlin so far has been unwilling to make concessions on the critical "northern territories" issue which is of greatest interest to Japan, its diplomatic posture toward that country has warmed considerably. In Southeast Asia, Hanoi with apparent Soviet support has continued its aggressive behavior in Kampuchea and seems unlikely to be willing to withdraw its forces in the near future. In exchange, the Soviet Pacific fleet enjoys excellent port facilities at Cam Ranh Bay and has deployed long-range bombers at Da Nang. In Southwest Asia, the Soviet pursuit of hegemony in Afghanistan has ravaged the country and resulted in renewed pressures on Pakistan.

In sum, the environment in Asia, as well as other parts of the Third World, is fraught with potential for crises. As a result, the Third World will remain the most likely area of conflict between the United States and the Soviet Union. This suggests, at a minimum, the need for dialogue between the United States on one hand and the United States and its allies on the other to clarify interests and search for mechanisms to manage relations with the Soviet Union in the Third World. Efforts should be undertaken to encourage the Soviet Union to play a constructive role in resolving the many political and economic problems that plague Third World countries. One area of mounting concern has been the ever increasing flow of arms to Third World countries. Many of these countries can neither afford the burden of larger military forces nor the instabilities that frequently attend increases in armaments. The United States and the Soviet Union should explore means for controlling and reducing arms sales to the Third World. It is clear as well that while seeking the cooperation of the Soviet Union, the United States in conjunction with its Atlantic and Pacific allies must recognize the increasing importance of the North-South dimension of inter-state relations and continue to pursue vigorously a relationship of constructive interaction between the Third World and Western nations. This relationship should be founded on development assistance, trade, and investment and the peaceful settlement of disputes. In many ways this latter line of policy is more fundamental and constructive. Both for its own direct results and to lessen the opportunities for Soviet exploitation, the rewards for enlightened Western efforts will be greater than from the continued pursuit of the more sterile East-West confrontation.

At the same time that the Western states work to improve the confidence and viability of Third World states, they should encourage the democratization of geopolitically "friendly" but internally authoritarian Third World regimes. They also should attempt to understand and deal more effectively with governments of a radical, dictatorial, expansionist, socialist, or communist hue that are interspersed throughout the Third World. As an earlier Atlantic Council Working Group concluded, "The West cannot afford to preclude opportunities for patient, quiet relations which may help to prepare the way for the acceptance of more moderate policies as time goes by and conditions change".[18]

International Terrorism

International terrorism may be defined as premeditated violence—including murder, assassination, kidnapping, hostage-taking, and intimidation—conducted against governmental, civilian, or private sector targets by individuals, subnational groups or state agents not constrained by the rules of law.[19] When terrorists are deliberately aided and abetted by the government of a sovereign state, it could be considered an act of belligerence.

For some years, there has been evidence pointing to Soviet support for terrorist activity. While the Soviet Union cannot control all of the activities of the many groups it supports, improvement in U.S.-Soviet relations should include a firm commitment to reduce and ultimately withdraw support for terrorist activity.

Some will contend that any possible agreement between the United States and the Soviet Union will flag on the issue of definition. This ought not, however, preclude the possibility of reaching an agreement with Moscow on certain issues where we have common interests. Indeed the history of aircraft hijackings, the seizure of Soviet diplomats in the Middle East in mid-1985, and Gorbachev's address at the 27th Party Congress suggest that some common ground may exist. Thus, the agenda for expanded U.S. talks with the Soviet Union should include efforts to find common grounds for Soviet-American cooperation in stemming the growing tide of terrorist activities.

To improve chances for success, talks on the control and elimination of international terrorism should be in a forum separate from existing arms control negotiations, avoiding linkage to more controversial issues. The talks could first focus on establishing principles for joint action to prevent the acquisition and use of weapons of mass destruction by terrorist groups. Ultimately, they should address the full range of potential terrorist activities, including such issues as the misuse of diplomatic missions for terrorist activities, hostage taking, abductions, and bombings.

The Working Group suggests that a most useful approach might initially concentrate on what constitutes a terrorist act. A sharp differentiation could be drawn between the violent action against innocents and the political sympathies of the perpetrators. To the victims of terrorism the consequences are the same regardless of the "purity" of the terrorists' objectives in some abstract sense. Thus, the hijacking of an aircraft from East to West which places innocents at risk would be as criminal as a hijacking from West to East or anywhere else. Likewise, the taking of an American, Soviet, or any other diplomat as hostage would be condemned by both superpowers equally.

Human Rights

Perhaps the greatest strengths of the Western world derive from its fundamental respect for human rights. Indeed, the guarding of individual human rights and freedoms is one of the principal duties of Western governments.

This commitment is driven not only by the belief that it is a moral imperative, but also by the demonstrated experience that societies which protect the rights and freedoms of the individual are best able to advance in face of the complexities of the modern world. Ultimately it is the cultivation of the human resource upon which the future depends.

The issue is how to advance the cause of human rights in a world where they are so often subject to extraordinary abuse. Here idealism must be tempered with realism if real progress toward our ideals is ever to be achieved. The pace of improvements within the Soviet Union on the individual rights of its citizens cannot be the *sine qua non* for an improvement in U.S.-Soviet relations. However, the Working Group believes that the Soviet Union should be encouraged to fulfill its obligations as set forth in the UN Declaration of Human Rights and the Helsinki Final Act, for failure to fulfill its obligations is likely to pose obstacles to the long-term improvement of relations between our countries. The rhetoric of a moral crusade is not likely to be helpful and should be avoided. More promising is consistent and quiet diplomacy designed to encourage the Soviet Union and others to moderate their policies. In any case, it must be increasingly apparent to all that failure to stimulate human creativity and incentives will inevitably result in a permanent competitive disadvantage in an increasingly dynamic world.

The United States should also appeal to the Soviet Union to use its influence with its allies, quietly urging them to compliance with human rights accords. As one example, the USSR might be encouraged to use its influence to halt the Bulgarian government campaign of enforced assimilation of the ethnic Turkish minority in Bulgaria. Such actions by Bulgaria are in contravention of a number of international agreements as well as the Bulgarian Constitution.

CONCLUSIONS AND POLICY RECOMMENDATIONS

Future U.S.-Soviet relations seem certain to be characterized by the simultaneous existence of conflictual and cooperative dimensions. There is no foreseeable escape from this complexity. By the year 2000, the two nations will still be the world's only superpowers. Their ideologies and political and economic systems will remain radically different and in competition. Neither side will "collapse" nor fail to maintain strong and effective defenses. Rival alliances will remain intact. Differences in history and outlook will continue to make each side mistrustful of the other.

Furthermore, the drama of U.S.-Soviet relations will be played out against a backdrop of rapid technological change, continued instability in the Third World which could entail superpower confrontation, and an increasing recognition of the fragility of the environment upon which we all depend. Technological advance will offer opportunities for dramatic improvements in the human condition, while also adding a dimension of uncertainty not only in the superpower balance, but also in the balances elsewhere around the world as dramatic increases take place in the lethality and firepower of modern weaponry. Within this context, there is a paramount need to reduce the chance of confrontation, miscalculation, and the risks of nuclear war. Thus, while recognizing that some of Moscow's predispositions have deep historical and ideological sources, agreements to minimize such risks may be possible in light of the Soviet Union's oft evidenced caution and pragmatism. Furthermore, in spite of the soured relations of the past decade, opportunities exist for cooperation in other aspects of relations in the political, military, and economic realms which may help to serve as building blocks for a more general improvement in U.S.-Soviet relations. Such opportunities should be vigorously identified, explored, and negotiated.

The Working Group believes that the policy recommendations outlined below, if implemented, will provide a firm foundation for improved U.S.-Soviet relations. Equally important, the Working Group believes that if the recommendations are followed, the United States would go a long way to closing the gulf between it and its Allies that now exists. The recommendations have been the product of an interaction with the Atlantic Council Working Group on strategic stability, co-chaired by Brent Scowcroft and R. James Woolsey, which conducted its work in parallel with this effort. The recommendations also take into account extensive discussions in Washington and in Western Europe among a wide variety of statesmen and scholars as well as in Moscow with Soviet representatives. Of course, the future of U.S.-Soviet relations will depend greatly on Moscow's willingness and ability to convert words to deeds. The task of U.S. policy is to encourage the Soviet Union to do so. Accordingly the following policy recommendations are made:

General Policy Recommendations

The United States must continue to seek an active and productive dialogue with the Soviet Union. This dialogue should be carried on with consistency and regularity and include explicit delineations on our part of critical U.S. and allied interests and our firm commitment to resist any Soviet attempt to extend its influence by military means. The dialogue must also emphasize America's determination (1) to reduce the risk of war by enhancing our ability to maintain a stable environment during crises; (2) to reduce and stabilize armament levels through sound and verifiable agreements, and ultimately to ease the burdens of military spending; (3) to improve bilateral relations on the basis of reciprocity and mutual interest; (4) to manage and resolve regional conflicts based on the principles of non-intervention and the self-determination of peoples; and (5) to seek improvements in human rights and encourage the Soviet Union to recognize the advantages of joining us in this effort. A willingness to engage in a dialogue with the Soviet Union must be an unalterable aspect of U.S. foreign policy.

Specific Policy Recommendations

Military/Security

1. The military/security dimension of U.S.-Soviet relations will remain the foremost consideration by policy makers well into the next decade. Superpower military parity will remain an essential factor for stability. Successful dialogue demands that both side approach negotiations from positions of adequate strength, confident in their capabilities and in their positions in the international order. Thus, while avoiding the impression that it seeks an arms race with the USSR, is pursuing military superiority, or is uninterested in reaching equitable arms reduction agreements, the United States must maintain the credibility of its nuclear and conventional deterrent forces through appropriate force modernizations and improvements in command, control and communications (C^3).
2. To avoid instability, the result of surprise advances in the field of military technology, and to strengthen the deterrence of nuclear conflict by defensive means, if such proves feasible and desirable, the United States should continue to pursue in concert with its allies a research program on antiballistic missile defense technologies.
3. It is of paramount importance to strengthen stability at the strategic and theater nuclear levels, and also at the conventional level where there is perhaps an even greater potential for a clash between U.S. and Soviet forces. Efforts to this end must not be held hostage to events in peripheral areas.
4. Arms control is central to the process of improving U.S.-Soviet

relations. The United States should continue its efforts to seek genuine and verifiable arms limitations and vigorously explore the possibility of limiting the military use of space to those uses which reinforce stability. More specifically, the United States should seek reductions in or the elimination of those weapons systems with characteristics that pose the greatest threat to stability—theater or strategic, conventional or nuclear. In this regard the following bilateral arms control approaches merit further consideration:

- a reduction in MIRVed land-based strategic systems and their replacement by single warhead systems;
- a move away from fixed site land-based systems and the prompt development of mobile systems;
- an increase in the proportion of warheads at sea;
- an overall sizeable reduction in vulnerable time urgent hard-target kill capability;
- a ban on terminal-homing ICBM and SLBM warheads;
- a ban on depressed trajectory SLBMs;
- a capping and subsequent reduction of non-strategic nuclear tipped missiles deployed by the superpowers in Europe; and
- a comprehensive ban on chemical weapons.

5. Moreover, the Working Group believes that the United States and the Soviet Union must begin to take a longer-term view of arms control if stability is to be truly enhanced in the future. To this end the United States should engage the USSR in talks designed to outline the strategic environment desired in the early decades of the next century. Specifically we should jointly:

- examine concepts of deterrence and crisis stability;
- delineate those weapon systems characteristics considered potentially destabilizing in the future;
- define in broad terms the preferred balance of strategic and theater forces of the future.

6. The United States and the Soviet Union also should explore means of reducing arms sales in the Third World.

7. The United States should attempt to engage the Soviet Union in talks designed to limit terrorist activities around the world. Such talks should be separate from existing arms control negotiations and focus first on establishing principles for joint action to prevent the acquisition and use of weapons of mass destruction by terrorist groups. Ultimately, talks should focus on the full range of potential terrorist activities. While the USSR cannot control all of the activities of the many groups it supports, improvement in U.S.-Soviet relations should include a firm commitment to reduce and ultimately withdraw support for terrorist activity.

Political

8. Consistent with the call for broad ranging dialogue with the Soviet Union based on realism, strength and flexibility, the Working

Group believes that the search for shared interests will be best served by consistency and regularity in the negotiating process. Thus the Working Group recommends that U.S. and Soviet leaders meet regularly in summit session, perhaps biennially*. Foreign Ministers and other relevant cabinet-level officials should meet their counterparts one or more times every year.

9. With the long-term goal of eliminating the division of Europe in mind, the United States should continue to seek a gradual transformation of the Soviet imperial relationship in Eastern Europe through a policy of contact and dialogue with East European peoples and governments. This process should include the maintenance and expansion of:
    • contacts and dialogue with East European regimes across the spectrum of activities;
    • trade and investment;
    • Western radio and TV broadcasting;
    • professional and cultural exchanges, travel, business contacts, and other non-state relations.

10. The United States must also recognize that it cannot by itself play a decisive role in accelerating the process of change in Eastern Europe. It should work closely with its allies and encourage a refinement in the Western consultative, coordinating, and crisis management machinery with the aim of a flexible harmonization of policies.

11. In Asia, the United States should expand economic and cultural ties with the PRC and encourage China to play a constructive role in enhancing stability, while offering continued quiet support for Chinese efforts to reduce Soviet military and political pressure. The U.S. should not, however, attempt to inflame animosities between the USSR and the PRC.

12. In the Third World, differing and competitive interests suggest that the potential for great power friction and confrontation will remain. As a minimum, the United States should engage the Soviet Union to clarify interests, establish limits of behavior and search for mechanisms for crisis management. Real social and economic progress in the Third World will require a stability built upon the pursuit of a new dynamic and constructive interaction between the Third World and Western nations. This relationship should

---

*Malcolm Toon comments: "I have reservations about summitry as a way of doing serious diplomatic business. If we must have summit meetings—and they are probably inevitable given the nature of political process in both countries—they should be well prepared by experts, preceded by close and comprehensive consultations with principal allies, based on a specific agenda, and geared to agreed political objectives. Reykjavik met none of these desiderata and thus was a near disaster. Summitry of the Reykjavik type should be avoided like the plague."

be founded on development assistance, trade, and investment and should be coordinated to the extent possible with the political and economic policies of our allies.

13. The United States should encourage Soviet leadership to recognize that the nature of improvements in human rights does not constitute a win/lose situation between West and East but that improvements will indeed create circumstances from which all parties will benefit.

14. Perhaps the greatest strengths of the Western world derive from a fundamental faith in human nature. The United States, however, should not make the improvement of the individual rights of Soviet citizens the *sine qua non* for an improvement in U.S.-Soviet relations. The United States, without excessive hyperbole and in close consultation with its allies, should encourage the Soviet Union to fulfill its obligations under international covenants, including the Helsinki accords, to which it has freely agreed.

Economic

15. The United States should take a broad and comprehensive view of trade with the Soviet Union. Recognizing that the USSR is a permanent fixture of the world landscape for the foreseeable future, and that it has very considerable human and natural resources of its own, the United States should normalize trade with the Soviet Union and thus permit the sale of a variety of civilian use goods to the USSR on a commercial basis. Working in conjunction with our allies, the U.S. government, however, should avoid subsidizing U.S.-Soviet trade.

16. The USSR, provided it is prepared to respond on a *quid pro quo* basis, should be granted Most Favored Nation (MFN) status through mechanisms similar to the 1972–73 trade agreement. This will inevitably involve a difficult political process in the United States, but the Working Group believes that linking MFN to Soviet emigration policy serves neither the ends of increased emigration nor improved U.S.-Soviet relations. MFN status should be primarily, but not solely, an economic determination.*

17. For security reasons, the United States must continue to prohibit the export to the USSR of military goods and technologies essentially designed for military purposes.

18. The United States should also continue to work with its allies through COCOM to limit Soviet access to technology likely to significantly enhance the military capability of the USSR—even if there are non-military uses which predominate in the West. The United States however, should not attempt to use COCOM for other foreign policy purposes.

---

*Brent Scowcroft comments that MFN status has not been and should not be based primarily on economic factors.

19. Trade, security, and criminal regulations should be strictly enforced and the cooperative efforts of other countries should be carefully sought.

Cultural/Social/Technical

20. The free flow of ideas and peoples should be encouraged as a means of enhancing the awareness of mutual concerns, adding to the understanding by each of the nature and national culture of the other, and—as a guiding aim—developing common interests and points of view. Hence the United States should seek an increase in government–to–government contacts at all levels, including:

    * a dialogue among U.S. and Soviet military personnel at various levels (e.g. Joint Chiefs of Staff, Service Chiefs, and field commands);
    * an increase in exchanges of citizens from educational, fraternal, and cultural groups;
    * greater numbers of scholarship programs, improved language studies, and a greater number of courses in each other's history and culture; and
    * a reduction in restrictions on travel and communication.

21. The United States also should seek, where security interests are not jeopardized, to expand U.S.-Soviet scientific and technical cooperation. In the wake of the Chernobyl disaster, a range of cooperative initiatives should be undertaken in the fields of disaster control, environmental protection, and medical assistance.

22. The United States should improve the quality of its information programming both in sophistication and in awareness that Soviet disinformation is becoming more effective at a time when a younger generation of allies and friends in the West may be more susceptible. The United States should also seek an end to deliberate disinformation.

23. Whatever the problems that may be anticipated during the remainder of this century, the United States should place its confidence in the basic strength of the democratic institutions and open societies that it and its allies possess. U.S. policy must go beyond attributing all evils to Soviet interventionism or merely accepting continuing confrontation in order to gain and maintain the support of friends and allies around the world. The United States should offer a vision of the future based on human freedom, dignity and creativity.

ENDNOTES

[1]Murray Feshbach, "Between the Lines of the 1979 Census", *Problems of Communism*, January–February 1982, pp. 27–27. See also John M. Weinstein, "All Features Grate and Stall: Soviet Strategic Vulnerability and the Future of Deterrence" in Robert Kennedy and John M. Weinstein, eds. *The Defense of the West: Strategic and European Security Issues Reappraised.* Boulder: Westview Press, 1984, pp. 50–52.

[2]See Robert F. Byrnes, "The USSR in the 1980s and Beyond", Chapter 6 of the present book.

[3]See John P. Hardt, "Soviet Economic Constraints on Defense to Year 2000," Appendix to Chapter 8.

[4]Seweryn Bialer, "St. Mikhail and the Dragon".

[5]See Barry Blechman and Douglas Hart, "The Military Dimensions of U.S.-Soviet Relations", Chapter 4.

[6]See Robert Kennedy, "The Changing Strategic Balance and U.S. Defense Planning" in Robert Kennedy and John M. Weinstein eds. *The Defense of the West*, pp. 23–29.

[7]See Timothy W. Stanley, "Western and Eastern Economic Constraints", Chapter 8.

[8]See Brent Scowcroft, R. James Woolsey, and Thomas Etzold, "Defending Peace and Freedom; Toward Strategic Stability in the Year 2000." Atlantic Council Policy Paper, May 1987.

[9]See John P. Hardt, "United States-Soviet Economic and Technological Interaction", Chapter 5.

[10]President Reagan, "A Mission for Peace." Address to the nation, Washington D.C., Nov. 14, 1985, reproduced in Current Policy 765, U.S. Department of State.

[11]Lincoln Gordon, Atlantic Council Working Paper.

[12]See Guo-cang Huan, "Sino-Soviet Relations to the Year 2000: Implications for U.S. Interests", Chapter 7.

[13]Ibid.

[14]"After Afghanistan—The Long Haul", Atlantic Council Policy Paper, Washington, D.C., March 1980, p. 9.

[15]See Martin J. Hillenbrand, "U.S.-Soviet Political Interaction", Chapter 3.

[16]Ibid.

[17]See Guo-cang Huan, "Sino-Soviet Relations", Chapter 7.

[18]"After Afghanistan—The Long Haul," p. 49.

[19]For a fuller treatment of the subject see "Combatting International Terrorism: U.S.-European Cooperation and Political Will," Atlantic Council Policy Paper, November 1986.

Chapter II

THE EMERGENCE OF THE USSR AS A WORLD POWER

Herbert J. Ellison

A. ENDURING FACTORS IN THE U.S.-USSR RELATIONSHIP

1. Historical

Before the 20th century there was little interaction between the United States and Russia. Visionaries such as de Toqueville predicted the future power and rivalry of the two continental giants in the early 19th century. Throughout that troubled and creative century, however, there was little contact between them. They were separated by two great oceans, and the United States, preoccupied with the settlement and development of its vast continental empire, was determined to remain aloof from foreign entanglements. Individual Americans— diplomats, explorers, and occasional specialists serving the tsarist government—came to know the Russian Empire. Only late in the century did contacts begin to expand—first as a result of the dynamic outward drive of commerce, colonization and empire (in Alaska, California and Hawaii), and then with the entry of American entrepreneurs into the trade and investment opportunities opened up by Russian development.

The names of American manufacturers (Singer, International Harvester, and others) were widely known in early 20th century Russia, though America was far behind Europe—especially Germany, France, Belgium and Britain—in trade and investment there. The American interest in Russia went beyond investment and trade. There was a fascination with the vastness of the country, and with its unique social and political institutions. The interest was nourished by the great figures of Russian classical literature, and by the accounts of American and European travelers and commentators. As in Europe, and partly through European reports, Americans became increasingly aware of the flowering of Russian culture, not only literature but in music, art, dance, scholarship, and science.

There was also a growing interest in Russian politics. From the perspective of American liberalism it seemed the natural thing that the Russian absolutist monarchy, like earlier European counterparts, must give way to popular rule. It was simply a matter of time and opportunity. The great Russian liberal thinker, Paul Miliukov, found interested and sympathetic audiences wherever he went on his American tour in the early 1900s, detailing liberal plans for a Russian democracy. American press reports of the persecution of Russian Jews, both before and after that tour, deepened the conviction that the autocratic power must be replaced.

Except between quite limited strata of Russian and American society, there was relatively little chance for contact and little basis for understanding. Like Russia, America was still predominantly rural, with a large element of a colonizing, frontier-oriented society. But America's rural society was dominated by farmers, independent agricultural proprietors, whereas Russian peasant communalism still bore the marks of the landowner-serf era. Not until the aftermath of the 1905 revolution did the Stolypin reforms seek to remake Russian rural society— to follow what Lenin astutely observed was the American pattern of rural social renovation. If any part of America resembled landlord-peasant Russia, it was the rural, post-slavery south. However that was regional America, not the mainstream with its combination of dynamic industrialization and the rapid conquest and development of the virgin lands of the frontier.

Russian eastward migration, much accelerated by the opening of the Trans-Siberian railroad in the 1890s, bore many similarities to its American counterpart. And expansion and settlement in thinly populated frontier regions was an experience that Americans and Russians shared. But Russia was also one of the great European empires, and a rapidly expanding empire in the last century before World War I. In the west it had acquired, from the seventeenth century forward, an immensely varied and mostly unassimilated potpourri of peoples— Finns, Swedes, Germans, Estonians, Latvians, Lithuanians, Poles, Jews, Ukrainians, Romanians—some of whom dreamed of separate nationhood by the late 1800s. Expansion southward had incorporated the lands of the Georgians, the Armenians and the Azerbaijani, and an enormous Moslem empire in Central Asia was the fruit of an era of remarkable imperial expansion comparable to the simultaneous effort of European states in Africa and East Asia. Russia had also expanded rapidly into East Asia from the 1850s forward, annexing massive territories from China along the Amur and Ussuri rivers and building a protectorate in Outer Mongolia.

American expansion bore some similarities to that of the Russians: agricultural colonization of the lands of thinly settled nomadic or seminomadic peoples; the conquest of the territory of a neighboring state (Mexico), even a small enterprise in overseas colonialism. In contrast to Russia, America was an immigrant nation and, whatever its racial, cultural and religious variety, it was linguistically and institutionally a relatively cohesive nation. Moreover, its political legacy was the cosmopolitan republican statehood of the 18th century, eschewing alike the dynasty-centered statehood of the Romanovs and the nationalism developing in late 19th century Europe with its emphasis on race.

On the eve of World War I and the Russian Revolution, the dominant American expectation was that Russia would continue the path extending from the emancipation of the serfs through the 1905 revolution toward a free society and self-government. Russian liberals and democratic socialists held similar views, and it was a mix of admiration for both democratic France and Britain, with which Russia was allied, that led them to support the government's war effort. They were unprepared for the horror of Europe's first modern war and the military power of industrial Germany. They were equally unprepared for the responsibilities of power which the collapse of the monarchy in early 1917 thrust upon them, or for the onslaught of Lenin's Bolshevism and the collapse of their hopes for Russian democracy. The disappointment was shared by contemporary Americans; the long-term challenge of the Bolshevik revolution was only dimly perceived, if at all.

2. Geographic

There have been five enduring factors in the structure and application of Soviet foreign policy—all of them related or similar to factors which have operated throughout much of Russian history. These are geographic, demographic, economic, military and ideological.

The main geographic fact about the Soviet Union is its domination of the central position on the Eurasian land mass. That position is the essential foundation of Soviet power today, providing actual or potential access by land to the whole of the Eurasian continent. In periods of Russian weakness that position—with the world's largest land frontier—has been a liability. In periods of strength it has been an immense asset—as today when it facilitates control of the East European states and makes Warsaw Pact military power, or Soviet troops on the Chinese frontier, potent political levers in the Soviets' international dealings. The enormous territorial additions in Europe and Asia in the 19th and 20th centuries, both incorporated territories and dependencies, and the scope of contemporary Soviet influence in bordering states from Norway to Korea, both derive from this unique geographic position.

Geography has also greatly influenced the U.S.-Soviet relationship, it has isolated the two states from one another through much of their history, and greatly complicated the American postwar task of countering Soviet direct or indirect expansionist initiatives, because of the relative remoteness of the United States from the strategically important areas of Western Europe and East Asia threatened by Soviet power. The American disadvantage was offset until the 1960s by Soviet logistical limitations which confined military action to contiguous regions, and by virtual invulnerability to Soviet military attack. But that advantage was compromised by the advent of Soviet parity in strategic weaponry in the late 60s, and the building of powerful Soviet naval and long-distance air support forces in the 70s. Meanwhile the expansion of Soviet strategic bases abroad—from Cuba to Ethiopia, South Yemen and Vietnam—was accompanied by a reduction of the counterpart positions in some of the same regions by America or American allies. Though geographic positions remain constant, other factors—especially the new logistical capacity—have greatly amplified the Soviet geographic advantage.

3. Demographic and Ethnic

The populations of the United States (241 million) and the Soviet Union (281 million) are not sufficiently different in size to make a substantial difference in actual or potential power, and the difference has narrowed substantially over the course of the 20th century. The dominant Soviet ethnic group, the Great Russians, comprise about 50 percent of the total, but the closely related Belorussians and Ukrainians bring the share of the East Slavic group to about 75 percent.

Since most of the many minority nations within the Soviet Union are located along the nation's borders, the government has been historically very sensitive to the danger of nationalist movements, and hence fearful of encouragement or manipulation of national aspirations by enemies, as was done by the Germans in both world wars. Though it has not been U.S. policy actively to encourage resistance by minority peoples to Russian rule, the national question has figured in U.S.-Soviet relations. The large numbers of refugees and immigrants in the United States (Estonians, Latvians, Lithuanians, Ukrainians and Jews, in particular) with strong feelings about Soviet policies toward their homelands or people have led them to seek to influence American foreign policy in various ways. Thus treatment of minorities, and particularly of Jews, in both pre-revolutionary Russia and the Soviet Union, has often been an important factor in formation of American attitudes toward the Soviet Union, and has repeatedly affected U.S. relations with that country.

4. Sociological/Cultural

American difficulties in understanding and dealing with Russia did not begin with the Bolshevik Revolution. The memoirs of American, as of other foreign travelers, diplomats and businessmen in the 19th century, are full of descriptions of the Russians' ponderous bureaucracy, their xenophobia, and other familiar themes. The contemporary relevance of the Marquis de Custine, for example, is often noted. However, the fact is that understanding did broaden as social contact expanded in the late 19th and early 20th centuries. In this regard, St. Petersburg had tens of thousands of foreign residents (50,000

Germans alone), and a very active commercial and cultural interchange with Europe and the rest of the world.

There remained a great gulf between the Russian educated class and the mass of the population, and the latter doubtless retained much of the traditional worldview of the village—were more "Russian" in that sense than the Westernized and cosmopolitan elite of the cities.

The popular worldview of today is formed by the Soviet system of mass education, and the attitudes and values it inculcates are quite specific, with important implications for international relations. The values taught stress the primacy of community and state interests over those of the individual, the notion of persistent class warfare, not only internally (where the eventual achievement of full socialism is expected to remove its basis), but also in the international arena (where the struggle with capitalism and imperialism will only end when socialism triumphs universally). It is this ideologically-derived worldview, universally and constantly repeated throughout the Soviet educational and communications process, that established the notion of two competing, irreconcilable worlds. This is strengthened and complicated by the limited contact between the two societies, which derives from the Soviet limitations on travel and of all forms of communication and information. This is a formidable addition to the usual difficulties of understanding and communication in international relations. Its most important consequence is that there is almost no independent public opinion to challenge or correct official presentation of the issues and conflicts in international affairs. A quick lesson on this subject is provided by the very one-sided Soviet press commentary on the war in Afghanistan.

5. Economic

Marx perceived in the middle 19th century that capitalism was rapidly drawing the nations of the world together. Whether they were in the vanguard group of industrial states or the less developed states which provided raw materials and markets, they were increasingly drawn into the vortex of the growing international capitalist trading and industrial economy. Certainly Russia in her first period of rapid industrialization—roughly the quarter century before World War I—illustrates the point. Foreign investment and investors multiplied rapidly, beginning with the new railroads and continuing through banking and joint stock companies and a wide range of industrial activities. Russian foreign trade expanded rapidly.

The economic system of the Soviet era functions in a way that is almost the opposite of that of the era of Russian capitalism—that is, it has a strong autarkic tendency. A combination of high costs and low quality of manufactures has set sharp limits to exports, while the lack of a convertible currency has also severely limited international trade. Meanwhile the lack of competition and profit motivation have discouraged organizational efficiency and technological innovation.

Hence the periodic pressure, from the 1920s to the present, for major imports of foreign technology, and the heavy dependence upon foreign sources—capitalist countries—of new technology. The result is that the Soviet economy has become an inefficient, technologically backward economy whose exports consist mainly of energy and raw materials.

The other side of the centrally planned economy—whatever its internal inefficiencies—is the capacity of the state to use international economic relations as an instrument of its diplomacy, holding out for example, important export opportunities as carrots when seeking favorable political terms. Carefully targeted, such measures can play an important part in diplomatic relations with American allies, though (except for grain purchases) this has less impact in American-Soviet relations. In general, it seems clear that, without significant modifications, the Soviet economy is unlikely to become a major factor in the trade of most capitalist states, or of most developing countries. On the other hand, the sheer size of the economy, and the enormous resources of energy and raw materials provide the basis of Soviet power, especially military power, and give the Soviets the capacity to make crucial contributions to the economic viability of allies and thus maintain their support. These are vital factors in the Soviet-American rivalry.

6. Military

Soviet diplomacy inherits from Lenin a strong conviction of the importance of force in achieving revolutionary objectives, and it has used it extensively, first to conquer power in Russia, and then to extend that power to neighboring states. Soviet Russia set the pattern, followed by most communist states since that time, of employing universal peacetime military conscription, enormous expenditure on war industries, and huge standing military forces. What is important—and a continuing theme of Soviet policy—is the persistent view of military power as a political instrument at the service of the revolution.

None of the major states of the modern era has placed greater emphasis upon military power than has Russia. The Muscovite "service state" of the 15th and 16th centuries bound all classes of the population to obligations whose main purpose was to sustain the power of the rulers and protect and expand the territory of the state. Land possession and state service, chiefly military, were closely bound together. The structure was transformed by Peter the Great and his successors in the 18th century, giving the Russian Empire a huge standing army, and a new navy, on the model of the absolutist monarchies of Central Europe. The modernized Russian military power was the key instrument of an enormous territorial expansion in the 18th and 19th centuries, as it is a central factor of Soviet power today, and the Russian armed forces have been Europe's largest for most of the past two centuries.

The functions of the military organization, and its relationship to society, show substantial similarities in the pre- and post-revolutionary periods. The functions were both defensive and offensive. Russia's vast territory and her long and vulnerable border exposed her to foreign attack, the main examples in modern times being the Napoleonic invasion and the German invasions in two world wars. But the armed forces have been equally important in the expansion and control of Russia's vast imperial domains. Military power was essential to the remarkable Russian expansion of the 18th and 19th centuries—in Europe, Transcaucasia, Central Asia and the Far East—adding territories more than double the size of the present territory of the United States. Military power also played a vital role in the internal defense of the empire, as in the suppression of periodic rebellions of the Russian Emperor's Polish subjects during the 19th century. Nevertheless, throughout the imperial era the financial costs of the military system, not to mention the social costs of permanent compulsory military conscription, bore heavily upon a state which was exceedingly poor by the standards of the major European powers.

The Soviet period began with noble proclamations of commitment to the abolition of empire and imperialism, and the traditional state and military organizations which sustained them. The proclamations were sincere enough, but the ideology of the new revolutionary state created conflicting imperatives. If the communist party was to monopolize political power, as Lenin insisted it must, domestic opposition to that power could only be suppressed by military means. The tiny military forces which buttressed the Bolshevik coup of October 1917 became a conscript army of 3.5 million by the end of the Civil War. Foreign invaders, to which contemporary official histories give such prominence in describing the Civil War era, were either bought off with large concessions, as with the Germans at Brest-Litovsk, or were only an occasional and unreliable source of support for domestic opponents, never acting in earnest to overturn of Bolshevik power, as in the case of the Allies. The real purpose of the massive military mobilization was to defeat anti-communist Russian and non-Russian internal forces and to establish communist power in as much of the prewar empire as circumstances would allow.

Since the Civil War the Soviet economy has been on a permanent wartime footing, mobilized not just for general expansion but for expansion of military power in particular. Certainly the conventional problems of state security have continued to be important, especially before and during World War II. But in the postwar era as well military power has expanded enormously and at very great cost—so great that the central preoccupation of the Gorbachev leadership is to reduce the burden of the military on a faltering economy. As before, there are conventional security requirements, and these have grown with the U.S.-Soviet global competition, itself a function of periodic expansion of American armaments in response to perceived security challenges from the actions of the Soviets or their clients.

But most of the actual postwar use of Soviet arms has been to control the new empire in Eastern Europe and Afghanistan, and the largest postwar buildup of conventional forces was occasioned by the conflict with China from the 1960s forward. Otherwise, the central role of Soviet arms has been to provide a protective cover and aid for Soviet clients (as with Cuba in 1962 and Egypt at various times in the 60s and 70s) or to reduce or eliminate the capacity of the U.S. or other rivals to block Soviet actions on the international scene. The pattern of economic organization and state power, combined with the Soviets' perception of themselves as the supporting center of an international revolutionary enterprise, provides rationale and motivation for the constant maintenance of a major military power.

B. PRE-WAR SOVIET POLICIES

Competition and conflict between the United States and the Soviet Union became the central factors in international relations at the end of World War II. They remain the central factors today, and are likely to remain so for the indefinite future, though conceivably with a diminished military component.

The war was the turning point because it shattered Germany's drive for hegemony in Europe and Japan's drive for hegemony in Asia, creating a power vacuum in both regions. That vacuum was soon filled by Soviet and American military power and alliance systems, but not without much conflict and the tendency toward political, ideological and military polarization of the globe. Social and economic revolutions in many parts of the globe have continued to change the political landscape, creating both dangers and opportunities for the two sides in the continuing competition.

Although the Second World War set the stage for a global U.S.-Soviet conflict, the First World War and Russian Revolution introduced the ideas and institutions that would inspire and guide it. Woodrow Wilson articulated the American view of the new global order: self-determination of states, democratic governance, and the peaceful rule of law among nations regulated by the League of Nations and its related institutions. Lenin also talked of democracy, national self-determination and peace, but his definitions of these terms—in word and deed—bespoke a vision opposite to that of Wilson. Democracy meant not popular sovereignty and parliamentary government but the dictatorship of a single authoritarian party. Self-determination was interpreted to justify military intervention by the Red Army, or Russian support of internal insurrection in neighboring states, on the grounds that only proletarian (i.e., communist) political power could properly exercise that right. Peace meant refusal to fight in the armies and wars of "bourgeois" states and willingness to fight for socialist revolution, while peace in the conventional sense of the term was an objective achievable only at the end of a global revolutionary process leading to socialism and communism.

It is these ideological differences represented by Wilson and Lenin that have motivated and dominated the American-Soviet relationship of the post-World War II era. The competing ideologies received very different implementation in the interwar years. Leninism prevailed in Russia and in most of the border territories of the prewar Russian Empire, ultimately through the victories of the Red Army. Beyond the borders of the Soviet Union the revolutionary mission was entrusted to a remarkable new strategy which combined "conventional" diplomacy with a variety of front movements and foreign communist parties.

The Communist International (Comintern) established the obligatory ideological and organizational model for foreign parties by the early 20s, and regulated their affairs through the Comintern executive committee in Moscow. The interwar years brought the development and testing of a variety of revolutionary stratagems—for the industrial societies of Western Europe, North America and Japan, or the agrarian societies of much of the rest of the globe. The central point is that the Soviet government endorsed and employed both direct armed force and clandestine support of foreign communist parties to advance the cause of communist power. The communists thus exhibited, despite many errors, an impressive strategic and tactical virtuosity, borrowing from the experience of the Russian revolution and adapting themselves both to alliances with leftist parties in parliamentary democracies and nationalist movements in colonial or semi-colonial dependencies of the European states.

The policy was fraught with potential for diplomatic conflict. French, British and Dutch complaints of Soviet links with revolutionary movements in their colonies were frequent, and complaints of internal subversion led in the late twenties to an Anglo-Soviet war scare and to the severance of diplomatic relations by Britain, as well as a short border war with Nationalist China. The disruption of relations with other states because of Soviet support of revolution abroad was a well-established pattern of the interwar years, a pattern that was merely continued after World War II in a new context and with new actors. Equally clearly established was the emphasis upon military power, the Soviet Union being the most heavily armed state in the world by the 1930s. At that point, however, the defensive rationale for such power was clear.

U.S. involvement with the Soviets during these years was relatively remote and limited. The democratic model of the victorious World War I allies was widely and spontaneously emulated after the war, especially in Central and Eastern Europe and in Latin America. But most of the new democracies proved to be frail structures, giving way to a variety of authoritarian regimes or the new fascist power that conquered first in Italy and then in Germany and Spain. Disappointment in the Wilsonian vision, and retreat into isolation, tended to insulate America from the conflicts with (and from the understanding of) the

Soviet Union experienced by closer neighbors in Europe and Asia. Wilson had been disappointed in the collapse of the Provisional Government in 1917, and with it the hopes for a Russian democracy. However, even during the Russian Civil War he had refused to endorse military action aimed at overturning Bolshevism, endorsing only strategic military action indicated by the continuing struggle with the Central Powers and by his desire to block Japanese expansion in the Russian Far East. Lenin's overturn of the Provisional Government, his repudiation of the Russian government's prerevolutionary debts, and his revolutionary attacks on all "bourgeois" regimes sufficed to maintain the U.S. policy of diplomatic non-recognition until November 1933.

The effort to end U.S. isolationism did not come with or because of the diplomatic recognition of the Soviet Union in 1933. It came with the appearance of the aggressive, expansionist policies of Germany and Japan in the 1930s, policies which led to war in China in 1937, in Europe in 1939, and to world war through German invasion of the Soviet Union and the Japanese attack on Pearl Harbor in 1941. Meanwhile, the global economic depression had shaken confidence in capitalist economies, leading many, particularly intellectuals, to take a new view of what appeared a dynamic and rapidly developing socialist economy in Stalin's Soviet Union. The tendency to form a new and more positive view of the Soviet Union was also aided by the vigorous Soviet initiatives from 1934 through 1939 for the formation of a popular front against Germany and Japan, an activity which cast Stalin as the leader in the struggle against fascism in Germany, Italy and Spain. Much of this good will was lost with the Nazi-Soviet Pact in 1939, the occupation of Poland and the Baltic States, and the Winter War (1939-40) against Finland. Yet these events seemed to be quickly forgotten following the German invasion of the Soviet Union in June 1941.

C. IMPACT OF WORLD WAR II

American gratitude for the Soviet resistance to Hitler, and for the major role in his defeat, served to dissolve many reservations and many negative memories of earlier years and thus to facilitate acceptance of the view held by both Roosevelt and Churchill during World War II that a broad and constructive postwar cooperation with the Soviet leadership would be possible. British and American scholarly specialists meanwhile emphasized the growing conservatism and nationalism of many of Stalin's internal policies of the 1930s, developments believed to demonstrate abandonment of revolutionary commitments. Wartime reopening of churches and reestablishment of the Orthodox Patriarchate, as well as the dissolution of the Comintern, greatly strengthened such views, views which both Roosevelt and Churchill found highly encouraging.

From the Soviet viewpoint, the interwar years, though difficult in many ways, had brought valuable experience and valuable gains which would serve them well during and after the war. Communist parties were intact and active in much of Axis-occupied Europe and Asia, using political and military strategy and tactics developed through experiences extending from the Bolshevik Revolution to the civil wars in China and Spain. These parties, and their Soviet patron, had also acquired both experience and skill in influencing public opinion and governments through their links with trade unions and other mass organizations and movements. Meanwhile, the conflicts in Europe and Asia (assuming eventual participation in the Pacific war) held promise of direct Soviet contact and support for revolution beyond the Soviet borders, an opportunity recalling the aftermath of World War I in Central and Eastern Europe.

How far this promise would be realized—and how pursuit of such goals would affect Soviet-American relations—would depend very heavily on British and American attitudes and policies towards the Soviet ally. In addition to the massive Anglo-American aid effort, a variety of specific wartime policy decisions were encouraging. There was the silence of Anglo-American leadership about Soviet occupation of the Baltic states, the acquiescence in Soviet demands on the Polish eastern boundary at Teheran, the shift of British support from the Royal Yugoslav government and its resistance representative Mihailovic, to the communist resistance leader Tito, and the urging of Stalin by Roosevelt for Soviet armies to enter the Pacific War at the conclusion of hostilities in Europe. Such measures gave Stalin and his European communist allies a number of important advantages and indicated a generous mood of cooperation on the Western side. Meanwhile the advance of the Red Army into Eastern Europe provided many opportunities for direct Soviet influence upon the postwar political arrangements for that region.

Beginning with Poland during the war, however it was Western opposition to the emerging nature and scope of Soviet purposes in Central and Eastern Europe that ultimately precipitated the conflict and collapse of the wartime alliance and established the postwar pattern of East-West confrontation. From the withdrawal of recognition of the Polish London government in April 1943 to the formation of the nucleus of a Soviet-sponsored Polish postwar government at Lublin in January 1945, the Soviets made clear their intention to control Poland's political future. Conflict over Soviet action in Poland—the very country whose invasion had been the *casus belli* in September 1939—was one part of the larger process of Sovietization in Central and Eastern Europe.

The process unfolded slowly. Most countries passed through real or bogus coalition governments to monolithic communist control, a procedure which helped obscure the Soviet influence and the main trend. Churchill's efforts from late summer 1944 to shift Western policy decisively by moving to occupy the maximum possible territory, including the whole of Germany and Czechoslovakia, in order to bargain effectively with the Russians, was rejected by the American side. American policymakers preferred to work for continued cooperation with the Soviets, seeking their commitment to enter into the Pacific War (and hence into opportunities for direct military/political intervention in Manchuria and Korea on the East European model). And when, at the moment of victory in Europe in the spring of 1945, the Sovietization process continued, the Western response at Potsdam in July 1945 was to demand free elections in Eastern Europe within a year. This was a renewed commitment both to cooperation with the Soviets and to the Western vision of a democratic postwar order throughout Europe, east and west, but it could be no more than a futile gesture. By February of 1948, with the communist coup in Prague, the Sovietization process was complete throughout Eastern Europe.

From the Soviet viewpoint the process was generally a success, though not without its shortcomings. The vigilance of democratic leaders saved Finland in early 1948 from Czech-style communist subversion, and British and American military support enabled the Greek government to resist a powerful communist guerrilla effort to gain control of postwar Greece. Other Soviet disappointments were the success of the Anglo-American airlift in preventing full absorption of Berlin, West as well as East, into East Germany through the blockade of 1948-9, and the break with Tito in June 1948, a failed effort to bring the Yugoslav communist party leadership and policy under Stalin's control.

Stalin clearly also hoped for larger gains from the war in Turkey and Iran. His unsuccessful efforts to extract strategic and territorial concessions from Turkey in the spring of 1945, and the necessity of abandoning the second effort to Sovietize the Azerbaijani territories of Northeastern Iran (1946), also contributed to the increasing strain in relations with the United States. The Truman Doctrine of March 1947 offered U.S. aid for countries threatened by communist subversion, though effectively it applied only to countries outside the orbit of Soviet power and was directed initially at Turkey and Greece. The Truman Doctrine, combined the Marshall Plan which aimed at the economic reconstruction of Europe, and in 1949 the creation of the NATO military alliance, which eventually (1954) included Western Germany among the European allies, became the cornerstones of "containment" as articulated by George Kennan in February 1947.

Stalin undoubtedly saw the offer of the Marshall Plan aid to all of Europe, including the Soviet Union, as a scheme to use U.S. economic power to buttress non-communist political forces in Eastern Europe. Hence he rejected it, not only for the Soviets but also for the other East European states under his direct or indirect control.

By 1950 the division of Europe—and the division of Soviet and American spheres of influence in Europe—had been completed. The

western portion, with Marshall Plan aid and under democratic governments, accomplished perhaps the most remarkable reconstruction and
sustained economic growth in history, developing a growing system
of economic cooperation through the EEC and a broad structure of
European political cooperation. Within twenty-five years the partners
of the EEC alone had become the world's most productive economic
unit, accounting for a quarter of global economic output—slightly more
than the U.S. share and double that of the Soviet Union. Economic
progress combined with political stability and an effective NATO
alliance security structure to allay anxiety about the future of Europe.
    In the Far East the defeat of Japan opened up remarkable oppor-
tunities for Soviet influence in that region in the early postwar era.
Entering the war on August 8, only two days before the Japanese sur-
render, Soviet armed forces occupied Manchuria and Southern Sakhalin
immediately, subsequently taking North Korea and the Kuriles. From
their positions in Manchuria they were able to aid the Chinese communists. They used their position in North Korea to carry forward a
communization similar to that in East Germany. Though denied the
position they sought in the occupation of Japan, they found opportunities to influence the postwar development of East and Southeast
Asia through local communist parties.
    The pattern of application of Soviet influence in postwar Asia had
three variants. In the first, the Chinese communists were assisted with
transfers of surrendered Japanese arms and by the Soviets delaying
Nationalist military occupation of Manchuria while the communists
occupied much of the country and prepared to resist the Nationalists.
The second variant was the communization of North Korea under a
communist leadership consisting mainly of Koreans arriving from the
Soviet Union—many of them with military and political training
acquired there. The third was indirect influence applied through communist parties, especially those which had become powerful in wartime resistance movements, such as the Vietnamese, Indonesian, Malay-
sian and Philippine communist parties. Without assuming total Soviet
control and coordination, it is possible to note a broad pattern of communist offensives beginning globally in 1947-8, probably with Soviet
political coordination.
    The crucial years were 1947-8 during which the non-communist
political parties and their leaders were largely absorbed, neutralized
or destroyed in Eastern Europe and North Korea, communist parties
in Western Europe (most importantly France and Italy) and in Japan
abandoned all cooperation with non-communist parties and organized
massive strikes, demonstrations and other disruptions. Moreover,
parties with influence or control of guerrilla forces organized major
insurrections aimed at acquisition of political influence or control by
military means (e.g. Philippines, Indonesia, Malaya, Vietnam and
Burma).
    The climax of these events in Asia came with the proclamation of

the Chinese People's Republic in October 1949 and the North Korean invasion of South Korea in June 1950. Clearly, the U.S. decision to meet the North Korean challenge succeeded. The war reached a stalemate by 1951 with the fighting concentrated north of the 38th parallel.

In Asia as in Europe the postwar communist offensive had mostly exhausted its resources by the early 1950s. The question of how the vacuum left by German and Japanese defeat would be filled had thus been settled. Communist regimes ruled in Easter Europe,, China, North Korea and (from 1954) in North Vietnam. Already in November 1952 at the Nineteenth CPSU Congress it was acknowledged that the time had come for a "relaxation of tensions," and with Stalin's death the following year the signs of change appeared quickly: the truce in Korea (July 1953); the agreement for the division of Vietnam (1954); the Austrian State Treaty (1955). Furthermore, during the same years most of the communist insurrection leaders abandoned their offensives, many achieving settlement agreements with the new nationalist regimes they had lately sought to overturn.

D. SOVIET-AMERICAN RELATIONS SINCE 1953

1. The General Situation in 1953

Soviet-American relations in the post-Stalin era have followed a complex course and the central threads are easily lost, particularly if one fails to pursue the analysis with due attention to the Soviets' own perception of the relationship and their goals within it. The main point for Stalin's successors, and one already noted before Stalin's death at the Nineteenth CPSU Party Congress, was that a position of stalemate had been reached—that the revolutionary opportunities and the opportunities for extension of Soviet power that had come with the political dislocation of World War II were at an end and a new period of stability had arrived. Meanwhile, the U.S. had built, or was building, a system of alliances ringing the Soviet territory; the new nationalist regimes that had succeeded the colonial powers had stabilized their political power; and in the capitalist states, economic recovery from the war was underway bringing political stability.

What was now required was a policy similar to that pursued by Lenin in 1921 when postwar stability returned to Europe—formally to terminate the revolutionary offensive, to end Soviet diplomatic isolation, and to allow opposition to subside. The language of the early post-Stalin foreign policy commentary, beginning with Malenkov's major foreign policy address in August 1953, recalled both the concepts and policies of the early 1920s. It spoke of a need for "relaxation of tensions" and of "peaceful coexistence." And soon the communist parties of Western Europe were being urged to adopt the policy of "united front" (i.e., to abandon revolutionary attack in favor of alliance with socialist and other left-wing parties).

The main aims of Soviet policy as a whole at this juncture, and their connection with policies toward the U.S., are not difficult to discern. Europe was a central focus of Soviet problems and concerns. In the east there were already rumblings in Czechoslovakia and East Germany which were rooted in the Stalin policy of forcible transformation of the political, social and economic institutions of Eastern Europe on the Soviet model and anticipated the greater explosions of 1956. Pressures had to be relaxed and efforts made to gain greater support for communist leaderships and to lessen popular hostility to their policies. Such efforts would lead even to the renewal of ties with Tito and to the acceptance of the potentially dangerous notion of many paths to socialism.

In Western Europe the chief concern was the success of the U.S. in the formation of the NATO Alliance, as well as the movement toward European economic and political unity. Malenkov's speech noted the "internal conflicts and contradictions" that persisted in the relations between the European states, and between Europe and the U.S., suggesting that once the tension in relations with the Soviet Union subsided these would revive. A related concern was the weakness and isolation of the major West European communist parties, mainly the result of their failed political offensive in the Cold War era.

New policies were also badly needed for the non-aligned states. Soviet policy statements had heaped contempt upon the major new nationalist leaders of Asia and the Middle East, treating them as lackeys of the former colonial powers, docile instruments of a successor system of "neo-colonialism." Even where such a policy made sense—as part of an effort to undermine and weaken nationalist leaderships with which communist parties or communist-led alliances struggled for power—the political stabilization of such countries no longer justified it. As with the communist parties of Europe, a "united front" policy seemed best suited to the circumstances. Communists could enter such fronts to broaden their support and to work for suitable domestic and foreign policies. A central objective both of Soviet policy and of the policy of local communist parties was to weaken the prestige and support for the former colonial states and of the U.S. For this effort it was essential to portray the U.S. as the arch-imperialist power. The absence of visible colonies was no obstacle to the line; the notion of neo-colonialism had its twin—neo-imperialism.

Soviet policy toward the U.S. was also badly in need of readjustment. The former wartime ally had become the major Soviet adversary and competitor in eight short years. The *coup de grace* had been delivered by the Soviet side—Stalin's approval of the invasion of South Korea—an invasion which precipitated an enormous acceleration of U.S. armament, aided the passage of the U.S.-Japanese security treaty, and generally tightened the structure of U.S. alliances from Europe to the Far East. The aim of Soviet policy had to be to change the atmosphere of U.S.-Soviet relations, reducing the tension in the relationship and, as possible, U.S. commitment to armaments, alliances, intervention—all of the elements of the U.S. policy of containment that reduced Soviet options and effectiveness. The broad aim of the policy, then, was to dismantle, to the degree possible, the organizational and ideological structure of U.S. containment policy.

2. The Soviet Leadership

The main architect of Soviet policy for most of the first decade of the post-Stalin era was Nikita Khrushchev, a man of considerable imagination and intelligence who would also acquire a justified reputation for impulsiveness. The main purposes just outlined, and the traditions and objectives of Soviet policy remained in place; Khrushchev added a variety of unusual touches—his personal diplomacy, his destalinization, his revision of relations with other communist states, his efforts to reduce the military budget.

Khrushchev operated with a revised concept of the U.S.-Soviet relationship. Determined to achieve direct personal contact, he traveled widely in the U.S., taking the measure of its industry, its agriculture, its cities and its people. More realistic—and certainly more knowledgeable—about America than Stalin, he nonetheless believed in the Soviet capacity to overtake and surpass the American economy, as his 1962 Party Program confidently forecast. At the same time, following the example set by Stalin, Khrushchev further downgraded the concept of the inevitability of war with the capitalist states. In his *Economic Problems of Socialism of 1952* Stalin had abandoned the notion of capitalist encirclement—and its attendant notion of inevitable conflict with capitalist states—in favor of the idea that conflict of socialist and capitalist states was not inevitable, that in fact conflicts among capitalist states were more likely. Khrushchev added the notion that the age of thermonuclear weaponry made general war unthinkable because of the huge destructive power of such weapons.

The U.S.-Soviet relationship during the Khrushchev years underwent important changes. In addition to the close personal contacts with presidents Eisenhower and Kennedy, the establishment of a variety of exchange contacts (cultural, educational, scientific), and the renewal of trade, Khrushchev did much to give the Soviet Union a less forbidding image in the United States, as among American allies in Europe. He thus laid the groundwork for the change in East-West relations in the 60s and early 70s.

The Brezhnev era brought a gradual but steady retreat from the internal liberalization of the Khrushchev years—in dealings with intellectual dissent, in general cultural controls, in the vigorous reevaluations of the experience of the Stalin era. During the Brezhnev era there was a degree of continuity with the foreign policies of the Khrushchev years, though it began with a vigorous though ultimately abortive effort to patch up the quarrel with China. Brezhnev's main foreign policy emphases with regard to U.S.-Soviet relations, were four: 1) an enormous military buildup aiming to expand Soviet capacity and Soviet power, especially in the competitive relationship with the United States; 2) a vigorous European policy aiming to strengthen Soviet influence in all spheres and to reduce the effectiveness of the American alliance structure; 3) a much broader and more aggressive policy in Asia, particularly East Asia, combined with military buildup in that region comparable to Europe; and 4) a very energetic forward policy in the third world.

3. Military Developments

No factor is of greater importance in the emergence of the Soviet Union as a global power than is the military. Lenin clearly understood the importance of the military instrument for the seizure and maintenance of Bolshevik power, and the first Soviet government used the Red Army not only to defend its power in Russia, but also to reconquer much of the former empire and to attempt to spread the revolution even beyond these limits. Soviet victory in World War II would not have been possible without the enormous investment in military power from the 20s to the outbreak of the war—an investment not only in the world's largest army but in the massive new military industrial plant that equipped and supplied it.

As with all states, the first task of the military organization was defense. The defensive priority dominated through much of the Civil War which the Bolsheviks fought to maintain power from 1918-20, and again in the struggle with the Axis powers in World War II. But just as the use of the army against internal or foreign military opposition was seen as "defense of the revolution," to send the army abroad and to use its power to establish communist political control in other countries was a legitimate service to the extension of the revolution, and Lenin began to do so as early as January 1918 with the invasions of Finland and the Ukraine. Soviet commentators speak proudly of the revolutionary mission of the military during and after World War II when the Soviet Army helped the weak communist parties in East Germany, Poland, Czechoslovakia, Hungary, Romania, and Bulgaria to take power and initiate a gradual social transformation.

It is, of course, precisely this dimension of Soviet policy that aroused the fear and hostility of the Soviet Union's wartime allies and precipitated the Cold War. Therefore the enormous increase in Soviet military power in the post-Stalin era—and the development of the military prerequisites of global power—became a central factor in the U.S.-Soviet relationship. A few comments on the development and uses of Soviet military power since the 1950s are needed as background to the discussion of the political applications of that power.

The most important new development in Soviet weaponry in the 1950s was the rapid accumulation of strength in strategic (i.e., nuclear) weapons. Soviet power in Europe after the war was based on a preponderance of conventional forces and weapons. These forces were important not only to "initiate a gradual transformation" but also to discourage Western intervention in the process, since the massive Soviet ground forces appeared constantly to threaten the security of Western Europe and there was little wish to provoke them. Early Soviet advances in the technology of strategic weaponry were impressive: the launchings of the first ICBM in August 1957 and the first space satellite only three months later. But Soviet leaders were painfully aware of the advantages which the U.S. retained from its continuing superiority in nuclear weapons during the fifties. The caution that underlay their bluster over Berlin (in 1958 and after), and Soviet efforts to restrain Chinese aggressiveness toward the U.S. in the same period, reflected an understanding not just of the potential costs of nuclear war but of the American superiority in nuclear weaponry.

The early 1960s brought first a debate on Soviet strategic weapons needs, then a decision to pursue their priority development within a new military unit called strategic Rocket Forces. After 1960 the priority shifted from medium-range ballistic missiles (MRBM) and intermediate-range ballistic missiles (IRBM) to intercontinental (ICBM) missiles. Khrushchev's abortive attempt to deploy short-and intermediate-range missiles in Cuba in 1962—creating *ersatz* ICBMs, as one analyst put it—and thus move more rapidly and cheaply toward a strong position vis-a-vis the U.S., was only an interval. His successors recognized the necessity of challenging the American ICBM superiority directly and in kind. But their military program rejected exclusive emphasis on strategic weapons in favor of a comprehensive program of theater and strategic weapons and conventional forces, land and sea, as well as anti-air defense and a strong program of civil defense.

The results of their efforts over two decades are an enormous achievement with profound political consequences. By the end of the 1960s the Soviets had acquired what James Schlesinger called "essential equivalence" with the U.S. in strategic weaponry. Yet in spite of U.S. appeals for cooperation on setting weapons limits, beginning in 1964, it was not until 1972 that the Soviets agreed to limits, meanwhile building steadily. The SALT agreements of the 70s tended to stabilize deployment of strategic (intercontinental) weapons, but excluded theater weapons in which the Soviets proceeded to amass an enormous superiority in Europe and in East Asia, triggering the NATO Council decision of December 1979 to deploy the Pershing II and Cruise missiles if Soviet deployments were not reduced. Meanwhile, the enormous buildup and modernization of conventional land and naval forces proceeded apace. By the 1970s the Warsaw Pact forces had acquired a 2-to-1 margin over their NATO counterparts, and a similarly powerful deployment of land forces was underway in the Far East, especially along the Chinese border.

The Soviet challenge to the U.S. position has nowhere—not even in Western Europe—been more profound than in East Asia and the Pacific. The buildup was first visible in the expansion of the forces concentrated along the Chinese border—now some 51 divisions. At present these forces include strategic nuclear weapons with the capacity to reach any part of Asia; a theater nuclear force with 150 SS-20s and a fleet of 70 Backfire bombers; 2,000 combat planes; and a Pacific fleet with 128 submarines, including 31 nuclear ballistic missile SSBNs. Japan, which as been repeatedly rebuffed in its efforts to secure return of the southern Kurile Islands, has been challenged with growing Soviet military forces near Japan, including permanent bases in the Kuriles. Soviet Far Eastern forces are presently second only to those which face NATO.

The expansion of Soviet military power has done much to equalize the Soviet-American relationship, even to shift the power balance in the Soviets' favor. The Soviets now have the military power not only to defend the Soviet Union against all competitors, but the ability to project their power globally. It is instructive to consider capacities which derive from that power by examining their specific applications.

One of the most important uses of the Soviet power is control of the empire. This was evident in East Germany in 1953, in Hungary in 1956, and in Czechoslovakia in 1968. Even where that power has not been exercised, its mere existence acts as a powerful controlling force, as it did with the Poles in 1956 and in 1980-81. It has also discouraged Western states from direct meddling in Eastern Europe in times of crisis.

At the moment it is more problematic what will be the political uses of the enormously expanded Soviet power in Europe and East Asia. For Europe the combination of Soviet strategic and theater nuclear weaponry has greatly transformed its relationship both to the United States and to the Soviet Union. The December 1979 NATO Council decision on theater missile deployments was a response (originally a European response) to fears that the advent of Soviet strategic parity with the U.S., combined with Soviet European theater preponderance in nuclear and conventional weapons, would lead to a U.S. "decoupling" from Europe. The four-year interval for discussion and negotiations between the decision and the actual deployment were powerfully exploited by the Soviets to sow discord among the allies and to magnify European anxieties about nuclear warfare. The simultaneous increase of pressure upon Scandinavia—including the submarine harassment of Sweden—served further to demonstrate the new Soviet power in Europe.

4. Western Europe

For both the Soviets and the U.S., Western Europe continued to be the zone of maximum importance and maximum competition. Efforts to weaken the NATO alliance were central to Soviet policy. Khrushchev's "relaxation of tensions" of the 50s and early 60s made some gains, though these were offset by the unpleasant image of Soviet troops in Budapest and Soviet intransigence over Berlin, including the building of the Berlin Wall. But during the years of American involvement in Vietnam, a war in which American policy received little support in Europe, a number of developments combined to weaken the cohesion of the alliance and especially to increase criticism of American leadership.

The first of these was the new Soviet policy with its emphasis upon peaceful coexistence and trade, a policy which did much to relax European fears of Soviet military danger. The second factor was the growth of Soviet power in strategic weapons—especially the deployment of ICBMs capable of striking North America. This development raised the possibility that the United States, newly vulnerable to Soviet missiles, might prefer to abandon Europe in a crisis rather than risk a missile exchange with the Soviets. Other frictions in NATO—over the implications of U.S. policies outside Europe and the lack of European control of the American Strategic Air Command—added to the concern over the American commitment, and led France to remove NATO forces and NATO headquarters from France in 1966.

The late 60s and early 70s brought the German *Ostpolitik* and the general détente between the NATO states and the Soviet Union. They also brought new problems for the alliance—the Greek withdrawal from the military structure (1974) on charges that Britain and the U.S. had failed to support her against Turkey over Cyprus, and the overturn of the Caetano dictatorship (1974) in Portugal which was followed by a period of internal turmoil that looked for a time likely to produce a communist dictatorship to follow on fascism.

But the NATO alliance survived. France remained a member and still wants and requires U.S. protection; Greece rejoined the military wing in 1980, and Spain joined in 1982, having made a remarkably successful transition from dictatorship to authentic democracy. But the new Soviet military power—described elsewhere—posed fundamental challenges, especially when combined with a powerful and well-orchestrated campaign using regular diplomatic channels and a much broader structure of communist party, front organizations and other channels to attack the security policies of the NATO governments from within.

The protracted Euromissile crisis lasted for four years from the NATO Council decision on Pershing and Cruise deployment in December 1979. The strain within NATO was great, though in the end Soviet refusal to make concessions, and a European propaganda campaign of unprecedented dimensions failed to block the deployment decision. The aftermath was marked by continuing and serious problems—dissatisfaction of sizable groups in Europe with the deployment decision; the division of the Social Democratic parties; and the formidable and still growing Soviet theater strategic and conventional forces, not just in Central Europe but in Northern Europe as well.

Meanwhile, however, the evidence of Western solidarity, the threat of the American plan for the SDI, and the Gorbachev leadership's concern for the mounting strain of military costs upon a faltering economy, appeared to underly a new Soviet interest in negotiating the reduction of intermediate range missiles in Europe. Whatever their motives, it was clear that the Soviets could create as severe divisive pressures within NATO by a policy of concessions as by one of intransigence.

5. East Asia

One of the most important modifications of the Soviet-American relationship in the post-Stalin years has been the transformation of that relationship in East Asia. In South Asia the Soviets succeeded brilliantly in their effort to establish close ties with India, taking advantage both of Sino-Indian and of Indo-Pakistani conflicts to become India's major supplier of arms and a major patron in economic aid. America meanwhile maintained a strong system of bilateral alliances, military forces and bases extending from South Korea and Japan to Taiwan and the Philippines. Until the mid-70s this structure remained intact, though the collapse of South Vietnam, and of the American support structure there in the mid-1970s combined with other changes to alter radically the security system in East Asia.

America had had little or no success in building a regional treaty structure to match that of NATO in Europe. The Southeast Asia Treaty Organization, formed in September 1954, included Australia, France, Great Britain, New Zealand, the Philippines, Thailand, and the United States. Pakistan was also a member until 1973, but the main treaty group never became really effective and was dissolved in 1977. It had failed to secure the membership of the largest Asian nations—India, Indonesia and Japan—and those states which were members could not agree on the seriousness of the communist threat (the containment of communist expansion was to be the main purpose, following on the French defeat in Indochina in 1954). Only Australia, New Zealand and Thailand joined the U.S. in sending troops to support South Vietnam during the Vietnamese war.

In the last stages of the Vietnamese War it appeared that there was a major revolution underway in the structure of strategic power in East Asia and that it was moving mainly in the Soviets' favor. The ability of the Soviets to continue supplying North Vietnam with the war materiel essential to its victory was itself a measure of the change in Soviet power. Their postwar assumption of the role of Vietnam's major patron and protector, and their support of Vietnam's conquest of Laos and Kampuchea, as well as the acquisition of military and naval facilities in that country, went with their overall military buildup in East Asia to shift the power balance significantly. Talk of withdrawal of American forces from Korea during the Carter administration seemed to complete the American withdrawal from the East Asian mainland, even as Soviet air missile and naval forces threatened American naval and offshore security systems.

There was, however, another crucial change underway, brought about by the revolution in China's diplomatic posture and by the spreading reaction throughout East and Southeast Asia to the growing Soviet military power, the Soviet-Vietnamese collaboration, and the Soviet invasion of Afghanistan. The Chinese shift in the early 70s, brought renewed contact and reconciliation with the United States, and eventually diplomatic relations with both the U.S. and Japan. An informal structure of tripartite cooperation emerged. Japan meanwhile moved toward a new security relationship with the U.S.—an alliance in all but name—and began steadily to expand its military and naval forces. The American recommitment to East Asia at the end of the 70s combined with other changes to rebuild a somewhat stabler power relationship in East Asia. Still the structure contained the potential for serious problems. China was effectively encircled by Soviet power— along the northern border, in Vietnam and Afghanistan, and in the seas washing her shores. Japan, now the world's second economic power, was still extremely weak militarily vis-a-vis the Soviets, as an island power exposed to overwhelming Soviet naval, rocket and conventional forces. The Soviet naval forces controlled the three strategic straits (Soya, Tsugaru and Tsushima) and were developing a capacity to control the Strait of Malacca as well.

American sea, air and strategic weaponry still held the Soviets' power frontier to the Western Pacific, but the Soviets were busily probing weak points—the Philippines and Micronesia—for possible new avenues of advance.

6. Revolutions in Both Worlds: Impact on U.S.-Soviet Relations

The Soviets have had to develop policies toward revolutions of two kinds in the post-Stalin era: revolutions within their bloc and revolutions outside it. Soviet actions with regard to the former appear to have caused less conflict in U.S.-Soviet relations than the latter, though both have complicated relations.

Though the label "Brezhnev Doctrine" developed from Leonid Brezhnev's statements at the time of the Czech crisis in 1968, the assumption of the Soviet right to intervene by every means including military to defend faltering communist regimes was clear in Soviet actions in 1953 and 1956. In spite of talk of "rollback of the iron curtain" in American political circles, no action was taken beyond protests. This reflected a tacit recognition that Eastern Europe was in the Soviet sphere and that the combination of overwhelming Soviet military power there and the danger of U.S. action—even if possible— would be too great. A similar—even more explicit—acquiescence prevailed at the time of the Soviet invasion of Czechoslovakia in 1968.

The detente years of the 70s had essentially contradictory consequences for Eastern Europe—particularly Poland. On the one hand the Helsinki Agreement of 1975 (following on important agreements with the Germans in 1969 and 1970) affirmed the territorial changes deriving from World War II, and seemed to accept Soviet hegemony in Eastern Europe. On the other, the detente years encouraged many East European leaders to pursue innovative economic policies, and their subjects to feel freer to press for political reform (especially in East Germany, Poland and Czechoslovakia). Similar expectations of detente existed in the U.S. and in Western Europe, so that the termination of Polish reform with the Declaration of Martial Law in December 1981, and the outlawing of Solidarity the following August, were a rude shock and brought a sharp U.S. response.

The events in Poland followed by just two years the December 1979 Soviet invasion of Afghanistan. That action too was undertaken to strengthen a faltering communist regime which had been placed in power with Soviet support in April 1978 but faced growing internal opposition to its policies, as well as a leadership split. The Soviets were probably genuinely surprised and annoyed by the U.S. response—termination of the grain agreement and a U.S.-led boycott of the Moscow Olympic Games—since there had been no comparable response at the time of the 1978 coup. In the interim, however, the overturn of the Shah and the Islamic Revolution in Iran had enormously increased U.S. concerns both about stability in the region and about Soviet intentions. An increasing Soviet military presence near the Afghan-Iranian border was a grave concern. Subsequent U.S. statements on the Soviet war in Afghanistan, and the military and diplomatic support of the opposition and of Pakistan, added to the tension in U.S.-Soviet relations.

It is significant that the Soviet actions in Czechoslovakia, Poland and Afghanistan have had major repercussions for Soviet relations with both governing and non-governing communist parties. The Soviet invasion of Czechoslovakia was denounced by the Chinese, already fearful of the Soviet military buildup on their borders and anxious about possible Soviet intervention in their affairs, and the Chinese expressed even sharper opposition to Soviet Afghan policy, becoming a major arms supplier to the Mujahedin. Both invasions were also denounced by several of the "Eurocommunist" parties—especially the Italian, Spanish and Japanese. For the Italians the Polish martial law was a crucial issue; Poland's transformation represented for Berlinguer and his colleagues the crucial test of the reformability of a Soviet-type system—a test whose failure was described as evidence that the potential of the Russian October Revolution was exhausted.

More crucial for U.S.-Soviet relations was Soviet policy in many areas of the Third World, independently and in cooperation with other bloc partners, especially Cuba. Egypt—from the Czech arms deal in 1955 to the ejection of the Soviets in 1972—was a constant source of friction. It was the focus of three major regional wars, and in 1973 provided the occasion for a U.S.-Soviet confrontation. The Egyptian-Israeli Peace Treaty of 1979, the culmination of a five-year-long process, represented a major change in the region.

Soviet operations in Egypt demonstrated—especially the rapid resupplying of the Egyptian forces by air in October 1973—the new Soviet logistical capacities for action in the Third World. The first thrust into Africa in the Congo in 1960 had lacked such backup, but the second major effort, in Angola and Mozambique following Portugal's abandonment of her African empire, once again demonstrated airlift capacities—the transportation of the Cuban troops which made possible MPLA victory in 1975, the same year when the communist-organized Frelimo took control from the Portuguese authorities in Mozambique, opening up a crucial region of Southern Africa to Soviet and Cuban influence. Meanwhile the U.S., just emerging from the Vietnamese conflict, and apparently convinced (notwithstanding Soviet protestations to the contrary) that detente meant an end to Soviet support of "wars of national liberation," lectured the Soviet leadership on the "linkage" between detente and Soviet behavior elsewhere, especially such provocative actions as those underway in Africa.

But the hectoring had little effect. Following British withdrawal from South Yemen in 1967, the government headed by the National Liberation Front, to which power was passed, was soon controlled by a Leninist regime and the country became the People's Democratic Republic of Yemen. During the mid-70s the Soviets gave strong support, including military, to communist consolidation of power. Similar Soviet actions in Somalia and Ethiopia in the mid-70s were seen in Washington as ominous signs that the detente process did not work. Soviet and Cuban action in support of revolution in the Caribbean and Central America has been an important irritant in U.S.-Soviet relations, and is likely to continue to be. The establishment of Leninist regimes in both Nicaragua and Grenada, followed by extensive support of the guerrilla insurrection in El Salvador from Nicaragua, were the central factors. The overturn of the Grenada regime in October 1983 by American armed forces, and the apparent stabilization in El Salvador following the June 1983 election of President Duarte, appeared to control the conflict. But the Soviet/Cuban armament of Nicaragua continued and U.S.-Soviet friction increased as well.

E. THE PAST AND THE FUTURE

There is an impressive continuity of problems and perceptions in the history of the U.S.-Soviet relationship. The first is the continuing ideological competition between two worldviews: the Wilsonian and the Leninist. Were the competition solely ideological, it would appear that the Wilsonian ideal is winning. Certainly, the number of democracies in the major states of the globe is growing, and the list of communist political victories since Stalin's death is unimpressive both in number and in content. Meanwhile the share of communist states in the global economic product continues to decline. Further-more, the Soviet Union itself, whose population and resources would justify a first place in the world economic ranking as Khrushchev predicted in 1962, has lately lost the second place position to Japan, a state with half its population and a small fraction of its land area and natural resources.

Yet the old problems and anxieties of the early postwar era persist: the concern with Soviet military power and the connection between the Soviets and communist revolution in a variety of areas of the globe. The central Soviet objective continues to be to make the world safe for revolution—revolution on the Soviet model. To break out of the American postwar containment system has been the continuing pre-occupation, and it has led to the largest and most sustained military buildup in history. To be sure, the scale of the buildup has generally (though not always) borne some relationship to the scale of American arms. American arms have in turn been a function both of the scale of Soviet arms and the perception of Soviet international aims.

Probably the Soviet arms buildup should be a greater concern than the danger of communist revolution, except where the latter occurs in strategically important territory. Moreover, the concern about Soviet arms should be more than a concern for peace, more than the fear of nuclear war which has dominated Western discourse on the subject. The important point is the present and future political implications of the scale and character of the Soviet arms buildup. One should be concerned about the preponderance of Soviet power in Europe©and East Asia—about the effective Soviet military hegemony in Eurasia, and how that hegemony might be used in the future. One should be con-cerned too about the evident Soviet aim to develop a series of vital strategic positions and strategic bases: the control of the Sea of Okhotsk and the Sea of Japan, the control of the straits around the Japanese archipelago, the possible future control of the Strait of Malacca from bases in Vietnam; the developing Soviet strategic positions in Ethiopia and South Yemen, in Southern Africa, and in the Caribbean and Cen-tral America.

The Soviets have wedded the administrative and military apparatus of an enormous empire to the rhetoric of an internal revolutionary movement. It is scarcely surprising that the power and intentions of that apparatus have become as much a matter of national security con-cern for non-governing communist parties (the Italian, Spanish and Japanese, to name some of the more important) and communist states (China and Yugoslavia, among others) as for leaders of the democratic states. It is significant that Soviet military action since World War II has been against East Germans, Hungarians, Czechs, Chinese and Afghans—all of them peoples who have already had a communist revolution. It has been noted by specialists on the Warsaw Treaty Orga-nization that a main purpose of the Soviet forces in Eastern Europe is to maintain Soviet control in that volatile and reluctant empire. It is also clear that the major Soviet conventional military forces in East Asia are deployed against China.

Perhaps a few concluding propositions are in order about what the past of U.S.-Soviet relations says about the future, especially about the likely continuity or change in the aims and form of Soviet policy. A few such propositions follow:

1. It is probably wise to take the Soviets at their word, to understand that they operate today on essentially the same worldview as did Lenin in 1917 and that they believe their mission is to spread their ideology and system globally; that they are prepared to work indefinitely, with very long-range planning, and with unstinting commitment of resources and human talent, to that end. Western commentators— politicians, journalists, academics, and others—have repeatedly produced analyses, ever since the Bolshevik Revolution, that insist that such purposes have declined in priority or even disappeared in Soviet policy. They have proven wrong.

It would be wise to devote more attention to this question, with particular focus on the complex ways in which the Soviets manage their ties to the communist movement abroad. There is a powerful impulse in Western analysis to project the structure and aims of Western foreign policymaking upon the Soviet Union, an impulse which Soviet policy encourages. It is significant that the Gorbachev presentation of Soviet foreign policy at the Twenty-Seventh CPSU Congress omitted entirely the kind of comprehensive presentation of the course of global communist revolution on which Brezhnev focused at the Twenty-Sixth Congress in 1981. The new leadership was well aware of the political costs of Brezhnev's glasnost' on this matter. Soviet support of third world revolution had combined with expansion of Soviet arms to derail the policy of detente.

2. The Soviets appear to seek overwhelming military power, but avoid war. They believe that the advance of communism will come in the future as it has in the past. First, it will come from revolutionary situations within countries in which an established power is overturned and the communists gain power, immediately or eventually, through control of the political and military/police apparatus to which the revolution gives rise. Such revolutions can be the product of a quick coup or a sustained guerrilla war. Tactical considerations—potential foreign intervention or internal opposition to communism—may require disguising the fact of communist control for some time, but the control of the levers of power is essential. Second, the advance of communism will come from the insertion, from outside, through military aid in the form of the troops of a communist state—for example, the Soviet troops entering Eastern Europe and North Korea, the Cubans in Angola, or the North Vietnamese in South Vietnam, Laos and Kampuchea. Such troops may have local political and military allies (e.g., local guerrilla forces), but the main point is that the power of the regular military forces of the foreign communist state is decisive.

There has never been a communist party come to power by victory in a democratic national election. The Soviets have allowed for this possibility, though clearly without much optimism. They have repeatedly stressed the need to gain control of the instruments of coercion—the-army, the police and the judiciary—in such situations, and to avoid "punctilious observance of parliamentary procedure." The elections and the parliamentary process are merely instruments in the revolutionary process, not an end in themselves.

In all of these situations the ideal arrangement is to have a sufficiently credible Soviet military power that no external opponent, including the U.S., will feel it is either feasible or safe to intervene. The Soviets have consistently shown great caution in such matters; they have erred only in situations in which the United States gave confusing signals, as in the case of Korea before the Korean War.

3. The U.S. role remains central in containing the outward thrust of Soviet power, and the extension of communist revolution either by the Soviets or by Cuban or other surrogates. The NATO alliance remains a viable structure for this policy in Europe, but the growing Soviet military power in Europe, and the continued absence of an effective European capacity to manage a separate European defense structure, means little change in the American role. Both the American public, and the European publics, are inclined to forget the role and importance of the NATO alliance, particularly in periods of relatively friendly relations with the Soviets. In Asia, without a NATO counterpart, the responsibility continues to fall more heavily on U.S. shoulders and the security structure remains weak compared to the importance of the region and U.S. interests.

4. It has been Soviet policy to search for the weakest point in the American and Western system of alliances and associated states, and probe there. The Soviets, for example, were quick to seek cooperation with President De Gaulle when they perceived his differences with the U.S. and with NATO. They perceived and sought (unsuccessfully) to exploit the instability of Spain and Portugal during the transition from fascist power to democracy.

The management of the long controversy over nuclear arms in Europe demonstrates a consistent effort, under Gorbachev as under his predecessors, to give priority to maximizing the strains of the controversy upon internal European politics, and upon the relations of the European NATO powers with the United States, rather than to achievement of an equitable agreement. Similarly, the Soviets have sought to exacerbate the Greek-Turkish dispute, so divisive for NATO, and have appealed to the anti-American sentiments unleashed in Japan by U.S.-Japanese trade tensions.

The crisis situations around the globe which offer some short-term prospect of expansion of the company of communist states are relatively few—the Philippines, South Africa and Central America. But there is a host of other crisis situations where longer term prospects exist, and where the task is to exploit opportunities for a reduction of Western and an increase in Soviet influence.

5. The Soviets are, in recent years, doing much more in the field of "inter-societal" relations. They are seeking to build more direct links with individuals and organizations for the purpose of gaining acceptance of Soviet foreign policy views in order to put pressure from within upon their governments. This is not a new policy, but it is recently applied more broadly and effectively. The massive propaganda effort in Europe during the first phase (1979-83) of the Euromissile debate is an impressive example of this policy in its recent form. A similar example is provided by the international propaganda program mounted in support of Soviet and Cuban initiatives in Central America and the Caribbean in the same period.

The Gorbachev leadership has refined both the organization and the policies for such efforts in a most impressive fashion, meanwhile greatly diminishing the Brezhnev-era emphasis upon Soviet military power and upon support for third-world communist revolution.

Clearly the second half of the eighties represents another of the periodic phases of Soviet foreign policy in which the emphasis is upon "relaxation of tensions". Soviet spokesmen address appeals for a united fronts to foreign socialist parties, while Soviet foreign policy emphasizes "interdependence" and "mutual security" and offers a veritable shower of disarmament proposals. Meanwhile, Soviet policy seeks also to cope with the legacy of problems inherited from the earlier period of aggressive political and military expansion—the strained relationship with China, the war in Afghanistan, the world-wide insurrections against the new communist power in Central America, Africa, and Southeast Asia, the NATO deployment of Pershing and Cruise missiles and the U.S. commitment to SDI.

Certainly no phase of Soviet policy is an exact replication of an earlier phase. Yet there is compelling evidence of a structure of alternating phases of offense and detente. The evidence today is of a new phase of detente. In the last phase the Soviets sought to consolidate recent gains, reduce the cohesion of opposing alliances, and refurbish the national economy with large importations of Western capital and technology. In the current phase the structure of objectives is very similar. In the interim between phases Soviet global power has substantially increased, in both political and military terms. The Soviet capacity to influence opinions and perceptions among publics in the major opposing states has also increased. But the Soviet economy suffers grave internal weaknesses, and these extend to the communist states of Eastern Europe, creating formidable political problems for the present and the future.

One is reminded of another series of alternating phases of Russian history—the emergence of Russia alternately as an irresistible colossus (as at the end of the Napoleonic wars or after World War II), followed by accumulating evidence of Russia's failure to reform and modernize her political, social and economic system to remain competitive with the larger world (the era of the Crimean War and that of Brezhnev immobilism). For the long term Gorbachev is doubtless right in stressing that internal reform is the essential requirement of the future power of the Soviet Union in world affairs. Much less certain are the concept of reform which guides him and the means at his disposal for its implementation.

Chapter III

U.S.-SOVIET POLITICAL INTERACTION

Martin J. Hillenbrand

A. FACTORS THAT GOVERN U.S. POLICY RESPONSES

1. National Attitudes

Any useful discussion of future Soviet-American relations must necessarily involve a reasonably accurate assessment of where we are and how we got there. We might begin by asking whether the inter-related causal factors that have influenced U.S. policy towards the Soviet Union have helped or hindered the formulation of a rational set of priorities most consistent with basic American national interests. A cynic could argue that the way U.S. policy towards the Soviet Union has developed can hardly be described as a rational process and that if basic American national interests are served, this would be purely coincidental. Another view might be that, despite obvious mistakes, miscalculations, inconsistencies, submission to pressure groups and excessive rhetoric, the broad thrust of American policy in the post-war period has been essentially correct. Which of these is closer to the truth will emerge, I trust, from the discussion that follows.

Despite its continental size, the United States has been essentially an insular country. Since our Civil War, we have been spared the physical disruption and destruction that the countries of Europe, East and West, have experienced in successive wars. Our soldiers have fought and died far from the home front, and when the wars had ended, our economy emerged strong and ready for rapid transition to normal civilian production. Those realities have added an ambivalent note to our involvement in Europe. It is fair to say, however, that engagement in two World Wars, and particularly in the post-World-War II period, has seemingly exorcised much of the strong isolationist impulse that has been traditional in this country.

American insularity spared the United States from participation in the frenetic race for imperialistic acquisition of colonies through military force to which most European countries succumbed in the 19th and 20th centuries. Historians would note, however, that the Mexican War, the Spanish-American War and periodic incursions into Central America were seeming exceptions. In any event, the United States was in a position after World War II to lead the anti-colonial fight and was therefore in a strong moral position to criticize Soviet colonial expansionism in Eastern and Northern Europe. Large ethnic groups in the United States representing earlier immigration from Eastern Europe added their protests against the post-war order in Soviet-controlled Europe. The commemoration in 1985 of the 40th anniversary of the Yalta Conference revived the heated debate among academicians and journalists about the implications for Eastern Europe of the agreements reached there by Churchill, Roosevelt and Stalin.

With the decline in influence of the old Eastern Establishment as political and economic power has shifted to other regions of the country, a concomitant decline of interest in Europe has been noted both in universities and among the public at large. Whether or not this is a permanent phenomenon, it has certainly added to the degree of general ignorance about Europe, including the Soviet Union—an ignorance tempered somewhat by an awareness that basic American values are threatened both by the prospect of nuclear war and, more specifically, by Soviet military strength, a tendency towards expansion of the communist system and adventurism when targets of opportunity open up. This has made it relatively easy for successive administrations in Washington to obtain broad support for a strong defense effort, including a major military presence in Europe, to prevent possible further Soviet expansionism.

2. Basic American Values

What are those basic American values which have seemed threatened? As most concretely articulated, they derive from the Declaration of Independence and the Constitution of the United States. The theoretical bases stem from natural law and Lockean philosophy. The formulations of these documents continue to play an important role in the identification of our values. In theory, at least, the decisions of the Supreme Court are only a logical extension of constitutional language. We have also benefited from our British heritage of parliamentary institutions and individual freedom. Countries seldom, of course, live up to their highest ideals, but most Americans, at various levels of sophistication, will accept the desirability of their government's doing so. Despite consistent strains of cynicism and protest, we are essentially an idealistic people who expect the best of other people. When our values are clearly and overtly rejected, we are seldom prepared to accept this as anything but morally reprehensible.

An important part of the American value system is both a theoretical and practical dedication to free enterprise as the way of best organizing economic life. While the United States has accepted most of the premises of the modern welfare state, this has not weakened the conviction of the large majority of Americans that a competitive economic environment is most likely to maximize productivity, initiative and general progress, as well as provide the widest measure of freedom and opportunity.

3. Domestic Politics

American politicians are very much a product of our culture, vary as they may between regions and states. If they do not always practice what they preach, few will openly break with the broad expectations of the public as to what is desirable conduct. Attitudes of politicians towards the Soviet Union tend to reflect the general values of our society. No one is likely to win many votes running on a pro-Soviet platform. The Communist Party has had a consistent record of significant failure in the United States. While liberals in the Executive branch and the Congress may sometimes be critical of American policy towards the Soviet Union as too negatively rhetorical, all varieties of opinion not of the extreme left can be counted on to unite in bipartisan support of governments, whether Republican or Democratic, which have found themselves in a confrontational situation with the USSR seen to be necessitated by the protection of important interests of the United States and its people.

B. CONFLICTS OF AIMS, COMMON INTERESTS, AND THE WAR OF IDEAS

1. Eastern Europe

Conflict of aims between the Soviet Union and the United States has been a constant reality in the post-war period. It would be strange if this were not the case given the ideological aggressiveness of a Communist government which claims to be the ineluctable wave of the future destined to engulf the world with its institutional forms. Whether the leaders of the Soviet Union are still true believers or merely cynical manipulators of power is not so important in this context as whether they continue to act as if they were the former, asserting the right to intervene around the world in support of insurrectionary movements with which they claim ideological affiliation. Even if this ideological factor did not exist, there would probably be a continuing natural rivalry between two superpowers, one of them with a long tradition of imperial expansionism.

One of the primary reasons for the change of American attitudes towards the USSR which led to the Cold War was the growing conviction that, while gobbling up Eastern Europe, Stalin also aimed at bringing the economic and military strength of Western Europe, and especially that of Germany, within the Soviet sphere of influence. The creation of NATO reflected this concern—a concern shared by the European members of the Alliance. Whether or not the Soviets ever really intended to invade Western Europe, there was a real fear in those early post-war years that they might, and that they could and would use their greatly preponderant military power to coerce and dominate the countries of Western Europe.

While the West prepared and then maintained its defenses, Eastern Europe came completely under Soviet dominance. During the first Eisenhower campaign, there was much talk of a rollback, but in 1956, events in Hungary and Poland demonstrated that this was essentially loose talk. The Soviets had organized their Warsaw Pact and COMECON and had no intention of permitting what they considered dangerous change in the direction of lessened Soviet control over their satellites. Western observers had feared that, with the passage of generations, younger and thoroughly indoctrinated cohorts would become firmly committed to the Communist status quo in Eastern Europe. As it turned out, it was the younger men and women who were to become the most vigorous proponents of change—a reality that the Hungarian Freedom Fighters demonstrated in 1956. Americans took a long time to learn that, even under Communist regimes, distinctive national characteristics and yearnings for a greater measure of liberty and economic freedom could, in fact, manifest themselves.

During the sixties and seventies American policy towards Eastern Europe developed several ambivalences. We obviously wanted the kind of change which would weaken Soviet ideological and physical hegemony, but recognized that any direct encouragement of such change might merely incite further Soviet repression. When Chancellor Willy Brandt pressed forward with his *Ostpolitik*, the Nixon White House became alarmed that our Allies were moving too rapidly and might be falling into a trap by conceding too much. Later we jumped on the bandwagon and participated in the process that led to detente. It seems clear that the West Germans, as well as other Europeans, believe that they know more intimately what is happening in Eastern Europe today, and are therefore in a better position to pursue policies which can induce further change while not unduly alarming the Soviets. The conceptual gulf between the United States and Western Europe on the best way to deal with the military regime in Poland illustrates the point. We have only recently come to see the futility of economic sanctions against that country as inimical to our broader purposes.

While the Soviet Union is obviously concerned about trends in a number of Eastern European countries, it does not seem sufficiently confident at this point simply to abort those trends by force as it did in Czechoslovakia in 1968. The Soviet leaders are also sophisticated enough to know that it is not the United States which provides the primary impetus for change, much as Soviet propaganda continues to fulminate against Radio Free Europe in Munich. One may assume that Soviet concern about Mr. Honecker's behavior in recent years (which led them to pressure him not to visit the Federal Republic) does not reflect any belief that the United States is really behind the new relationship which seems to be developing between the two Germanies. The Kremlin is sufficiently well-informed to be aware that at least some officials, in Washington as well as in Paris, are themselves concerned as to where all this is leading. The Germans themselves are puzzled by Mr. Honecker's smiling face, although it is easy enough to postulate strong economic motives for the GDR leader to want a closer and more cooperative relationship with the subsidy-and credit-bountiful Federal Republic. Some see undercurrents of Pan-Germanism flowing in both parts of divided Germany as the GDR not only tolerates but evokes the symbolism of German historic figures such as Luther, Frederick the Great and Bismarck. It is too early yet to see in all this any significant new impulses towards national unity, however.

The one lesson that should emerge, humbling as it may be, is that the United States is not destined to play an independently decisive role affecting the future of Eastern Europe. The slow process of favorable change which many Europeans hope for will either take place, or be frustrated, with limited American input. Wise policy will recognize this, leaving to the Europeans, especially the Germans, the influencing of change at a pace not likely to precipitate Soviet repression. Such awareness in Washington will not only permit Soviet-American relations in other fields to develop at their own pace, but is also most likely to be conducive to the achievement of our objectives in Eastern Europe.

2. Western Europe

Apart from its interest in Eastern European developments, the United States must never forget that, in the peaceful contest between the two superpowers, Western Europe remains of prize importance. There has been some talk in Washington about the need to shift priorities away from the old continent to an Asia rapidly growing in economic importance. Even purely in economic terms this does not make much sense. Western Europe is a significantly more important market for American exports than East Asia, and with the current depreciation of the dollar, this market will expand. The Soviet Union would still like very much to incorporate the economic and military strength of Western Europe into its own sphere of influence, not necessarily by force of arms, but by gradual extension of its political influence. A constant aim of Soviet propaganda has been to separate the United States from its European Allies. Often this propaganda has been clumsy and counterproductive from the Soviet point of view, but Gorbachev has demonstrated a new flexibility and sense of public relations that is having an impact in Europe. It would be unrealistic to pretend that European views of responsible policy and behavior towards the USSR do not differ from those of the U.S. Government in some important respects, and that a more subtle form of Soviet propaganda could not exploit such differences.

Related areas that might be subject to Soviet exploitation in this sense are those of strategy and arms control. Although the INF deployment issue quickly lost its intensity and represented a Soviet failure, the lingering suspicion that American military planners proceed on the assumption that we can fight and win a war involving use of nuclear weapons—a war that could leave much of Europe in ruins—continues to give Soviet propaganda a convenient peg on which to hang arguments that the U.S. and not the USSR is the real threat to peace. This doubt about American strategy is linked to the suspicion entertained by some that we are not really very much interested in arriving at arms control agreements in Geneva. In the aftermath of the Reykjavik summit, Gorbachev seems, at least temporarily, to have captured the high ground with a series of arms control initiatives to which the American response has reflected the divisions on the subject within the U.S. government and NATO. Some real success in the Geneva negotiations would, of course, change the mood, but even here the discussion of complete withdrawal of intermediate range missiles has, ironically enough, revived fears of decoupling and the development of further imbalance in nuclear delivery systems in Europe as long as shorter range Soviet missiles are not included. The most recent Soviet proposal indicating their willingness to withdraw their shorter range missiles as well, linked apparently to a further proposal for the removal of all tactical nuclear weapons from Europe, has added a new fluidity to the whole situation. It is impossible at the date of writing to foresee where this will all come out. The Strategic Defense Initiative proposed by President Reagan is still open to Soviet manipulation in the context of arms control, although they have now indicated a willingness to detach this issue from the negotiations on intermediate nuclear weapons.

Too often U.S. officials seem to think that winning verbal battles and eventual support in the NATO Permanent Council or at Ministerial meetings is all that is needed. For the kinds of European publics developing today, this is not enough, although broad popular support remains for the Alliance which we and our European Allies have constructed and maintained. Our supporting propaganda efforts—the attempt to tell our story—however, have not been as persuasive or as skillful as ideally they might be, and significant segments of European populations, especially among the young, are now, in effect, turned off by these efforts. We have relied too much on Soviet clumsiness

rather than our own adeptness, and the basic strength of our ideals.
Given the long-term Soviet objectives vis-a-vis the area, it is difficult
to find any Soviet-U.S. common interests in Western Europe other than
avoiding its physical destruction as part of the larger superpower interest in maintaining the peace and avoiding mutual destruction—
although these of course are not inconsiderable. The issue of extended deterrence and to what degree it continues to protect Western
Europe merges into the reality that a badly destroyed Europe would
serve the interests of neither the USSR nor the United States.

Looking ahead, one may ask whether the kind of Pan-Europeanism
expressed in the concept of a European Peace Order (*Europaische
Friedensordnung*), which has a certain appeal to a segment of intellectual youth, particularly in Germany, is likely to grow in attractiveness.
Such an order envisages a gradual coming together of Western and
Eastern Europe as superpower presence and influence diminish both
in the East and the West. This hardly seems realistic today, but in the
long-run, if there is ever to be a settlement of the European question
and a final line drawn under World War II, it must presumably be in
such a direction. Should that day ever come, the dissolution of the
current alliance system would no longer be the disaster for the West
that it clearly would be under present circumstances.

Although the new and highly interesting relationship developing between the German Democratic Republic and the Federal Republic of
Germany has a number of causes, one has surely been an incipient
revival of a common feeling of Germanness, with the leaders of the
GDR, in their quest for a greater measure of legitimacy, now seeking
to evoke symbols out of the German historic past. Despite frequent
predictions both in the United States and Germany that the goal of German national unity was a dead issue, particularly as a new generation
took over with no personal experience of a unified nation, a more
perceptive view would recognize that the appeal is still there and will
continue, even if in realistic terms the achievement of such unity could
only come in the long run. Only a basic shift by the Soviet Union in
the assessment of its own security requirements in a changing Eastern
Europe would make it possible. This was a long-term objective of the
Eastern Policy *(Ostpolitik)* of Willy Brandt, though the precise
modalities of the changes to be sought were left somewhat vague. The
CDU/CSU willingness to take over this policy involved a recognition
that movement was under way which it would be self-defeating to attempt to abort.

A question which will obviously affect Soviet success or failure in
detaching Western Europe from its close ties with the United States
is where the advanced industrial countries of the West are heading
economically. Those countries face a period of difficult and often painful structural change as comparative advantage in many of the old-line
industries (the so-called smokestack industries), as well as in some
technologically more advanced industries such as consumer elec-

tronics, shift elsewhere in the world. It is unlikely that this process can be reversed. Apart from other economic pressures, since many of the old-line industries such as coal-mining, steel, ship-building, metal-working and even textiles have traditionally been associated with the production of arms or at least the clothing of soldiers, no country which considers itself a military power is likely to acquiesce in the disappearance of these industries. The pressures to resort to various forms of protectionism will mount. Under these conditions, one may ask to what extent the old economic complementarities between Europe and the United States are breaking down. Another aspect of this general problem is the collapse of the former triangular patterns of trade with Europe buying more from the United States but selling more to the developing world which, in turn, would sell more to the United States (thus maintaining a rough triangular balance of trade). The heavy debt burdens of the developing world plus the collapse of commodity prices have upset this equalizing mechanism along with the impact of dollar overvaluation until late in 1985. The developed world must now face the serious adjustments required by a depreciated dollar.

The years ahead are therefore likely to be years of strain and growing economic competition between Europe and the United States. This will not only have political consequences for the Alliance but will, at least in theory, open up new possibilities for Soviet propaganda and divisive tactics. With wise leadership, the United States could presumably do much to mitigate the strains ahead. At this point, however, few Europeans are impressed with the capacity of the United States to manage its own internal budgetary imbalances or to regain for its export industries the markets lost because of over-valuation of the dollar. The fact that in 1985 the United States became a net debtor country, and is now the world's largest external debtor, adds an unprecedented and troubling new feature to an already muddled international economy. That the richest country in the world should be a net importer rather than exporter of capital runs counter to all past experience and conventional economic theory.

The Soviet Union, as the other superpower, itself faces mammoth domestic economic and social problems the solution of which Gorbachev has stated to be his primary objective. Whether he can succeed, even in part, remains hidden in the future.

3. Middle East

After the Soviet invasion of Afghanistan, there were genuine fears in the United States that this could prove to be only the beginning of an eventual Soviet sweep to the Persian Gulf in fulfillment of the old Tsarist aspiration for warm water ports. The Carter Doctrine followed with its seemingly open-ended commitment to defend the Persian Gulf region against any outside force. Whatever the reasons, apart from its intervention in Afghanistan, the Kremlin has played a relatively passive role during recent years in the Middle East—perhaps as much confused as American policy-makers by the turbulence and unpredictability of events in that troubled part of the world. The Soviets have, of course, given much aid in the form of arms to Syria and Iraq, but few who know the region would describe those countries as totally subservient to Soviet policy. Nor have close American ties with Israel made it possible for the USSR to play the kind of role in the Arab countries that one might have expected. The Soviets do vote, of course, for all anti-Israeli resolutions proposed in the United Nations or related organizations, and will systematically encourage the Arab countries in their opposition to Israel or to any settlement that does not involve Israel's withdrawal to its pre-1967 borders.

It seems clear that the Soviet Union would like to have a larger voice in the Middle East, and had hoped that participation in the Geneva process would make this possible. American unwillingness to revive the talks in Geneva has so far been successful in excluding the Soviets from participation in the various initiatives and meetings that have dealt with aspects of the Middle East in recent years. There are some who believe that the USSR could be constructively engaged in trying to achieve some sort of Middle East settlement, but a succession of American policy-makers, beginning with Henry Kissinger, have felt it to be in our overriding national interest to keep the Soviets out. The U.S. refusal to accept the Hussein initiative in 1985 follows in this tradition.

The two oil shocks of 1973 and 1978-79 added importance, at least in the eyes of some Europeans, to Soviet oil and natural gas reserves. These have now become one of several significant sources of energy for Western Europe. Conservation and slower economic growth in oil-importing countries has reduced overall demand down to a point where the entire crude oil market is soft with continuing downward pressure on prices. The Soviet Union has both suffered from this trend in terms of the foreign exchange which it can expect to harvest in the short term, and gained from the degree of stability (if at considerably lower levels) that OPEC, at least temporarily, was able to impose on crude oil prices by fairly drastic reductions in production. If, as most experts believe, including those in the International Energy Agency in Paris, continued economic growth in the world will again bring upward pressure on crude oil prices sometime in the 1990s, the Soviet Union will be in a position to play an important role in the world both as a source of oil and natural gas.

If one were searching for some common interest that the United States and the Soviet Union might share in the Middle East, one would presumably find it in the desire to prevent the fundamentalist Islamic Revolution from exploding in such a way as to dominate the entire region. With its large Moslem population, the Soviet leaders cannot help but view with some anxiety any spread of Islamic activism that might move across their borders. How effectively to deal with the Iran of the Ayatollahs must be as much a puzzle in Moscow as in Washington. It is difficult to imagine, however, any concrete circumstances that would bring the two capitals together, either formally or informally, in furtherance of the common interest they might share in this matter.

4. Latin America

The current divisions in Washington over Central American policy make difficult any precise definition of desirable policy. If most Latin American countries are viewed as critical of the Reagan Administration's policy in Nicaragua, and to a lesser degree, in the rest of Central America, this is obviously an important fact. The Soviet leaders clearly would like to encourage what they perceive to be growing resentment of the United States—a resentment that, of course, is not new but perhaps more intense in our time. The growing respectability and acceptance of Fidel Castro being reported in the Latin American press is undoubtedly a derivative of that resentment as well as a feeling in some Latin American capitals that American policy has gone off the rails. The fact that a sizeable segment of the overwhelming debt burden borne by Brazil, Mexico, Argentina and other countries is held by American banks adds to the problem, since it is easy for their politicians to focus blame on greedy U.S. banks rather than on their own rising consumption standards as the cause of present austerity and social and political stress.

Since the Soviet Union is not prepared to rush in with generous offers of aid or loans under more favorable terms, its field of maneuver is limited to propaganda and encouragement where possible of political parties and potential regimes sympathetic to its interests. The burden of supporting the Cuban economy has been a heavy one over the years. The Kremlin cannot help but be gratified that Castro's influence seems to be growing, even though the price of respectability that he must pay is a less activist and subversive role in Latin America. An interesting question to which we do not have a definitive answer is whether the Soviet leaders view Latin America as a whole, with its enormous population growth and widespread poverty, as being in a pre-revolutionary stage. Experience should have shown that Latin American regimes, whether they are essentially military dictatorships or democracies, are not very stable, and that somehow or other the revolutionary impulses do not work themselves through to the point of fundamental societal change. That may in the future no longer be the case, but the Soviets cannot be sure. Hence they must be cautious lest they simply create more Pinochets.

If Gorbachev sees widespread alcoholism in the USSR as a problem requiring urgent measures of reform, he cannot be unhappy about the role which some countries of Latin America are playing in adding to the drug problem in the United States—a debilitating factor that corrupts the youth and weakens the national fiber and will to action. This does not necessarily mean the KGB is secretly encouraging cocaine and heroin production in Colombia, Bolivia or Mexico, but stranger activities have been charged to that organization.

In any event, it is difficult to find any significant area of common interest which the Soviet Union and the United States might have in Latin America other than the prevention of nuclear proliferation in such countries as Brazil and Argentina. Here the worldwide interest that the two superpowers have in minimizing the spread of nuclear weapons coalesces with the specific interest in keeping Latin America as a nuclear free zone.

5. Africa

Ever since the decolonization of Africa—itself a chronologically irregular process—the two superpowers have competitively sought influence over the emerging new countries. During one period, the People's Republic of China was also in the competition. The supposition was that Africa is a strategically important continent and that its future would largely be determined by the way in which individual countries aligned themselves. The first arena in which this competition manifested itself in a major way was the Belgian Congo. Following extensive rioting, the Belgian government granted independence on June 30, 1960. The struggle between Patrice Lumumba (favored by the Soviets) and Joseph Kasavubu (originally favored by the United States), with Moise Tshombe and Joseph Mobutu initially on the sidelines, seemed to divide along ideological lines. After a tangled and confused period involving, *inter alia,* the United Nations and Secretary General Hammarskjold, Mobutu finally emerged as the strong man who would obtain U.S. support. Whether the subsequent not particularly distinguished history of Zaire under Mobutu justified the strenuous diplomatic and other efforts of the United States is at least a question worth asking, and assessing, in relation to the available alternatives.

It was perhaps only natural that the regimes that came to power in many of the poor countries of Africa, which had emerged into an independence for which they were inadequately prepared, should find in some form of Marxism, adapted to African conditions, a congenial ideology to justify the essentially dictatorial practices they imposed. Western educated elites exposed to left-wing doctrines in Western European or Soviet universities brought back with them strong antipathies to international capitalism, and the multinational corporations and banks which were its institutional embodiment. It was relatively easy for these elites, who provided the basic leadership in Black Africa, to lean towards the Soviet Union with its police state techniques rather than to the United States as a model and anticipated source of aid.

It has been the fate of Africa in the post-colonial period not to live up to expectations, whether Soviet or American. To some extent the continent has been plagued by an overestimation of its strategic importance on the part of the two superpowers, and at one stage the People's Republic of China as well. Despite the potential riches of the country, the contest over Angola and the resources invested in that context, particularly by the Soviet Union and its Cuban surrogate, seem out of proportion to any possible gain. The confused situation there has now arrived at the absurd point where Cuban troops maintain security for the Chevron production facilities in the Cabinda Concession. A good case could be made for the contention that, despite the built-in advantage of left-leaning elites, most of the Soviet ventures in Africa have turned sour. On the other hand, the U.S. government has perhaps displayed undue anxiety about Soviet and Cuban activities in Black African countries. A policy of patient restraint and of giving such aid as we can for famine relief and agricultural improvement, while leaving the main burden of self-development to the countries themselves, and the basic tasks of diplomacy and political influence to the French in Francophone Africa, and to the British in their former colonies, is likely in the long-run to be most productive and consistent with American interests.

If the past has taught any lessons, it is that while the Soviet Union is willing to deliver arms, frequently at market prices, its economic aid is meager and often misguided. The appeal of Marxist-Leninist doctrine to educated but corrupt ruling elites, now often dominated by the military, is likely to wane in the absence of more tangible forms of assistance, just as it did in the Guinea of Sékou Touré.

South Africa, of course, presents especially difficult policy problems for the United States. The Soviet Union has been able to seize the propaganda advantage in Black Africa and the United Nations by charging the U.S. with too permissive a policy toward that country. The "constructive engagement" approach of the Reagan Administration has failed to stimulate the kind of movement, either in Namibia or South Africa itself, that would satisfy both domestic and foreign critics and provide some counterweight to Soviet propaganda. Whether any U.S. policy could be devised which takes account of basic security interests, and at the same time copes adequately with the moral and political implications of South African behavior, is an open question.

The Northern Tier or Mediterranean countries of Africa in turn present another set of unique problems. For many years, they were within the competency of the Bureau of Middle Eastern Affairs in the U.S. Department of State. The Libya of Colonel Qadhafi is obviously the most troublesome and unpredictable. Even at his worst he is unlikely to become a reliable supporter of Soviet policy. On the whole, starting with the prime example of Egypt, Soviet activities in North Africa have essentially failed to achieve their purpose. While there are some serious problems of stability and political succession in the Northern Tier countries, the United States can be reasonably satisfied with the current situation as far as rivalry with the USSR is concerned. If the two superpowers have any common interest in this area, it would be to prevent Libya from acquiring a nuclear capability.

6. Asia

Asia is an enormous continent even reserving China as a separate country for consideration. For the convenience of analysis, this section will begin with West Asia—essentially the Indian subcontinent and Afghanistan—and then discuss East Asia including Japan.

Ever since achieving independence, India has had a mixed role in the development of U.S. policy. It has been a thorn in the side of the United States with its public criticism, its holier-than-thou preaching and its close alignment with the Soviet Union. This has not hampered the flow of large amounts of U.S. aid, however, and at levels other than the political, relations have not been all that bad. There had been some hope that Rajiv Gandhi, the new Prime Minister, would be less prejudiced than his mother, but his choice of the Soviet Union for his first foreign visit and the verbal love feast which ensued in Moscow did not augur well.

Any American visitor to India will hear a great deal about the Islamic Bomb that Pakistan is alleged to be building. This is immediately followed by the threat that, if Pakistan goes nuclear, India will inevitably have to follow (though it is easily possible that India, having conducted a nuclear "explosion" has already done so). Some of the Indian resentment rubs off on the United States because of our past support of Pakistan. One sometimes even has the feeling that, over time, they have attributed to us some of the British responsibility for partition in 1947.

Continuing Indian flirtation with the USSR is something we shall probably just have to live with. As outrageous as the behavior of Indian officials may sometimes be, we have little to gain by displays of irritation and agitation. India is no direct threat to American security and she is not in a position, even if she were inclined to do so, to add to the military strength of the Soviet Union. Nor does it seem likely that the Soviets can devise any way to use India against U.S. interests beyond what the country and its leaders have done in the past. There has been a considerable tendency in the United States to exaggerate the significance of India on the world scene.

This does not mean that the United States must accept a purely passive role. An adept and resourceful diplomacy, and propaganda, of limited scope, can moderate aberrational behavior. Moreover, in their hour of need, the Indians tend always to turn to the United States, for they know the Soviets cannot deliver the goods, other than military equipment, whether grain or technology.

Pakistan is the sort of partner with whom one does not feel entirely comfortable. We hope for continuing political stability in the country although we do not particularly like the means by which that stability is maintained. It is clear that, in open conflict, Pakistan is no match for India; the creation of Bangladesh was evidence of that reality. However, Pakistan under its present leadership is firmly anti-Soviet, and has played an important role vis-a-vis Afghanistan both as a haven for refugees and a transmission point for supplies and manpower for resistance groups. It also provides the United States with the opportunity to have a friendly involvement in the Islamic world not confused by the ambiguities of the Near East.

The Soviet invasion of Afghanistan was a brutal use of power to safeguard against any regime that might not be subservient to Moscow. Although drawing strict analogies with Vietnam can be misleading, the Red Army has obviously encountered more resistance over the years since 1979 than the Soviet leaders had counted on. Washington has never seemed able to define with precision how much of our reaction derives from an assessment of American security interests in Afghanistan and how much from sheer moral indignation. Our propaganda can make and has made good use of the opportunity which the invasion has provided to stress the fact of flagrant Soviet misbehavior, and we have been a principal source of supplies for the freedom fighters.

Gorbachev does now seem to be seeking some solution in Afghanistan that would permit Soviet military withdrawal without too much loss of face. Whether he can find it, and to what extent if any the West should attempt to help him in his search, are still open questions.

Bangladesh is, unfortunately, one of those potential basket case countries, the future of which is, at best, clouded and, at worst, dismal. We shall provide our share of the aid that will be ineluctably necessary for humanitarian reasons over the years. We can be reasonably certain that the Soviets will not do likewise.

Observers of the contemporary East Asian scene have noted that the actual situation is, in some respects, better than one might have expected in the immediate aftermath of collapse in Vietnam. Thailand, Malaysia, Singapore, Taiwan, Hong Kong, Indonesia and South Korea continue independent and, in most cases, prosperous, while Vietnam, Cambodia and Laos are impoverished and under the heel of Hanoi. The Soviet Union has continued to support Vietnam, but the age-old hostility between the Vietnamese and the Chinese has quickly reasserted itself. Communism, if with a distinctively indigenous flavor, obviously won a major victory in Vietnam, and American prestige suffered greatly, apart from the fissures in our society that the war revealed. But the United States has emerged from all this in a relatively stable political position vis-a-vis most of East Asia. It does not seem that the Soviet Union can do very much, at least in the short-term, to change this.

Unwise American economic policies could, however, do much to alienate these presently friendly countries which depend to a major extent on access to U.S. markets. If a wave of protectionism should sweep over the Congress (as seems more and more likely), this could have substantial political consequences.

Japan is, of course, of prize importance. Partly because of Moscow's obduracy over the Kuriles and partly for ideological reasons, the Soviet

Union has had meager success in improving its relations with Japan. The Japanese will do business with the USSR and accept juicy sales and construction contracts, but they will be wary of any undue Soviet influence. As in the case of other Asian countries, one development that could sour the still very good U.S. relationship with Japan would be major restrictions on Japan's access to the American market. Not that this would drive the Japanese into the arms of the Soviets, but it would stimulate new trends in Japanese diplomatic and economic policy that could be adverse to American interests in Asia. Some accommodation to American trade complaints on the part of Japan will also be necessary if confrontation is to be avoided; the kinds of imbalance on trade account that the United States now runs with Japan seem statistically untenable to many members of the U.S. Congress.

Some have also questioned the wisdom of American pressure on Japan to rearm, given the formidable demonstration of Japanese military prowess in World War II at a much lower level of national technological capability. Other Asian countries clearly fear the potential of a rearmed and remilitarized Japan.

The Philippines remain a distinctive problem for U.S. policy in the aftermath of the corrupt and despotic Marcos regime. The Communist movement on some of the islands is a good investment for the Soviets but, for optimists at least, the democratic forces in the country remain sufficiently strong to retain power in the post-Marcos era. If a hostile regime were to seize power from the well-intentioned and democratically inclined Aquino government, it could seriously damage American security interests, if loss of our air and naval bases in that country were to result.

Korea, like Germany, remains a divided country, and the two systems that have developed in the North and the South have become increasingly disparate. The North Korean Communist government continues to make threatening noises from time to time, but given the state of relations between the USSR and the People's Republic of China, any repetition of the aggression of the late 1940's seems unlikely. The American presence in South Korea will, however, be a continuing necessity for some time both for psychological and military reasons. Our position would be morally strengthened if the South Korean government were to become less repressive, but a realistic appraisal would not indicate this to be highly likely. The Olympic Games to be held in Seoul next year will provide a good test of both Soviet and North Korean intentions: if they decide to participate it will indicate willingness to accept the reality of South Korea.

If one looks for common U.S. and Soviet interests in Asia, it is difficult to find any except a shared concern about nuclear proliferation, for example, in South Korea or Taiwan, which at least have the technical capability to go nuclear. Should the Soviet Union under Gorbachev move away from foreign adventurism, as he concentrates on domestic reform, the economically thriving countries of East Asia, especially Japan, could play a constructive role.

7. China

American policy since the Nixon Administration, openly or tacitly, has seen improved relations with China as an influence for restraint by the Soviet Union. It has, on the whole, worked in this way given the almost paranoid, if (in our view) rather unrealistic concern of some Soviet leaders about the long-term threat of China to the security of the USSR. However, in this triangular relationship, it has sometimes not been entirely clear who was playing which card against whom. The Chinese have probably had more success than the Soviets in taking advantage of the possibilities, but even very tentative Soviet efforts to improve relations with the PRC by sending senior officials to Peking cause watchful concern in Washington.

In any event, the improvement in Chinese-American relations during the past 15 years has been a development of historic importance. It has provided leverage against the USSR in many subtle and some not-so-subtle ways, apart from encouraging a general Chinese interest in stability in Asia. Although the potential of the China market has proved somewhat of a will-o'-the-wisp for the West in the past, recent Chinese economic reforms may open up new possibilities. Whatever may come of them, they are clearly in a direction away from the kind of Communism still found in the Soviet Union. The basically peasant nature of the economy always made the application of classical Marxism an obvious anomaly. Gorbachev obviously has the improvement of relations with China as an important objective of Soviet foreign policy. Whether or not he succeeds will probably depend more on Chinese judgements about the nature of the changes he is attempting to bring about in his own country rather than increased Soviet diplomatic efforts.

The People's Republic of China is a country with enormous problems which will grow with its population. Whether it can in our time reach the point of industrial take-off that some of the more prosperous Asian countries have already passed in a matter of conjecture. Given some continuity of policy in the leadership succession to the present gerontocracy, the United States will undoubtedly do what it can to help. A relatively stable, economically growing China is not only in our interest but that of all Asia. Recent reversals of the liberalization process in China, whatever they may mean in the long run, demonstrate that the process of change will not be easy.

C. ROLE OF INFORMATION/DISINFORMATION ON AMERICAN-SOVIET RELATIONS

Many have questioned the efficacy of American efforts in the propaganda war with the Soviet Union that has been under way for more than 40 years. It is true enough that our information policies and programs have sometimes been feeble or misdirected, whether they were intended to influence the population of the Soviet Union or the rest of the world. Compared to the Soviet Union, we suffer from two serious handicaps at least at the short-term, tactical level: the closed nature of Soviet society contrasted with the open nature of Western societies, and a certain regard for the truth in the West contrasted with the Soviet view that truth is manipulable in furthering the cause of communism. We have, of course, one great and fundamental asset in the obvious and serious political and economic flaws of the Soviet system. Whatever one may think of Eurocommunism, the days are over when Soviet propaganda could automatically count on reflexive support for its policies from communist parties around the world. It would be gratifying to think that this has happened largely because of our successful information programs. A more realistic assessment would be that, while those programs have sometimes had an impact, the major causal factor has been Soviet bad behavior or poor performance, coupled with fundamental flaws when compared to Western value systems.

Disinformation, or the propagation of deliberately falsified or invented news or rumor, is a practice at which the Soviets are masters. In wartime, we and our Allies have not hesitated to do the same in order to mislead the enemy, but in the absence of hostilities, we lie only with personal unease and, if we do, given the nature of our free media, frequently end up with great embarrassment. Our major concern must obviously be to prevent the confusion and even alienation that Soviet disinformation can bring to the citizens of free Western societies. To do this effectively, both the quality of our own information services and their reputation for veracity must be maintained at a high level, along with confidence that our own governments, while not revealing sensitive and strategic information, are basically honest in what they say about their judgments of a situation and their reasons for advocating specific ways of dealing with it. In the absence of such confidence, the field is open for the operation of Soviet disinformation. Needless to say, our behavior with respect to arms shipments to Iran has not enhanced such confidence as far as the U.S. is concerned. U.S. is concerned.

Since even with such instruments as Radio Liberty and the Voice of America, the United States can only marginally penetrate the information iron curtain that the USSR imposes on its population, we cannot hope to have a major impact on the average Soviet citizen. There are larger opportunities in the rest of Eastern Europe where our Radio Free Europe reaches many listeners from its Munich base. A more important factor, however, in exposing the populations of Eastern Europe to Western news, opinion and cultural life are the radio and TV transmissions from such countries as Austria and the Federal Republic of Germany.

Despite its frequent crudeness and tendentiousness, Soviet propaganda has had some successes in recent years in disaffecting segments of Western European populations against American policy. There is a generational problem here for a sizeable number of young Europeans provide a receptive audience for charges that the U.S. government is militaristic, is sabotaging arms control and is indifferent to European concerns. The kind of Washington rhetoric which American information agencies have often disseminated sometimes seems to confirm these charges. One might argue that a more skillful and sophisticated American information program could turn things around—but the problem is more deep-rooted than that. American policies and official behavior which seem to fall short of the ideals we profess cannot be sold to European publics. Lest one be too inclined to pessimism, however, it remains true that solid majorities exist in most Western European countries for continued alliance with the United States and for NATO as the institutional embodiment of that alliance.

The propaganda war between the superpowers will continue in the years ahead. Despite *glasnost,* the Soviets will not play by the same rules that we do, but that can be an asset as well as a liability for a professional information service that recognizes the propaganda of a democracy can, in the long run, never be better than the policies it is defining.

Chapter IV

THE MILITARY DIMENSION OF U.S.-SOVIET RELATIONS

Barry M. Blechman and Douglas Hart

The Soviet Union has been gradually—but steadily—improving the size, quality, and operational characteristics of its armed forces for more than twenty years. By now, this sustained military build-up has touched all elements of the Soviet armed forces, resulting in far more capable central nuclear forces, as well as greater theater-level and tactical nuclear capabilities. Soviet capabilities for chemical warfare have also been expanded and modernized. Meanwhile, Soviet leaders have not neglected conventional military capabilities: Soviet ground, air, and naval forces are all considerably improved as compared to their Western counterparts of twenty years ago.

This continuing military build-up has greatly expanded the options available to Soviet leaders in the event of international confrontations or threats to Soviet interests anywhere in the world. It also has provided a substantially improved measure of operational flexibility to Soviet leaders in normal times, making it possible for the USSR to consider involvement in a variety of international situations, even those for which it may understand that the local configuration of indigenous and outside forces might imply a degree of military risk.

Yet, the Soviet military build-up also clearly has had adverse effects on U.S.-Soviet relations and on the possibility of economic and political cooperation between the great powers. Moreover, it has triggered a major rearmament program by the Western nations, led by historic peacetime increases in U.S. defense spending during the 1980-1984 period. While this precipitate growth in American defense spending appears to have subsided, the United States, most other NATO nations, and Japan are continuing to improve their military capabilities substantially. These programs do not promise to regain the measure of military superiority possessed by the Western alliance during the 1950s and early 1960s—before the initiation of the Soviet build-up, but the United States and its allies do appear to have made clear their intent to assure that, at worst, the military balance remains ambiguous.

There can be little doubt that the military competition between the two great powers has had significant effects on their respective standing in international affairs, on the broad sweep of international politics, on the balance of power between the two blocs, and on the risk of conflict. The competition will almost certainly continue to have such consequences in the future. In this paper, we examine the implications for U.S. policymakers of the continuing military competition with the Soviet Union, particularly over the next fifteen years. Soviet and U.S. force structures and military doctrines are described and compared— both as they look today and as they are likely to look in the future. In addition to this objective analysis, we also describe each side's subjective assessment of the military balance and its effects on its options in world affairs. It is, after all, these subjective perceptions which determine how nations respond to changes in the military balance. The paper concludes by describing some of the strategic problems associated with the military balance which American policymakers are likely to confront before the end of the century.

EVALUATION OF SOVIET FORCES AND DOCTRINE

The current political-military environment is in large part a product of certain key shifts in the military balance during the last twenty years. Four major milestones in this continuing process are examined in this section:

- Soviet attainment of strategic parity with the United States in the early 1970s;

- Modernization of Soviet long-range, theater nuclear forces, beginning in the mid-1970s;

- Modernization of Soviet tactical nuclear weapon systems, commencing in the late 1970s;

- Modernization and expansion of Warsaw Pact conventional forces throughout the 1970s and 1980s.

Consequences of the Soviet Build-Up

The end of U.S. strategic superiority over the Soviet Union constitutes the major military watershed in postwar history. The impact of Soviet attainment of an unambiguous capability to withstand an attack and retaliate with devastating effect on U.S. military assets, industrial infrastructure, and population has not been lost upon Soviet leaders. Soviet spokesmen state that the achievement of strategic parity has brought about a major shift in "the global correlation of forces." As stated by then-President Brezhnev in 1970, "At the present time, no question of any importance in the world can be solved without our participation, without taking into account our economic and military might.''

The ending of U.S. strategic superiority meant that American strategic weapons were relegated to the sole function of deterring a nuclear attack on the United States. In particular, the loss of American strategic superiority meant that the U.S. could no longer be assured of ultimately dominating any escalatory process. When applied to calculations concerning European conflicts, this loss of "escalation dominance" greatly increased the credibility of the conventional threat posed to NATO by the Warsaw Pact, by making it more difficult for NATO to contemplate seriously the initiation of nuclear war in response to such an attack. It also called into question the NATO concept of how to threaten the use of nuclear forces credibly. Without confidence in its ultimate ability to emerge victorious, in some meaningful sense, from the most severe form of a nuclear exchange, NATO's plan to initiate any nuclear response with tactical or "battlefield" weapons was transformed from a rational military option to an irrational threat whose effectiveness in any future crisis would depend mainly on the Soviet Union's assessment of the alliance's resolve and political cohesion. And, finally, the loss of escalation dominance laid bare the inherent political tensions between the United States and its European allies stemming from their respective geographic positions relative to the Soviet Union, tensions which could be glossed over during the era of U.S. superiority.

The Soviet program to modernize longer-range theater weapons accentuated the disparity between the nuclear postures of NATO and the Warsaw Pact, and also increased the USSR's leverage vis-a-vis the United States in other sections of traditional American interest around the Eurasian periphery. Although, as we have noted, strategic parity partially discredited NATO's intention to make use initially of short-range nuclear systems, the political consequences were mitigated by the facts: (a) that the USSR's missiles intended for theater warfare were liquid-fuelled and therefore vulnerable to preemptive attack; and (b) that the ability of the Soviet Union's fleet of medium-range bombers to penetrate NATO's air defenses was questionable. The introduction of mobile SS-20 intermediate-range ballistic missiles and Backfire bombers, beginning in the late 1970s, ended this situation. Soviet theater-range nuclear forces are now survivable, operationally flexible, and significantly more accurate than their predecessors. Coupled with the attainment of strategic parity, these achievements suggest to some Western observers that the USSR might attempt to become a "sanctuary" in a future conflict, an inviolate base for nuclear systems that could strike Western Europe but, so long as they did not attack American soil, still deter retaliation by U.S., or even U.K. and French, strategic forces.

Furthermore, by 1990 the Soviet tactical nuclear modernization program will have turned a sector of traditional weakness into one of parity or superiority vis-a-vis NATO. The deployment of a new generation of tactical ballistic missiles (TBMs), fighter-bomber aircraft capable of delivering nuclear munitions, and nuclear-capable artillery is augmenting gains at the strategic and theater-level by challenging NATO's one remaining area of advantage. If NATO were to remain superior in battlefield nuclear systems, Soviet planners would be faced with some residual uncertainty about whether NATO would initiate a tactical nuclear exchange in spite of its parity (or inferiority) at the higher levels of the escalatory ladder. The Soviet tactical nuclear build-up thus appears designed to destroy whatever credibility may still be attributed to NATO's threat to initiate nuclear conflict. In addition, the increased ranges of the new Soviet tactical systems provide a significant hedge against the conclusion of an arms control agreement that would limit or constrain intermediate-range systems.

Perhaps the most important aspect of the new Soviet TBMs and fighter-bombers, however, is their conventional strike capability. The SS-21 TBM has been deployed with a cluster munition warhead, among other types, and has achieved accuracies, measured by circular error probable, as precise as 30 meters. The longer-range SS-23 and SS-22 have not yet been deployed with conventional warheads, but are likely to have them in the future—along with some form of terminal guidance. Moreover, Soviet aircraft like the SU-24 Fencer can carry significant loads of conventional ordnance deep into NATO territory.

The emergence of genuine dual-capable systems in the Soviet force structure may complicate command and control procedures and increase the vulnerability of those bombers and missiles which are equipped with nuclear weapons early in, or prior to, a war. This new capability, however, also serves as the linchpin for efforts to maintain the Warsaw Pact's conventional dominance over NATO. The new systems may allow Moscow to execute preemptive attacks on NATO's nuclear assets, utilizing only conventional forces, with high confidence of success. The new Soviet TBMs may be especially important in such missions as they would provide assured penetration, short flight times, and an ability to strike targets throughout the depth of the theater. The reemergence of the mobile group concept in the guise of operational maneuver groups (OMGs), task-organized formations of ground forces of varying size that appear intended to carry out rapid operations deep behind the enemy's lines, may also, in part, be intended to support this offensive strategy of seizing or destroying NATO's nuclear weapons before they could be used.

The continuing growth of Soviet and Warsaw Pact conventional capabilities exacerbates a situation which has long seemed likely to place the onerous decision to initiate nuclear war in the hands of Western decisionmakers. Yet, the cumulative impact of the coincident Soviet build-up in nuclear capabilities is that U.S. policymakers will find it increasingly difficult to contemplate the employment of nuclear weapons as a means of counterbalancing conventional inferiority. This calculus will apply not only (or even primarily) to NATO's central front, but also to potential Eurasian flashpoints like northern Norway, the Persian Gulf, and Korea.

Evolution of Soviet Military Doctrine

As the USSR gradually acquired a more diversified and capable force structure, Soviet planners expressed growing interest in the possibility of conflicts waged below the level of all-out nuclear war. Soviet writers had entered the 1960s espousing the concept of a single threshold war. Once conflict started, Soviet military authors maintained, escalation to general nuclear war would be inevitable. The notion of "war by phases" entered Soviet doctrinal writing in the mid-1960s. A major East-West conflict might not begin with intercontinental nuclear strikes, Soviet writers argued, but might progress to full-scale nuclear combat only after periods of warfare in which the two sides employed only conventional forces or tactical nuclear weapons.

During the 1970s, the Soviets devoted further attention to, and elaborated on, the concept of a conventional phase in East-West conflict. In the 1960s, Soviet analysts had described the conventional phase as a brief period, lasting perhaps one week, which would inevitably be followed by escalation to nuclear war. By the mid-1970s, the conventional phase had been lengthened to a "strategic operation," an appellation previously reserved for conflicts involving nuclear weapons, lasting up to thirty days. By the early 1980s, Soviet military spokesmen were discussing the possibility of entire wars between the great powers conducted without the use of nuclear weapons.

The foregoing is not intended to argue that the USSR has relinquished nuclear options at either the tactical, theater, or strategic level. Once weapon deployments provide a military option to a nation, it obviously will continue to exist regardless of changes in military doctrine and, indeed, will influence efforts to create additional options thereafter. The growing Soviet emphasis upon conventional options would not be viable if the USSR had not achieved rough nuclear parity. Parity also has made possible major changes in Soviet pronouncements on the utility of nuclear weapons. In retrospect, Brezhnev's renunciation of strategic superiority at Tula in 1977 appears to have been based on three major conclusions by Soviet policymakers.

1. The achievement of strategic parity at high numbers of nuclear warheads on each side makes additional investments in theater nuclear and conventional forces more attractive, in terms of political-military payoffs, than incremental gains in strategic capabilities.

2. The failure (at that point) of research and development programs to provide ballistic missile defenses capable of

significantly limiting damage from a nuclear exchange makes the price of victory in nuclear war unacceptably high.

3. Past Soviet statements concerning the possibility of victory in a nuclear war and the need for strategic superiority have been counter-productive in that they are used by "anti-Soviet elements" in the West as arguments for increased defense spending.

These three conclusions are probably also behind recent Soviet doctrinal pronouncements that espouse deterrence based on parity in strategic retaliatory capabilities and reject the possibility of either strategic defense or victory in nuclear war. This new Soviet obsession with deterrence, as opposed to nuclear war-fighting, can be found in recent formulations by some of their highest-ranking military leaders. These statements portray a core pessimism concerning the possibility of conducting a nuclear war successfully. Likewise, Soviet commentators argue the theoretical inadvisability of pursuing defensive weaponry; the Kremlin no doubt fears that U.S. efforts to develop strategic defenses will require a response that will bleed resources away from areas in which it sees greater political-military utility.

Future Soviet Weapon Programs

Over the next decade or so, it seems likely that the USSR will allocate significant resources toward the following three military force planning objectives:

• Continued modernization of conventional forces;

• Improved survivability of offensive strategic forces by deploying mobile ICBMs;

• A capability to suddenly and rapidly deploy ballistic missile defenses based on existing technologies.

The USSR can be expected to seek to maintain its conventional advantages in the European and Near East theaters of military operations. In all likelihood, these forces will not be expanded. The Soviets face severe demographic problems with respect to any further expansion of their force structure and, in any case, they could never hope to match Chinese manpower. Thus, conventional force improvements will probably entail more advanced equipment and measures designed to ensure success early in a conflict, given that structural deficiencies in the USSR's and Eastern Europe's economies would pose severe problems in any protracted conflict. The Soviet Union also will continue to streamline its force structure and organizational framework — building on a series of reorganizations begun in the late 1970s — in response to the conditions of modern warfare.

A major by-product of such efforts will be reduced warning time for NATO. Throughout the doctrinal changes of the last twenty years, Soviet writers have held steadfastly to the importance of the "initial period of the war." Originally, the beginning of a conflict was seen to be decisive because Soviet writers predicted that massive nuclear strikes would take place at the outset of a war and would determine its outcome. Today, the initial period is said to be important because such advanced conventional systems as the new generation of Soviet tactical ballistic missiles hold out the possibility of fighting and winning a war before NATO could employ nuclear weapons, or at least before it could employ them effectively.

The major addition to Soviet strategic forces in the late 1980s will be mobile ICBMs. The Strategic Rocket Forces (SRF) will probably acquire both a land-mobile and rail-mobile versions, fulfilling a longstanding perceived Soviet requirement for mobile missiles of greater than tactical (1000 km) range. The SRF will continue to maintain silo-based ICBMs as well, but unless the United States greatly increases its ICBM force and related facilities, deploys defenses around its ICBM silos, or deploys mobile ICBMs, there is no military reason for the number of silo-based Soviet ICBMs to increase. Mobile ICBMs will reinforce the Soviet strategy of attempting to win any war quickly, using only conventional weapons, by making escalation to the strategic nuclear level an even less attractive response for an opponent undergoing conventional defeat. Soviet writers have expressed considerable concern—some rhetorical, some legitimate—that the deployment of MX ICBMs and D-5 submarine-launched ballistic missiles will give the United States a preemptive first strike capability in the 1990s. Creating a reserve of mobile ICBMs will reduce this possibility significantly.

Although the USSR wastes no opportunity to attack the U.S. Strategic Defense Initiative (SDI), and has emphasized in the Geneva talks and every other forum, including the recent U.S.-Soviet summit, the need to ban or severely limit research and development of spaced-based defenses, it maintains a vigorous strategic defense program of its own. This program includes a major research effort for at least the weapon components of exotic missile defense technologies, and a much larger effort to develop and deploy new land-based missile interceptors guided by ground-based radars. In the fourteen years since the Anti-Ballistic Missile (ABM) Treaty was signed, the USSR has modernized all components of the GALOSH ABM system deployed around Moscow, as permitted by the treaty. Moreover, Soviet anti-tactical ballistic missile (ATBM) technology has continued to advance through the development of a new generation of surface-to-air missiles (SAMs), one of which is said to have some capability to intercept strategic reentry vehicles. These defensive capabilities remain minimal in the face of the West's large number of offensive warheads, but the USSR's apparent willingness to probe the limits of the ABM Treaty, to say nothing of constructing a large phased-array radar at Krasnoyarsk in apparent direct violation of the treaty, has heightened concerns about the USSR's ability and perhaps intention to expand its missile defenses rapidly at some future point.

The GALOSH ABM system, as well as Soviet air defense doctrine and pattern of deployments, indicate that the USSR's highest priority is to protect clusters of political targets, military command and control assets, and vital war-supporting industries. Unlike the United States, the USSR has shown little interest in defending its ICBM silos. A Soviet break-out from the ABM Treaty, if one occurred utilizing existing technologies, would probably be directed toward establishing dense deployments of endo- and exo-atmospheric interceptors whose targeting "footprints" constituted non-adjacent "bubbles" around concentrations of administrative facilities, military forces and bases, and military-related industries.

The extent of Soviet programs to develop more advanced missile defenses is not so clear. Although the USSR is usually credited with parity, and sometimes advantage, in directed energy technologies, it is clearly behind in such critical areas as electronics, computing, optics, and communications. If this assessment is accurate, the Soviets might be expected to adopt a brute force approach if they were to deploy advanced ballistic missile defenses. Initial Soviet efforts, similar to their early space program, could consist of a series of spectacular "firsts"—probably involving beam weaponry—of great propaganda value, but little military utility. Eventually, the Soviets might deploy massive ground-based laser complexes rather than seek to master the technologies necessary to deploy lasers in space. Computer inferiority might be compensated for by leaving more "men in the loop," perhaps through the deployment of manned orbital battle management facilities. Whatever the exact dimensions of Soviet missile defense research, the USSR's various ABM-related activities indicate that the United States cannot assume that it would be the only nation to deploy large-scale ballistic missile defenses.

EVALUATION OF U.S. FORCES AND DOCTRINE

Despite years of analysis, the consequences of the waning of American strategic superiority remain a major point of disagreement in the West. A great deal of attention has been focused on the putative vulnerability of silo-based ICBMs, but questions also have been raised concerning the future survivability of bombers and even strategic submarines. For the most part, U.S. strategic weapon modernization programs are designed to alleviate these possible vulnerabilities of strategic offensive forces. The Reagan Administration is more or less emulating the Soviets to relieve its vulnerable ICBM force, seeking to deploy both a heavy, silo-based missile (MX) and a reserve of lighter, mobile missiles (Midgetman). Bombers and submarines are being equipped with cruise missiles, greatly adding to their potential missions. "Stealth" technology and highly accurate submarine-launched missiles hold the promise, in the 1990s, of shifting some of the responsibility for attacking time-urgent, hard targets away from the ICBM force.

While these programs will maintain, or perhaps even shift the balance of strategic forces in favor of the U.S., they cannot in any sense restore U.S. strategic predominance. And the most damaging aspect of the Soviet achievement of parity relates not to central strategic forces and threats to U.S. territory, but to the confidence of European decision-makers in U.S. commitments to defend Western Europe. Extended, not central, deterrence is the major victim of the Soviet strategic build-up.

Faced with the refusal of the European members of NATO to pay the material costs of a conventional defense of Western Europe and American refusal to pay the political price at home (i.e., conscription), every U.S. administration since the early 1970s has sought to make American intercontinental forces relevant to European defense calculations. This effort has consisted largely of developing the weapons and targeting doctrines necessary for limited strategic options that could be employed, theoretically, in response to Soviet success in a war in Europe or Asia.

Many Western analysts, however, feel these efforts lack credibility. While limited strategic options are seen to be useful in deterring limited Soviet attacks on the continental United States, the great counter-force capability of the Soviet ICBM force is seen to make it very difficult for U.S. leaders to contemplate expending their own ICBMs, thereby provoking a Soviet counter-strike, in response to anything less than attacks on U.S. territory. As Soviet leaders must recognize this deficiency, the argument continues, the benefits of such limited options for the credibility of extended deterrence must be considered marginal.

The credibility of extended deterrence is reduced further by the growing mismatch between U.S. weapons and war plans. Most limited options would be executed most effectively by ICBMs given their speed, accuracy, assured penetration capabilities and—as compared to submarine-launched missiles—the greater reliability and flexibility of their command and control system. But ICBM warheads will be a shrinking portion of the U.S. strategic arsenal for at least the next ten years, if not indefinitely. And the deficiency is even worse if residual U.S. ICBM capabilities following a Soviet counter-force attack are considered. In such a situation, U.S. decision-makers would likely face a severe shortage of counter-force retaliatory assets, yet also would be reluctant to employ other systems, like submarine-launched missiles, which would constitute the vast bulk of surviving strategic forces.

The United States is currently seeking to alleviate the disparities among its strategic doctrine, war plans, and weapons inventory by modernizing all three components of its strategic forces. Of equal or greater importance, U.S. command and control capabilities are being modernized and made more survivable in order to allow national command authorities the flexibility to implement increasingly elaborate war plans with a variety of weapon systems.

The Reemergence of Ballistic Missile Defenses

While continuing the gradual embrace of nuclear war-fighting plans and doctrines initiated in the 1970s, the Reagan Administration also has accelerated and broadened research programs intended to explore technological avenues for defending actively against ballistic missiles. The SDI is the latest manifestation of popular and specialist concern about the durability and political consequences of deterrence based on mutual vulnerability. To paraphrase the President, the only way to truly protect ourselves from nuclear weapons is to develop defenses capable of rendering them "impotent and obsolete."

Two distinct schools of thought concerning the purpose of U.S. strategic defense efforts currently co-exist uneasily in justifications of the program. The first school—usually associated with President Reagan and Secretary of Defense Casper Weinberger—seeks a fundamental reorientation of the postwar strategic environment from one based on offensive striking power to one dominated by defensive systems. The second school, usually credited to civilian defense analysts, the technical community, and the armed services, envisions only a modification of deterrence. Nuclear war would be deterred by a combination of threatened retaliation and denial. Ballistic missile defenses would be used to complicate Soviet targeting efforts and to enhance the survivability of offensive forces, thus increasing Soviet uncertainty about the consequences of a first-strike.

Though not strictly mutually exclusive, these two approaches could lead in practice to very different preferences as to priorities in BMD research and procurement programs. The President's March 1983 speech clearly envisioned a comprehensive defense of the population of the United States and its allies. The most expeditious route to the comprehensive and very effective system required to defend cities and other urban-industrial targets involves the early deployment of weapons—necessarily involving components in space—capable of destroying missiles in their boost-phase, before they could release the multiple warheads, decoys, and other penetration aids that would greatly complicate the defender's task. But even an accelerated effort to erect space-based, boost-phase defenses could not be expected to achieve an operational capability until well into the next century, if then. This would give the USSR years to develop both offensive and defensive counter-measures (e.g., to deploy additional numbers of missiles and warheads, to develop new types of missiles that could withstand directed energy weapons and accelerate more rapidly through the boost-phase, to deploy traditional ABMs, etc). Since the Soviets could probably deploy a very dense ballistic missile defense system based on existing technologies far more quickly than the U.S. could deploy an effective space-based system, implementation of the President's objective for the SDI could mean accepting a Soviet defensive advantage for the next twenty years. Preliminary estimates of the cost of a comprehensive space-based system suggest, in addition, that expenditures on defenses would be so great as necessarily to divert resources from other pressing military needs, leading perhaps to additional Soviet offensive advantages as well.

Aiming for a defensive system intended only to reduce the vulnerability of critical military targets, particularly ICBMs and command centers, would alleviate the above problem, but would not achieve the President's objective of ending American vulnerability. Indeed, to the extent that such limited BMD deployments would seem to make possible the successful defense of key U.S. military assets, they might induce the Soviets to increase the size of planned attacks, thereby further blurring the distinction between counterforce and countervalue attacks. Deployment of limited BMD systems also would greatly complicate arms control negotiations, thus perhaps removing impediments to the expansion of Soviet offensive forces. Limited U.S. missile defenses thus may not discourage a reactive expansion of the Soviet offensive arsenal, even if they complicated Soviet targeting efforts by degrading the assured penetrivity of ballistic missiles that has undergirded the Soviet preemptive strategy since the late 1950s.

The emergence of SDI also will require a major reorientation in the two nations' approach to arms reductions. In fact, the effectiveness of a population defense version of SDI would depend in no small part upon the prior accomplishment of major reductions in offensive force levels—and continuing agreements which effectively and indefinitely bound the two sides to such reduced forces. Defenses made effective by deep cuts in strategic offensive forces also could help to solve the twin problems of stability and verification that necessarily accompany efforts to bring about steep reductions in offensive weapons. Such an altered strategic environment would lower first-strike incentives on both sides and provide a margin of safety against cheating.

Indeed, the inevitable interrelationships between SDI and arms control greatly complicate decisions about the program's future. In order for SDI to work, the Soviets must acquiesce in the same degree of limitations on ICBMs which they repeatedly rejected during the SALT and START processes of the 1970s and early 1980s. Being hostage to Moscow's veto is not an entirely negative situation, since supporters of SDI can argue for funding from Congress on the basis that SDI represents the ultimate bargaining chip. Unfortunately, bargaining chips must eventually be cashed, and the new, more adroit Soviet leader seems to be proposing the very reductions in Soviet offensive forces required for a viable defense system as a *quid pro quo* for American abandonment of SDI.

Deficiencies in Theater Nuclear and Conventional Forces

After a decade of ignoring the Soviet achievement of strategic nuclear parity, NATO finally began to address the previously noted nuclear and conventional imbalances at the theater and tactical levels during the Carter Administration in the late 1970s. In the 1980s, NATO began to implement force structure improvements and modernization initiatives in several areas.

- *Long-range intermediate nuclear forces:* The planned deployment of 572 Pershing II ballistic missiles and ground-launched cruise missiles in Europe will be completed by 1989, and will reduce the likelihood that the Soviets would consider initiating or threatening a nuclear strike on Western Europe in the belief that their own territory would be spared. (The USSR is responding to NATO's deployments with resumed deployments of SS-20s, as well as additional deployments of shorter-range tactical missiles in Eastern Europe. The latter appears to have caused some political difficulties within the Warsaw Pact reminiscent of those in NATO prior to the initial Pershing deployments.)

- *Short-range intermediate nuclear forces:* NATO has decided to remove several thousand obsolete and vulnerable tactical nuclear weapons from Europe, reducing its inventory from around 6,000 to nearly 4,000. At the same time, the United States is manufacturing enhanced radiation nuclear warheads for use on Lance missiles and artillery which, in the event of a tactical nuclear war, could limit collateral damage to friendly forces and territory. These weapons are stockpiled in the United States, but presumably would be deployed to Europe during a crisis or a conflict. Like the deployment of Pershings and cruise missiles, this step is said to make NATO's strategy of flexible response somewhat more credible.

- *General purpose forces:* Both U.S. and West European conventional force structures are being modernized substantially and slightly expanded. Increases in ammunition stockpiles, spare parts, maintenance schedules, and training time have complemented these modernization programs—although they remain far below stated objectives.

All these efforts are necessary, but not sufficient, to maintain an adequate military balance in Europe. NATO has yet to devise and implement a doctrine and strategy that credibly would be able to defeat a Warsaw Pact offensive without the use of nuclear weapons, and thus still, in the end, depends on the Soviets' fear of the unknowable consequences of any use of nuclear weapons to deter such an offensive in a crisis.

Rather than confront directly the Soviet concept of modern, high-intensity conflict as it has emerged over the last 25 years, NATO staked its defense upon two critical assumptions: adequate warning and stability of the rear. In the simplest terms, NATO's strategy boils down to the proposition that if the Warsaw Pact conducts the type of war the

West has prepared to fight, NATO could defend successfully. To be sure, each NATO member has developed and continues to perfect operational methods for utilizing the forces at its disposal—for example, the U.S. Army and Air Force's air/land battle doctrine. But the emphasis here must be placed on battle, revealing the tactical orientation of such efforts.

Should the Kremlin act to invalidate NATO's assumptions of adequate warning and rear-area security, the alliance's recent efforts could be undone. Without timely and unambiguous warning of hostile intent, and a political decision to act, NATO's nuclear forces could be vulnerable to attack by conventional forces and the West's superior mobilization potential would be taken *en passant.* Without rear-area security, NATO's surviving nuclear forces would be susceptible to further degradation and, far more to the point, troops airlifted from the United States would arrive to find their prepositioned stockpiles of weapons and equipment destroyed.

In the final analysis, NATO's current strategy remains dependent on the one course of action acceptable to all member nations—the threat of escalation to global nuclear war, should the Warsaw Pact successfully invade Western Europe. Regardless that these threats make no sense militarily, the uncertainties they introduce presumably provide some deterrent value. But, so long as this state of affairs continues, NATO will remain vulnerable to the effective implementation of the preferred Soviet option of a sudden conventional attack aimed at forcing the capitulation of key NATO members before nuclear weapons could be employed, or at least employed effectively.

OFFSETTING FACTORS: MILITARY INTANGIBLES

The discussion of the military balance up to this point has focused on capabilities and doctrines in the abstract. Such comparisons, while useful, suffer from several artificialities with respect to political, societal, and industrial aspects that would come into play should the two great powers actually face the prospect of open hostilities. Two intangible factors seem destined to play a special role: the reliability of allies and industrial flexibility. In addition, the quality of the two sides' officer corps and enlisted ranks, the intangibles of leadership, resiliency, and personal bravery would be important factors in any NATO/Warsaw Pact conflict.

Coalition Warfare and the Question of Cohesion

At the political-military level, a conflict in Central Europe could be viewed as a competitive process in which the two sides attempted to prevent themselves from disintegrating. Both NATO and the Warsaw Pact would experience centrifugal pressures as the result of a deep crisis and war. The side that was able to best manage the competition—that is, reinforce its own cohesion while accelerating the break-up of the rival coalition—would possess a major advantage.

The Soviet leadership is acutely aware of the twin aspects of opportunity and disaster that they must confront at the brink of war with NATO. The potential fault lines in the Eastern Alliance inform Soviet preferences for a rapid conventional dismemberment of NATO. From such preferences arise the military requirements for a preemptive attack launched by initially unreinforced groups of forces permanently located in East Germany, Poland, Czechoslovakia, and Hungary. While NATO has not kept pace with the Soviet general purpose force build-up, the West's efforts have forced the Soviets to rely far more than in the past upon the armed force of their East European allies for successful execution of their war plans. Thus, Soviet strategy for coalition warfare is paced by the fragility of the governments of the USSR's satellites.

Moscow has chosen an offensive solution to the problem of alliance cohesion: to bring about the collapse of NATO before its empire suffers a similar fate. The Soviets increasingly stress the political components of a conflict during all its phases. Recent Warsaw Pact exercises have demonstrated, for example, the importance of special operations forces—or Spetznaz—in conducting acts of sabotage, terrorism, and assassination. These exercises practiced the refinement of tactics that would seek to demoralize NATO's population and disintegrate civilian and military cohesion. Resources devoted to training and equipping Spetznaz units have been increased significantly and Spetznaz elements stationed in the USSR were recently deployed to Czechoslovakia and Hungary.

NATO faces a series of dilemmas in responding to Soviet political strategy for coalition warfare. Can the West successfully exploit the Warsaw Pact vulnerabilities that have such a decisive influence upon Soviet War plans? Is an offensive response suited to NATO's defensive *raison d'être?* Could efforts to exploit Soviet weakness in Eastern Europe actually accelerate the Warsaw Pact's slide toward preemptive attack by providing Moscow with what it could perceive as serious evidence of hostile intent on NATO's part?

There are no easy answers to these potentially vital questions, but it would seem highly imprudent to ignore their implications for NATO's defense. It is not clear that Warsaw Pact fault lines can be exploited during the period of maximum danger to NATO: the initial hours and days of a war. The history of partisan warfare and resistance during World War II indicates that disintegration of the Axis occurred only after a lengthy period of conflict during which the fate of Nazi Germany was sealed on the battlefield. Even accounting for a much shorter conflict than the Second World War, the case can be made that the cohesion of the Warsaw Pact will be strongest in the initial period of the war, and that NATO must demonstrate its ability to withstand the initial onslaught in order for divisive effects to become pronounced within the Eastern bloc. In short, successful defense appears to be an essential element in exploiting potential Warsaw Pact wartime vulnerabilities.

Threatening Soviet control over Eastern Europe prior to a conflict is fraught with escalatory consequences. During a severe crisis, threats to Soviet dominance, especially in East Germany, could tip the scales toward war by confirming the worst of Soviet suspicions. Such efforts could thus rob NATO of valuable time in which to mobilize for war. Even taking the logical steps in peacetime so that NATO could execute a counter-political control strategy rapidly once hostilities erupted could create dangerous tensions vis-a-vis Moscow and reinforce the Soviet offensive-oriented strategy. Finally, such efforts could well constitute a losing game; the porous nature of Western societies could allow the Soviets to preposition assets for political warfare in Western Europe and the United States while denying such an advantage to the West.

Economic Asymmetries

It has become conventional wisdom to juxtapose Eastern military strength against Western economic power. In peacetime, economic strength is a major Western advantage. But what about in a crisis or war; of what advantage would the West's economies be then?

The difficulty with Western and Eastern industrial power comparisons is that they do not take into account the temporal dynamics of a U.S.-Soviet conflict. In order to determine whether the industrial democracies could offset the established military forces of the Eastern bloc with latent industrial strength, an *a priori* question concerning the amount of strategic warning available to the West and the political capacity to act upon it must be addressed.

Although the Soviets may strive for, and perhaps achieve, tactical surprise, both sides have long assumed that long-term strategic warning of war would be evident to decisionmakers through their respective intelligence services. Unfortunately, it could well prove difficult for the Western democracies to place their economies on an integrated war footing (from which they would derive maximum military leverage vis-a-vis the East) significantly prior to the actual outbreak of hostilities. Since 1981, the Reagan administration has sought to increase the capacity of American industry to transition rapidly to a wartime footing, but these efforts probably have not reduced the change-over time to less than a year. Given the preceding analysis concerning Soviet planning for a rapid conflict, the West may not have time to bring its massive economic potential to bear.

In a short war setting, the command economies of the Warsaw Pact enjoy several distinct advantages. In many respects, Warsaw Pact economies are already on a wartime footing: central planning is a hallmark of a war economy, a larger percentage of the Eastern industrial infrastructure is devoted to military products than their Western counterparts, and the civilian sector depends more on heavy industry than that of the West. As in the case of allied reliability, the Soviets appear to be planning to mask their economic vulnerabilities by rapidly exploiting those of their adversaries.

Aristotle portrayed commercial polities as slow to take action but, once aroused, possessed of great capacity to resist conquest and eventually to secure victory against an adversary. This is the challenge facing the industrial democracies. In order to maintain the economic underpinnings of their power, the NATO nations and Japan could not impede their economies by imposing the strictures of wartime centralization until a conflict appeared inevitable. Enough military strength must be maintained in peacetime, however, to buy time to shift to an integrated wartime economy. By carefully planning for such a transition, the West could strengthen deterrence by forcing the East to bear a greater burden of its economic inefficiency.

CURRENT OUTLOOK: SOVIET UNION

The Soviet Union is no doubt highly desirous of retaining the political-military advantages which have resulted from its achievement of strategic parity with the United States. Faced with strategic stalemate, in true reflection of their respective military-industrial advantages, the great powers have chosen different paths of military competition. The Soviets are pursuing the "low road" of conventional and theater nuclear superiority based largely on overwhelming numbers of forces. The U.S. strategic modernization program, SDI, and emphasis on the "emerging technologies" of conventional forces constitute a "high road," so to speak, of the application of advanced technologies to solve strategic problems.

U.S. (and British and French) nuclear modernization programs are surely very worrisome to the Kremlin. By the turn of the century, the United States and its allies will have greatly increased the counterforce capabilities of their land- and sea-based forces. The Galosh ABM system around Moscow, never a serious problem for U.S. central forces, will be incapable of protecting the Soviet leadership from attacks by British or French nuclear forces, and perhaps U.S. Pershings deployed in Europe (to say nothing of the Chinese). Even the application of "Stealth" technologies to cruise missiles and aircraft has definite first strike implications from a Soviet point of view.

But far more troublesome to the Soviets is SDI. When combined with growing U.S. counter-force capabilities, even less-than-perfect defenses could be seen by the Soviets as placing them at a major disadvantage, permitting the U.S. to contemplate a first strike with the defenses in place to protect against a necessarily reduced and perhaps ragged Soviet retaliation. Even if such a dire situation failed to materialize, Soviet leaders probably would fear that SDI would eventually require a response-in-kind, diverting their resources from areas of greater political-military utility.

Soviet concerns also extend to the application of U.S. technology to conventional forces. Before his removal as Chief of the Soviet General Staff, Marshal Ogarkov noted in *Red Star* that "the emergence in developed countries of automated reconnaissance-and-strike complexes, long-range high accuracy terminally guided combat systems, unmanned flying machines, and qualitatively new electronic control systems make many types of weapons global and make it possible to sharply increase (by at least an order of magnitude) the destructive potential of conventional weapons, bringing them closer, so to speak, to weapons of mass destruction in terms of effectiveness." This observation reflects continuing Soviet concerns that Western technical superiority may eventually overwhelm the advantages in general purpose forces that the USSR has worked so hard to develop, and which they now seek to make more pertinent by neutralizing Western nuclear capabilities.

CURRENT OUTLOOK: UNITED STATES

If the United States maintain their strategic modernization programs as currently envisioned, more or less, and if modernization of British and French strategic forces proceeds as planned, many of the most troubling aspects of the strategic balance could be rectified by the mid-to-late-1990s. These prospects must be considered uncertain, however. Tightening budgetary constraints mean that nuclear modernization programs must be traded off increasingly against other military and civilian requirements—both here and in Western Europe. Moreover, the U.S. has yet to resolve the issue of how to assure the survivability of its ICBM force. With the MX now more or less rejected, both mobile systems and active defenses will come increasingly under scrutiny.

These problems notwithstanding, the major difficulty facing the West remains its inferiority in conventional military capabilities around the Eurasian periphery. Indeed, the balance on the central front in Europe may well suffer over the next fifteen years, as growing threats to U.S. interests in the Pacific basin and Southwest Asia, combined with a shift in the economic, demographic, and political basis of U.S. policy, continue to bias American procurement in favor of naval and air forces. In addition, facing only modest economic growth and structural problems of unemployment, it seems likely that West European governments will exhibit even greater reluctance to increase defense expenditures over the next ten years than they have in the past.

Moreover, there seems to be a greater popular awareness of, and participation in, security decisions in many West European nations, particularly those issues involving nuclear forces, and a slowly growing gap between U.S. and West European perceptions concerning requirements for an adequate deterrent posture. The political implications of these trends will place additional obstacles in the path of force modernization.

The challenge to U.S. policymakers over the mid-term is to correct existing nuclear and conventional weaknesses while holding open the possibility of a long-term dramatic breakthrough in defensive technologies and avoiding a Soviet decision to deploy missile defenses based on traditional technologies. A clever approach to arms control negotiations could aid in this effort, along with carefully balanced military programs and enlightened diplomacy. If breakthroughs in defensive technologies do not materialize, the need to correct nuclear and conventional weaknesses will persist, as the USSR can be expected to offset U.S. progress toward negating current Soviet advantages. Should a defensive breakthrough occur, however, the terms of the competition might be altered fundamentally. The key problems facing U.S. decisionmakers are discussed below.

ICBM Vulnerability

Unless the United States restores a measure of survivability to its ICBM force, or replaces those capabilities with other forces also capable of carrying out prompt attacks against hardened and relocatable targets, the types of warheads that theoretically could be used in the event of a Soviet breakthrough in a conventional or tactical nuclear war to support deployed U.S. and allied forces would have to be husbanded to deter Soviet attacks on the continental United States. Unfortunately, the options through which the United States might reestablish such a survivable counter-force capability for limited options are severely constrained.

A missile defense system might be able to defend silo-based ICBMs efficiently, thus protecting such capabilities, but deploying such a system would require modifying or terminating the ABM Treaty and would add to the likelihood that the USSR would deploy a nation-wide missile defense system based on existing ground-based technologies. Such a development could have serious adverse effects, not the least of which could be negation of the deterrent value of British and French strategic forces. The mobile small ICBM now in development might also provide a solution, but many problems of cost, survivability, and the political feasibility of deployments remain to be resolved.

The dilemma might be finessed by removing U.S. ICBMs from plans for central nuclear war, reducing their number, and earmarking them for use solely in limited contingencies. Such a move would establish a separate force dedicated to executing limited strategic options while shifting the retaliatory and major war-fighting burdens of possible central exchanges to a force composed of bombers and submarines. These latter would be beefed up explicitly to compensate for the loss of the ICBM force, unless it had proven possible in arms negotiations to bring about overall reductions in both sides' forces.

Although significant efforts have been expended on designing possible limited strategic options (LSOs) for nuclear forces, U.S. targeting plans, according to several sources, remain biased toward large-scale attacks. Targeting packages are apparently designed in a top-down fashion, reflecting the priority accorded to major retaliatory missions, resulting in LSOs that are not optimized either in terms of the number of weapons involved or the military value of the potential targets. Since ICBMs are the preferred instrument for executing controlled, discriminate, and time-urgent strikes, their dedication solely to limited roles would remove this preference accorded to major strikes and facilitate the design and execution of more effective LSOs, thus strengthening deterrence.

If this option were selected, the U.S. would need only to maintain enough ICBM warheads to execute LSOs (several hundred should be sufficient). This number would not be large enough to threaten a significant portion of the Soviet ICBM force, thus partially defusing arguments about U.S. first-strike capabilities (the Soviets are already complaining about the emerging counter-force role for U.S. strategic submarines, however). Indeed, it would be foolish operationally to use MIRVed ICBMs for LSOs, because multi-warhead systems drive up the attack density and diminish targeting flexibility. A dedicated limited strike system would use its payload to assure the accurate delivery of a single, low yield nuclear weapon through possible future Soviet strategic defenses. Reductions of U.S. ICBM warheads also would deprive the Soviets of the strategic leverage which is now associated with their ICBM force, by removing those weapons' most important targets, thus perhaps inducing the USSR to respond more favorably to U.S. arms control proposals that would place tight limits on missile throw-weight.

Accepting permanent ICBM vulnerability, however, would place the entire burden of second-strike missions on U.S. submarines and bombers. Weapon programs that would provide the requisite accuracy (Trident II) and penetrivity (Stealth) are already underway. The key question would be the adequacy of command and control systems. The flexibility, responsiveness, and—most importantly—survivability of existing command systems would have to be improved measurably. Eventually, the U.S. might wish to consider the active defense of command and control assets to maintain the level of assured connectivity necessary to carry out all second-strike missions with bombers and submarines.

Retarding Soviet Deployment of ABM Systems Based on Existing Technologies

Western observers have worried periodically that the USSR possessed a latent ABM capability in its large inventory of air defense interceptors and radars. These fears have been reinforced, at times, by circumstances in which Soviet air defense radars appear to have been tracking missile flight-tests and by related activities. In recent years, concern about the Soviet Union's potential to break-out suddenly from the 1972 ABM Treaty and deploy a nation-wide ballistic missile defense system utilizing existing technologies has been aggravated by a number of factors:

- Upgrading of the GALOSH ABM system around Moscow with a new generation of interceptors and radars indicates continuing progress in these technologies. Maintenance of a "hot" production capability for the new interceptors is particularly troubling.

- Construction of a large, phased-array radar near Krasnoyarsk is an almost certain violation of the ABM Treaty. While the U.S. and British intelligence agencies appear to believe that the radar is primarily designed for early warning purposes and is not oriented properly to perform an ABM battle management function, it nevertheless remains extremely troubling that the USSR would violate the treaty so flagrantly. In addition, the tracking data derived from the Krasnoyarsk radar could be "handed off" to mobile ABM engagement radars that the Soviets are currently developing.

Theoretically, the United States might seek to reduce these concerns by negotiating amendments to the ABM Treaty which would tighten relevant provisions, particularly those pertaining to verification and compliance. Insofar as it does not itself deploy any operational ABMs, the United States might even consider seeking an amendment which would prohibit the currently permitted deployment of 100 interceptors at a single site, as well as tightening controls on radar deployments. A number of conflicting aims in U.S. strategic plans will all but rule out such possibilities, however.

For one, the possible need to defend Western Europe against Soviet tactical ballistic missiles might make it more difficult to negotiate clarifications of existing treaty restraints or to extend those restraints to anti-tactical ballistic missile systems in order to remove certain existing ambiguities. Secondly, many in the U.S. believe that the deployment of point missile defenses may be necessary to assure the survivability of U.S. ICBMs. These beliefs will grow more important if technical problems emerge in the development of the mobile Midgetman ICBM, or if mobile land-based missiles were to be banned in an arms control treaty. Efforts to explore point defense technologies again would limit the United States' ability to tighten relevant restrictions in the ABM Treaty and, indeed, might persuade the Soviets that termination of the treaty was all but inevitable and that they should therefore take advantage of their current lead in conventional technologies by getting a jump on deployments.

Most importantly, so long as the central thrust in U.S. strategic policy remains the exploration of the technical possibility of effective ballistic missile defenses utilizing advanced technologies, any efforts to tighten ABM restrictions will be politically, and increasingly technically, crippled. This tension between U.S. objectives will not disappear; more likely, it will be aggravated over the years.

To the extent that the United States appears to be moving towards a decision to deploy a nation-wide missile defense system, the Soviet Union will perceive less incentives to even appear to be abiding by the constraints in the ABM Treaty. Soviet leaders, no doubt, would never afford the United States the advantage of renouncing the treaty; they will protest their adherence to the end. Instead, the USSR will seek as long as possible to mask its deployments of new missile defenses in the guise of new air defense systems or under other rubrics. Eventually, it is the U.S. which would have to renounce the treaty or, at least, because of its open political system, take explicit public steps that clearly would be in violation of the treaty's constraints.

Moreover, this entire process will be fraught with dangers for U.S.-European relations. The first casualties of a serious Soviet ABM system, should they deploy one, would be the deterrent value of the British and French (and Chinese) nuclear forces. The Europeans will also perceive the continued pursuit of missile defenses as: (a) complicating and, thereby, making less likely the achievement of meaningful arms control, and (b) presaging the decoupling of American military power from the defense of Europe. For these and other reasons, the Europeans will protest as the two great military powers move toward the eventual abrogation of the existing arms control regime. The United States must recognize this likelihood as it develops strategic defense technologies and seek in its arms control policies, diplomacy, and other military programs to delay the Soviet reaction as long as possible, while simultaneously aiming to ease friction in the Western alliance.

Countering the Tactical Ballistic Missile Threat to Europe

Not surprisingly, in Geneva and elsewhere, the Kremlin is seeking to exploit European fears concerning American research into ballistic missile defense. One result has been to complicate efforts to determine whether ballistic missile defenses in Europe might not offer the most effective hedge against the very accurate, conventional ballistic missiles now being deployed with Soviet ground forces in Eastern Europe. These new Soviet missiles threaten the heart of NATO's defense policy of flexible response; they endanger the Alliance's capacity to resist aggression at the conventional level and to threaten nuclear escalation credibly should the Warsaw Pact's military success demand it. Even if there were major reductions in long- and medium-range nuclear-armed missiles, Soviet tactical ballistic missiles will increase the risk, and the consequences, of conventional war in Europe.

Tied as they are to the Warsaw Pact's offensively oriented strategy of preemptive surprise attack, these new deep-strike Soviet missiles will create strong incentives for the Soviets to substitute military for diplomatic action early in a crisis, before NATO's vulnerable military assets can be dispersed to more secure field locations. Most of NATO's highest value military installations (nuclear storage sites, airfields, air defenses, and reinforcement depots)—a few hundred in number—are located within 300 miles of the inter-German border. Based in Eastern Europe, new Soviet tactical missiles could easily reach these critical installations (the SS-22 has a 560 mile range, while the SS-23's range is 300 miles).

There are several possible counters to this emerging threat. Some, however, like suppressive fire against Soviet missile launchers, could heighten the risk of war during crises by increasing Soviet incentives to launch a preemptive attack. Others, including such defensive hedges as improved capabilities for dispersal and mobility, can succeed only if political leaders believe strategic warning signals and react decisively. But fear of provoking a Soviet attack could inhibit such precautionary measures as dispersing nuclear weapons and, thus, paradoxically, increase the value of preemption from the Soviet perspective.

The development of active defenses against these tactical ballistic missiles, by comparison, would be entirely consistent with the historic premise that NATO is a purely defensive military alliance. And because they would not raise the tension between prudent military preparations and provocative actions, missile defenses would not raise questions of stability in crises. Most important, even if NATO leaders failed to react to warning and the Warsaw Pact successfully surprised the alliance, the effectiveness of ballistic missile defenses need not be seriously undermined. An anti-tactical ballistic missile (ATBM) system would constitute a major increment in NATO's ability to withstand the initial shock of a Soviet *blitzkrieg,* thus perhaps buying enough time for Eastern alliance cohesion and economic vulnerabilities to make themselves felt.

There are major political and technical barriers to the successful development and deployment of an ATBM system in defense of NATO, however. To begin with, such an effort would not be welcomed in many NATO capitals so soon after the "Euromissile debate." The West European domestic political climate also will set stiff technical challenges for ATBM technology. The deployment of hundreds of nuclear-armed ATBMs to the continent, for example, would clearly be imprudent. Conventionally-armed ATBMs, however, present a more difficult technical challenge. And the greater the degree of technical difficulty, the more resources would have to be drawn away from badly needed improvements in general purpose forces.

Consequently, rather than pursuing ATBMs as a high-priority program, thus duplicating the problems current plaguing SDI, NATO might seek initially only a limited self-defense capability for its air defenses. The alliance is devoting significant resources toward upgrading NATO's air defense network against modern Soviet strike aircraft. The new Patriot surface-to-air missile sites, however, are vulnerable to attack by conventionally-armed Soviet TBMs. By modifying existing hardware, Patriot could be upgraded to protect itself, even though the vast majority of European territory would not be defended. Endowing NATO air defenses with some self-protection capability would maintain pace with similar Soviet developments, and help deter a Soviet attack by seriously complicating the delicate timing necessary to coordinate missile and air attacks.

On a longer-term basis, the development of a new non-nuclear ATBM system might offer attractive opportunities for European scientific cooperation with the United States. The first phase might consist of only ground-based components: high-acceleration interceptors and supporting radars. In a second phase, airborne or space-based early warning sensors might be added to the system, substantially broadening coverage against a range of Soviet attack options.

Reducing Deficiencies in NATO's Conventional Posture

Even while pursuing the changes in its strategic and tactical nuclear forces described above, the United States and its West European allies will have to continue to work at improving the balance of conventional forces and capabilities. The "emerging technologies," if combined with necessary changes in tactics and organization, offer clear prospects for impressive gains in certain types of conventional capabilities. Still, one suspects that continued efforts will be necessary in the more pedestrian aspects of military strength: expanding stocks of ammunition and spare parts, reducing downtime required for equipment maintenance, increasing the interoperability of the different na-

Figure 1

DEFENSE SPENDING (% of GDP)
Non U.S. NATO

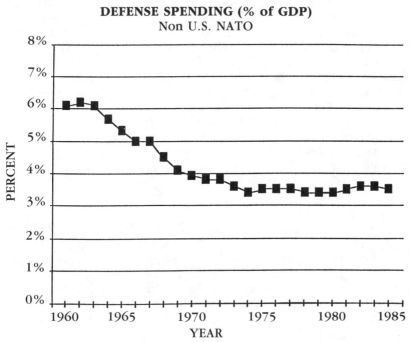

tional forces, and so forth. Steps like these could do much to improve the alliance's deterrent posture. Yet NATO faces serious problems in its efforts to remedy current problems.

Foremost among these is money. Since 1970, the military budgets of most NATO nations have stabilized firmly as a share of their gross domestic product (see figure 1). The United States increased its share sharply during the first Reagan term, but it too now seems to have leveled off and it may well decline during the second half of the 1980s. Given this history, the fact that public opinion in most NATO nations is firmly opposed to increases in defense spending, and the record of even conservative governments in refusing to make significant changes in budgetary priorities, it seems almost certain that future growth in NATO defense budgets will be limited. At best, NATO budgets might rise in step with growth in domestic economies; more likely, they will remain relatively stable for the foreseeable future. Short of a major crisis in Europe, conventional force modernization and the correction of existing deficiencies will have to be accomplished without an infusion of additional resources. The problem is aggravated, of course, by the continuing increases in the real cost of modern military weapons. In Britain, France, and the United States, the demands of nuclear modernization programs add an additional complication. And a special problem exists in Germany, in that the declining size of the German manpower pool will exercise a powerful constraint on that nation's defense choices in the 1990s.

None of this is to suggest that NATO's problems are hopeless; simply that the alliance must be realistic in settling its future plans. Choices have to be made; not all deficiencies can be remedied at once. The cost of alternatives have to be explored seriously and, at times, preference will have to be given to lower cost alternatives.

Finally, fiscal constraints on NATO's military postures emphasize once again the desirability of greater cooperation among the military establishments of the sovereign members of the alliance. To the extent that duplication can be eliminated, that national forces are enabled to operate together effectively, that national plans are coordinated and meshed into an overall strategy for the alliance as a whole, all the members will benefit. We may all hang together, but surely we will all hang separately.

CONCLUSION

In the winter and spring of 1987, the United States and the Soviet Union made rapid progress toward a treaty that would require the destruction of all intermediate- and medium-range missiles in Europe, and sharply curtail their deployment elsewhere. This progress resulted primarily from surprising concessions on the part of the USSR. First, shortly after the turn of the year, Soviet General Secretary Mikhail Gorbachev reversed the existing Soviet position, stating that it would be possible to "delink" an agreement on European missiles from other arms negotiations on central strategic offensive forces and strategic offensive forces and strategic defenses. (The issues had been linked, previously, by the Soviet side, following the Reykjavik summit in November 1986). Second, during Secretary of State George Shultz's visit to Moscow in April 1987, the Soviet leader stated that the USSR would be willing to "eliminate" within one year of an INF Treaty, all missiles with ranges between 300 and 600 miles, a category in which the USSR had more than 100 weapons deployed in Europe but the United States had none.

Although NATO had yet to take an official position on the Soviet offer at the time this paper was completed, and despite the clear uneasiness on the part of several European governments, it seemed evident that the Alliance had little choice but to accept the Soviet proposal. Persuading European publics that an agreement requiring the USSR to eliminate an entire category of missiles for which the West had no counterpart was not in their security interest would clearly be a hard (read impossible) political sell. Assuming that the details of the Soviet proposal accurately reflected the broad outlines sketched so far by Soviet officials, this meant that only verification procedures remained to be negotiated and that chances for an agreement within Ronald Reagan's remaining term of office would be high.

There are obvious risks for NATO in agreeing to eliminate all medium- and intermediate-range missiles from Europe, those pertaining to the danger of decoupling the defense of Europe from American central strategic forces being the most important. The likelihood that political factors will necessitate completion of the agreement despite these dangers has clear implications for the alliance's security planning:

First, it reinforces the desirability that NATO move forcefully to initiate and make progress in talks on the conventional balance in Europe. The Warsaw Pact's 1986 proposal in Budapest of up to 25 percent reductions in conventional forces, combined with the Atlantic Alliance's decision later that year in Montreal to pursue such far-ranging negotiations in a forum outside the stagnant Vienna talks on conventional forces opens the perhaps remote possibility of an agreement that could help significantly to rectify asymmetries in the conventional balance. But it is evident that it is essential for the Alliance to establish conventional forces as the preeminent item in the European arms control agenda. Assuming that an agreement on intermediate- and medium-range missiles is concluded, unilateral and negotiated reductions in nuclear forces have clearly gone far enough pending rectification of the conventional balance. The essence of NATO's strategy requires a balanced approach to conventional and nuclear forces; this pertains to force reductions as much as force improvements.

Second, the prospective agreement reinforces the long-standing need for the alliance to act decisively to improve its conventional force posture. While it would be nice to rectify existing asymmetries by negotiating reductions in the other side's force advantages, the expectation of such a development is hardly a sound basis for policy. Given its resource base and its technological advantages, there is little excuse for the Alliance's continued reluctance to take obvious measures to improve the conventional force posture; reductions in nuclear forces make this all the more essential.

Third, NATO must also review the other aspects of its nuclear force posture in light of the INF agreement, including battlefield nuclear weapons and air-delivered ordnance. The decision at Montebello in 1983 to reduce these forces may or may not still be sound—at a minimum, the changed external circumstances require a review.

Chapter V

U.S.-SOVIET ECONOMIC AND TECHNOLOGICAL INTERACTION

John P. Hardt

OVERVIEW

The 1985 Geneva Summit, in the words of both superpower leaders, initiated a "new beginning" in bilateral relations, projecting a continuing summit process and increased interaction in all facets of the U.S.-Soviet relationship. For commercial relations, this reengagement could signify the first step in the process toward full normalization of trade by the end of the century. More likely than full normalization, however, is an end to the decadelong downward trend in bilateral commerce with a modest revival of trade turnover levels by the end of the scheduled summits, approaching the $5 billion highwater mark of the mid-1970s. Such a development would fit the cyclical policy pattern of long-term relations that has been characterized by recurring fluctuations in each nation's commercial policies and, consequently, in levels of bilateral trade.

Commercial relations of East and West Europe have not experienced the same commercial fluctuations as the superpowers. Since the 1960s neither the Soviet Union nor the United States has dominated and unified East-West commercial policy. While Great Power relations have been diverging from the commercial relations of most of the other nations of OECD and CMEA, East-West relations have followed a consistently increasing pattern or trend line, toward expanded interconnections.

Superpower intercourse, though cyclical, has brought about relationships in each cycle that are broader in terms of economic interconnections such as non-trade transfers, including scientific communication through bilateral exchanges; direct enterprise involvement; and use of government and private credit. Moreover, the duration of agreed interconnections has been extended through long-term agricultural and industrial agreements.

The variations in policy for each side have turned on the perceived need to balance the benefits of trade against the political costs, i.e., the potential loss of security and diplomatic leverage. If the process begun at the summits is to change the historical cyclical pattern, each side will need to reach a domestic and alliance consensus on the stable and long-term delineation between trade for military and for non-military purposes, between the economic and political net effects of trade. This may not be either possible or desirable, depending on the terms of accommodation.

While political considerations continue to hold sway over economic factors in both Washington and Moscow, commercial policy has been increasingly influenced by economic considerations in both capitals as the value of grain, technology and credit have become more important to the respective trading partners. The United States' central, continuing concern, however, has been to avoid strengthening Soviet military capability through commercial relations or illegal transfer. On the other hand, Soviet security concerns have centered on minimizing the dependency and vulnerability that could result from broadened economic relations in the West. Industrial and and grain trade and credit policy have been special instruments of Western trade and diplomacy; energy exports may have provided the Soviet Union with some leverage of its own. While there has been some symmetry to superpower interaction, confrontation and restriction of trade have appeared, from the American perspective, to be initiated primarily by Soviet hostile actions at home and abroad.

Over time the economic and political stakes involved in trade policy have risen on both sides. Potential economic benefits have increased, alliance constraints on both sides have become more important, more complex, and more controversial. The appropriate and effective interrelationships of East-West policy on arms, international and inter-regional relations, human rights, and bilateral issues have become increasingly difficult to calculate and orchestrate.

To extend its policies on restricting trade for foreign policy and for security, the United States has enacted embargoes and export sanctions in East-West relations and imposed import sanctions and the use of extraterritorial jurisdiction in West-West interaction involving the East. Mechanisms designed to limit the use of trade as an instrument of foreign and security policy in the United States have included longterm agreements assuring contract sanctity and national legislation to limit the imposition of one ally's policy on that of another, i.e., blocking legislation limiting extraterritorial reach.

Despite the continuing political aspects of East-West trade, Soviet plans for modernization and improved efficiency in their economy under the Twelfth Five-Year Plan (1986-90) and the Fifteen-Year Plan (1986-2000) suggest heightened interest in importation of Western goods and technologies and expansion of exports to finance such imports. Potential improvements in their planning and management mechanisms, i.e., economic reform, might further increase the needs for Western goods and improve their effective use. Gorbachev's preferred commercial strategy would appear to be one of trade facilitation, based upon East-West consensus on economic and technological exchange policy and a more open, accessible Soviet economy. Soviet trade facilitation would require not only a priority for more imported goods and services, but also increased attention to obtaining the means to pay for imports given falling revenue from oil and gas exports. In other words, it would be necessary to increase the export of manufactured goods, countertrade, barter, nontrade transfer and credit. Bilateral U.S.-Soviet commercial relations may increase modestly through a shift of orders away from other Western industrial nations. However, substantial increases in the Soviet ability to import will likely be based on their ability to give priority to generating more competitive goods for the world market and to effectively cooperate with Western partners who may assist in export stimulation.

With declared interest in Washington and Moscow for expansion of bilateral commercial relations, history may seem to be repeating itself. Even were there to be a continuation of the cyclical pattern toward a summit-led trade upturn, a debate on the appropriateness and implications of change in U.S.-Soviet economic interaction is in order. With the Soviet Union among the largest of the U.S. grain markets, and given prospects for substantially increased U.S. sales of agricultural and energy industry products and technology, economic stimuli point to serious consideration of an American policy of trade facilitation. Resumption of bilateral economic and technological exchanges, including the revival of the umbrella agreement on U.S.-U.S.S.R. cultural, scientific and technical exchanges, may be possible outcomes of summitry. At the same time, revelations regarding the East's illegal acquisitions of technology, espionage, and unintended transfers through third countries raise serious questions about the form any upturn in economic and technical relations should take.

In spite of summit rhetoric by President Reagan and General Secretary Gorbachev on mutually desired increases in commercial relations, further restrictions are conceivable, especially if political and military agreements are not reached and the human rights record of the Soviet Union does not improve or deteriorates. Thus, a scenario of restricted commercial policy toward a "no trade" position must be considered a possibility. More likely, though, based on policy statements and actions to date of the Great Power principals, is a second scenario—facilitated commercial policy—that may find modest, but significant, increases in bilateral commercial relations toward the high levels of the 1970s. Facilitation or restriction in commercial relations will especially result from government policy on both sides to foster or inhibit exports, imports and credit relations. The process of commercial facilitation could proceed in time toward fully normalized commerce—a third scenario. However, very basic political-military changes and agreements, as well as concrete measures in each country to open bilateral trading relations, would be necessary. Secretary Baldrige noted in Moscow "we are closer to the beginning than the end in creating a fully normal U.S.–Soviet trading relationship. Yet we are on the right road. . . ." Although a potentially useful exercise in contingency planning, attaining full normalization seems quite problematic based on past Soviet performance and concrete developments to date, but worth exploring as a possible development pattern toward the year 2000. Without firm basis in a process of accommodation of political differences on arms, regional policies, and human rights, the countervailing process of offsetting commercial facilitation and restriction is likely to continue. Substantial, stable, predictable commercial relations must accompany, not precede, overall accommodations. Thus, full normalization in commercial relations is likely to occur only if it is part of a broader pattern of Great Power accommodation.

I. HISTORICAL PATTERN OF GREAT POWER ECONOMIC AND TECHNICAL RELATIONS

A. The Variable Pattern of Economic Interrelations[1]

Since 1917, the beginning of the Soviet period, U.S.-Soviet commercial policy has followed a cyclical pattern of high peaks of interchange alternating with deep troughs of mutual economic isolation or independence. The variations in policy on each side have turned on the perceived need to balance the benefits of trade against the political cost—that is, the potential loss of security and diplomatic leverage.

The Soviet Union used commercial opportunities in the early 1920s, on the eve of the first Five-Year Plan, as well as in the 1970s, to gain economic advantage and facilitate political accommodation. In each case, the United States was motivated by similar perceptions of both commercial and political advantage. Nevertheless, each time the pendulum began to swing toward increased economic ties and political accommodation, the upswing was reversed and tempered by the political and security concerns of each side.

Over the course of Soviet governance, the economic relationship of the U.S.S.R. with the Western economies has been both adversarial and cooperative. Ideologically, the conflicts of capitalism and communism provided the centrifugal impetus. Pragmatically, development of the Soviet economy and opening of the Eastern market provided

---

[1]For elaboration see: John P. Hardt and Donna L. Gold, "Changes in East-West Trade: The Policy Context," in East-West Trade in the 1980s: Prospects and Policies, Jan K. Fedorowicz, ed. (Boulder, Colorado: Westview Press, 1987).

a measure of mutual interest that stimulated the overall centripetal force toward selective economic interdependence.

In contrast with the cyclical pattern of U.S.-Soviet trade, East-West trade has moved along a steady trend line toward interdependence and normalization since the 1960s. In the immediate postwar period the United States and the Soviet Union dominated the respective commercial policies of the West and East. However, with increasing technological, economic and political power, differentiation and pluralism in both West and East, alliance understanding or agreements replaced domination, especially in the West. Particularly after the NATO pipeline embargo of 1964, the unified East-West relationship began to unravel in the West. On each side there were greater prospects for independent action and diversity of commercial and scientific resource deployments.

As a whole, for Soviet relations with the West, certain periods have been more conducive to economic isolation or autarky and others to interrelations. Autarky became a central feature of the restrictive Stalinist economic development, making that period a low point in economic relations. Again, the pendulum swung when the period of war alliance accompanied by Lend-Lease led to a return of a special economic interrelationship. The temporary wartime upturn was again followed by a downturn as the Cold War resumed after World War II then deepened during the Korean War and up until Stalin's death. This deep downturn was followed by de-Stalinization in the U.S.S.R. and a resumed opening to the West.

The periods of U.S.-Soviet commercial relations are very generally and briefly summarized below, indicating the variations downward and upward akin to policy cycles:

Up Cycles		Down Cycles	
1921-23	New Economic Period	1924-28	Industrialization Debate
1929-33	First Five-Year Plan	1934-40	Pre-World War II Autarky
1941-45	World War II Lend-Lease	1946-62	Post-World War II Soviet Autarky, Western Exports Control, Cuban Missile Crisis
1962-68	Kennedy Grain Sales of 1963. "Bridge Building" Johnson-Kosygin Glasboro Meeting	1968-70	Czech Invasion by the U.S.S.R. and Retrenchment
1971-74	Economic Detente	1975-85	From Detente to Confrontation
1987-90	?		

The periods 1929-1932 and 1972-75 were the highwater points in U.S.-Soviet commercial relations before and after World War II. These were times in which both the expectation of expanding commercial relations and the willingness to compromise on outstanding economic, political, and systemic differences were greatest in both countries. For the United States, these periods were characterized by a willingness to settle old credit and tariff issues and to develop means for bridging differences between the two divergent systems. For the Soviet Union, the perceived need for the technology and products of the West, especially the United States, was at its apogee. To obtain them, the Soviet Union indicated a greater readiness to negotiate outstanding economic issues and accept flexibility—even openness—of the system to American influences. Acceptance of a degree of dependency was a key factor in each period. Although there was some symmetry in the interactions, the subsequent downward swings in relations were primarily initiated by Soviet policies of isolationism and antagonistic military buildup.

In 1929-32 the Soviet Union accepted some dependence on American technology in order to develop the key, show case projects of the First Five Year Plan: the metallurgical complex at Magnitogorsk; the major energy project—the Dnieper hydro project; the auto facility at Gorki. In each case American capitalist giants were responsible for the design of those projects, e.g., U.S. Steel, General Electric, and Ford Motor Company, respectively. However, these were short-term American corporate commitments with limited systems transfer and each involved cash payment in convertible currency, i.e. no credit.

Efforts to settle outstanding debt issues were coupled with actions designed to limit the flow of credit. While the United States established the Export-Import Bank primarily to provide credit to facilitate trade with the Soviet Union and granted the U.S.S.R. provisional tariff privileges (MFN) to expand trade turnover, the Johnson Act was passed to limit trade by barring credits to governments with outstanding debts (Tsarist debts). Furthermore, the "forced labor" provisions of the Smoot-Hawley Tariff Act of 1930 were adopted, adding an unusual degree of trade restriction.

The Soviet Union, for its part, while relying on American and Western corporations, attacked them for "wrecking" and restricted their contractual relations with Western commercial enterprises. Thus, even in this upturn period of commercial relations, both countries pursued policies of trade restriction that counterbalanced, then reversed, the policies of trade facilitation.

Many decades later the Soviet Union and the United States again became willing to consider industrial cooperation in the 1972-74 gas development projects, i.e. "North Star" and Yakutia, with direct involvement of American engineers and technicians, American plans for construction, quality control in performance and product output (gas) in repayment. The degree of Soviet systemic flexibility was greater in the post-World War II than the pre-war period, as was the length of commitment and systems transfer over time. Terms of the settlement of Lend-Lease debt were agreed to. Large-scale U.S. government credits were proposed and accepted in principle. But, while provisional agreement was reached on large-scale cooperation, credit, debts, and tariffs, the period of increased U.S.-U.S.S.R. cooperation was quickly ended with the passage of the Trade Act containing the Jackson-Vanik Amendment and the Export-Import Bank Amendments of 1974 including the Stevenson amendment. Based on this restrictive legislation, the provisional trade agreements did not continue in force.

In both these high water periods of Soviet-American commercial and technological relations, it was as if the dialectic process were operating —for each new positive thesis in commercial relations, an offsetting negative factor arose. Thus, while long-term trade facilitating commitments were being arranged, simultaneous efforts were underway from both the Soviet and the American side to restrict, even terminate, trade.

Nevertheless, the quality of exchanges broadened and deepened over time. Initially the exchange was dominated by products of the technologically advanced United States, but in more recent years, the Soviet Union, recognizing the advantage of obtaining entire technological systems, expanded its imports beyond selected products. Likewise, Soviet exports in early periods consisted exclusively of raw materials while their imports were manufactured goods. In contrast, the recent policy has emphasized the diversification of trade by increasing manufactured goods exports from large, new auto and metallurgical complexes and permitting the import of agricultural products and material resources. Finally, credit and other non-trade factors in the balance of payments have emerged as significant elements in trade in the post-Stalin period.

Other forms of bilateral exchange, including a wide range of formal cultural, educational and political exchanges, have also developed over time, although they, too, have been subject to the fluctuations of overall U.S.-Soviet relations. Party Secretary Khrushchev's summit in Washington in 1958, for example, was followed by the signing of the Lacey-Zarubin agreement in 1959 which formally initiated a battery of educational, cultural and political exchanges. However, during the period from the U-2 through the Cuban Missile crises and again from the Czech invasion up to the Nixon-Brezhnev Summit, there was significant downturn in this pattern of interconnections.

With the Moscow Summit in 1972 bilateral relations and exchanges once again proliferated, including sister city exchanges, governor exchanges (Governor Reagan met Politburo candidate member Boris Ponomarev in California in one such exchange), and even citizen exchanges. The International Exchange (IREX) was the vehicle for educational exchanges, while the U.S. Information Agency and the U.S.S.R. Ministry of Culture handled the cultural activities.

As Soviet political relations with the United States deteriorated during the Carter Administration the momentum for exchanges slackened and, following the Afghanistan invasion sanctions in 1980, a sharp cut-back in bilateral relations took place. Still, the framework for interconnections was retained and many low visibility exchanges continued. With the revival of political dialogue leading to the Long-Term Grain Agreement of 1983, an exchange of ministers in 1985, and the beginning of the process leading to the summit, bilateral relations began to return somewhat to the *status quo ante* in Afghanistan. Importantly, at the Geneva Summit in November 1985 the two leaders signed a General Agreement on Exchanges and Cooperation in Scientific, Technical, Education, Cultural and other fields that in many ways went further than any previous bilateral agreements toward direct and extensive interaction between the superpowers in people exchanges.

If U.S.-Soviet economic relations continued their variable pattern, we may expect another cycle upward in the future; indeed, we may be on the eve of such a period. In that event, precedents of the past—a central feature of which was an offsetting negative force related to each positive initiative—will be instructive for the future.

B. U.S.-Soviet Cycle; OECD-CMEA Trend

In the immediate postwar period the United States and the Soviet Union dominated the respective commercial policies of the West and East. With increasing differentiation and pluralism in both West and East, agreements replaced domination, especially in the West. From the NATO pipeline embargo of 1964, to Ostpolitik in the early 1970s, the unified East-West relationship ended in the West. U.S.-led economic detente in 1972–74 reinforced the change. But as U.S. policy shifted in 1975, Europe did not follow. Each side used their greater prospects for independent action and diversity in a variety of commercial and scientific partners in East-West relations, with Europe trending toward broader and deeper interrelations.

Movement towards interdependence and normalization of East-West trade has been a trend for the OECD nations from the 1960s to the present. By contrast, as described above, U.S. government administration of East-West commercial relations has been characterized by cycles ranging from the trade promotion policy of the period 1971–1974—Nixon's economic detente—to trade restrictions under the Carter and Reagan Administrations, 1980–1985.

Commonalities in U.S.-Soviet trade cycles and OECD-Eastern commercial trends[2] could provide the basis for a Western consensus to develop a more normalized trading relationship with the East. In spite of multipolarity and divergent trade patterns, the basis for agreement in the West is wide and deep. If an agreement could be reached among Western allies on the objectives of East-West commercial relations and the appropriate use especially within CMEA of the mechanisms of law

---

[2]OECD and the CMEA or Soviet Socialist countries do not have formal agreements, although there have been discussions on developing formal Common Market-CMEA relations. The smaller countries are said to oppose such relations as they fear dominance of the larger trading partners.

and multilateral agreements, a consensus might be more easily achieved within the United States on how to implement the Export Administration legislation.

C. Political and Economic Significance of East-West Trade

During the early postwar years, overall trade between the OECD countries and the Eastern bloc held more political than economic significance for the West, providing leverage in East-West disputes such as the Berlin airlift. In recent years, however, Eastern trade has become economically important for the West, especially in certain key economic and geographical sectors throughout the OECD.

The economic importance of Eastern trade to the domestic economies in the West began to increase in the 1960s: in 1962 Italy exchanged oil pipe for Soviet petroleum products, in 1963 the United States concluded the first of its major grain deals with the U.S.S.R., in 1966 an automotive deal was concluded between Fiat of Italy and the U.S.S.R. By the 1980s, when the partial grain embargo and the gas pipeline sanctions were imposed by the United States, it was clear that trade with the Soviet Union had become a vital factor in determining acceptable levels of domestic production, employment, and profitability for American agricultural and European metal working and equipment industries. Key Western exports to the Soviet Union and Eastern Europe include grain (Canada, France, United States), metal processing, and machine tools (FRG, Japan, France, Italy). The 1983–88 U.S.-Soviet Long-Term Grain Agreement (LTA) establishing a minimum level of wheat sales was perceived to be of great importance to American farmers. In fact, consummation of the agreement was considered influential in determining the outcomes of several Congressional races in grain producing states. Energy equipment and pipe sales to the U.S.S.R. were likewise important to the factory workers in Le Havre, France, Glasgow, United Kingdom, and Dusseldorf, FRG, as demonstrated by local elections; for example, the continuation of Soviet pipe and equipment orders was a significant factor in the elections held in the depressed industrial areas of the Ruhr where incumbents lost seats in the 1983 German election.

Important as economic factors have become, it may nonetheless be argued that Eastern trade continues to have a significant political motivation in the West. The yearly "swing credit" extended by the FRG to the GDR will surely be spent on West German goods, but the larger benefits to the FRG are probably expected to be in political coin.

Limited credit prospects, constrained hard goods for exports, and moderate domestic growth plans will likely make competing for individual CMEA-country trade a decisive and divisive factor among the Western industrial countries. With economic recovery proceeding slowly in Western Europe, new expanding foreign markets are needed to spur on European growth. Continued Eastern requirements for energy equipment, metal products, and automotive equipment find competitive suppliers throughout the OECD. Where are there significant orders for steel and metal products as potentially large as those from the Soviet Union, Eastern Europe or the PRC? Metal for the industries of the East and grain for their "food programs" are thus special magnets for key exporting sectors in the West.

II. FORMS OF ECONOMIC RELATIONS: TRADE AND TECHNOLOGY TRANSFER[3]

In bilateral trade and trade between the economic alliance systems, (CMEA and associated communist states; NATO and CoCom) the Soviet Union and the United States have set up mechanisms to restrict and facilitate the flow of commerce and technology. In facilitation, steps have been taken to "normalize trade", i.e., move toward the use of the commercial practices and institutions of the world trading community. New mechanisms, such as agreements on bilateral balancing and long-term contracts, have been used to bridge the institutional differences of a market system and centrally planned economies. In restricting trade, concern has centered on the various means of transfer, including industrial espionage and third country transfer.

In periods of trade facilitation, commercial relations, scientific communication, and participation in the multilateral forums of the world market and the international organizations have been expanded and business promoted. In times of restriction, when goods and services for both military and industrial needs have been controlled, the Soviet Union may have relied more on illegal transfers rather than scientific communications, and bilateral, rather than multilateral, trade and transfers.

While interposing middlemen such as the KGB have been skilled in surmounting trade restraints and embargoes, their efforts have not generally promoted effective transfer in the industrial sector. Using illegal means to obtain goods and technology for the civilian economy places one additional barrier into the transfer process, inhibiting an already inefficient transfer mechanism. Civilian transfers, even when conducted through commercial channels, have been characterized as ineffective in terms of absorption, adaption, and diffusion, and uneven in improving productivity.[4] In contrast, transfers for the Soviet military's economic needs, characteristically satisfied through illegal channels, have probably been more precise in requirements, effective

---

[3]See *East-West Technology Transfer: A Congressional Dialog With the Reagan Administration*, Dec. 1984, one of a series of Joint Economic Committee publications that have included *East-West Commercial Policy: A Congressional Dialog With the Reagan Administration*, Feb. 1982, and *Issues in East-West Commercial Relations*, Jan. 1979.

[4]Bruce Parrott (ed.), *Trade, Technology, and Soviet-American Relations*, Bloomington: Indiana University Press, 1985.

in utilization, and have more likely shown results in productivity comparable to Western source-country effectiveness.[5]

Overall, the economic mechanism for commercial and technology transfer have been as effective as the Soviet Union and the United States would permit them to be. The difficulty in marriage between a rigid, technology-unfriendly, planned Soviet system and a technologically dynamic, global trading system has posed not only technical difficulties but, more importantly, political and systemic problems.

A. Commercial: Bilateral Trade, Credit and Industrial Cooperation

In trade facilitation, the use of normal commercial mechanisms has expanded over time. Nikita Khrushchev rediscovered the international division of labor or comparative advantage as a criteria of trade with the West. Necessary imports under Stalin were limited largely to industrial goods to meet short term bottlenecks, a policy based on absolute advantage. In 1963, Khrushchev broke with the Stalinist pattern by importing grain from the United States. Later, under Leonid Brezhnev, corn and other feed grains were imported to provide for the needs of a newly important sector—the feedgrain livestock economy. The break with Stalin's policy of grain independence echoed the English acceptance of Ricardo's argument more than a century earlier that importation of grain from the continent was economically desirable, even if trade raised political concerns of interdependence.

While Khrushchev initiated the break with Stalin's policy, he resisted establishing a modern basis for passenger cars and trucks by improving Soviet automotive technology through Western industrial cooperation. Under Brezhnev, though, automotive complexes based on Western systems were established at Toliyatigrad on the Volga (VAZ) and in the Kama River Truck Plant (KAMAZ) in the Urals. This moved comparative advantage to manufacturing import policy.

Likewise, a break with Stalin's no credit policy occurred with the Soviet acceptance of large government loans preferred for gas pipelines and agricultural imports. However, the U.S. credits for the gas pipeline did not materialize and credits for agricultural sales were short-lived. Commercial credits were sought and obtained. The terms of credit the Soviets sought were often considered preferential in the West. The terms obtained by the Soviets from Western countries were often considered discriminatory by the Soviet Union.

In contrast, the CMEA-Six plus Yugoslavia were offered both commercial credit and government loans and guarantees. Some felt that, should the East European nations become overextended, the Soviet Union would provide a credit umbrella or be the "debtor of last resort;" this did not turn out to be the case. The U.S.S.R. itself has

---

[5]*Soviet Acquisition of Western Technology*, submitted to Senate Banking Committee, April 1982, *An Update*, Sept. 1985.

become a major creditor nation and currently drives a fairly tough bargain with her politically allied debtors. When faced with the choice of becoming more dependent on Western creditors or delaying high technology imports, Soviet bankers seem to have won out fairly consistently over economic planners. Evidence of this is that the orders for the Kama plant were stretched out after 1976, the U.S.S.R.-Western debt was kept low and the basis of Soviet creditworthiness high. Moreover, the difference between gross and net debt remained wide with available hard currency used for a variety of purposes, including participation in Western credit syndications.

In conformance with this credit policy, the preferred industrial cooperation strategy for the Soviet Union with the West has historically been a pay-back arrangement such as that discussed in the U.S.-Soviet negotiations on the "North Star" pipeline—a gas for pipe arrangement. The Soviet-American project, as noted above, was to involve directly the U.S. company in construction, operation and management. Later European arrangements did not include such direct involvement.

More recently, the Soviet Union has moved away from investment in large new complexes to renovation or modernization of existing plants. The new Gorbachev-preferred strategy for Western commercial relations appears to be more targeted to these kinds of specific needs, more effective in application, and comparably more productive. Soviet trade institutions are being reformed to make possible direct contact between foreign suppliers and Soviet end-users, and to allow joint ventures in production, construction, and management in ways that permit the Soviets to develop competitive manufactured or processed goods for exports. New forms are developed within the International Chamber of Commerce and in bilateral, East-West contracts.

B. Scientific Communications: Exchanges, Professional Interactions, Emigration

Scientific communications have been encouraged through normal government exchanges—especially those under the umbrella U.S.-U.S.S.R. Agreement on Scientific and Technology Exchange. Under this agreement, participation of Soviet scientists in international meetings and through international institutions such as the United Nations was expanded. Through most of the 1970s, until bilateral programs were interrupted after the Afghanistan invasion, these exchanges were largely considered a mutually beneficial interaction between the Soviet Union and the United States.

During the 1980s, unplanned scientific communications and the unintended transfer of technology (industrial espionage) were thought by the U.S. administration to be out of control, i.e., "hemorrhaging." The resulting control of government-funded scientific research stemmed from the belief of both the Carter and Reagan Administrations that the nature of trade in "critical technologies" deserved special attention.

In this regard, in 1976 the Defense Science Board under Texas Instruments President Fred Bucy had found that scientific communications—people-related transfer—represented an active mechanism for the transfer of critical technologies. However, detailed, current reports on Soviet illegal acquisitions for their military indicate that product requirement lists prepared by those in charge of the core Soviet military programs have established the focus of Soviet industrial espionage efforts. To the extent that this is true, the older concept of product rather than critical technology control may be more appropriate for limiting illegal transfers. Moreover, there is wide agreement among CoCom and OECD countries on appropriate controls for high technology, directly military-related products. A Western policy characterized by tightening control on these specific militarily-significant products might receive wide support and effective administration.

Most Western observers argue that non-trade transfers of technology—industrial espionage—have played a significant role in the qualitative improvement of the Soviet military arsenal. Some in the United States, looking at both product and critical technology systems transfer, have even gone so far as to say that "when we see the Soviet weapons system, that is actually ours or a derivative of ours." While industrial espionage for core military programs is doubtless critical for relieving military bottlenecks, available information does not support the contention that broad Soviet military advances have been wholly or even primarily a product of clandestinely obtained technology.

It is also argued that some transfer of militarily relevant information occurs simply through the scientific openness of U.S. society. Non-trade, people-related technology transfers are not easy to stop. Measures to restrict the modest transfer that takes place through scientific communications have been discussed within the U.S. scientific, academic, and governmental communities. In September 1982, the National Academy of Sciences released the well-known Corson Report on Scientific Communication and National Security which recommended "security through accomplishments," and "tall fences around narrow areas." While the principle of these conclusions seems to have been widely accepted, its application continues to be adjudicated.

Resumption of U.S.-U.S.S.R. science and technology exchange programs depends upon agreement on the concept of appropriate scientific communications. The "umbrella" agreement in science and technology signed in 1972 established programs in chemical catalysis, electrometallurgy and materials, microbiology, physics, computer applications to management, science policy, and scientific and technical information. The general agreement served, furthermore, as a model for other agreements signed during 1972 and 1974 that dealt with energy, atomic energy, space, public health and artificial heart research, housing, transportation, environmental protection, the world oceans, and agriculture. The net benefit to the United States of these programs, if resumed, would likely be assessed according to the view that, in these specific areas, the United States gains more by having the bilateral programs than by prohibiting them.

The flow of information from the U.S.S.R. to the United States, promoting better understanding of the Soviet system in the West and in the United States, has been increased by an unprecedented emigration, some quarter of a million in the last fifteen years. Many of these emigrants brought with them a knowledge of the Soviet military and civilian system of scientific and technological research. The large Jewish emigration from the Soviet Union to the United States provided an especially valuable source of insight on Soviet economic needs and use of Western economic and technical transfers. In effect, this emigration provided to the United States an active communication mechanism. The Soviet Union's broad definition of security, under which many types of employment are used as an excuse for restricting emigration, represents an evident concern about unintentional scientific communication to the United States. The human treasure house of insights represented by these émigrés is only now beginning to be effectively exploited.

C. Third Country Transfer and CoCom

The problem of third country transfer of products and technology to the U.S.S.R. has motivated the Reagan Administration to advocate tightened CoCom controls on Western high technology goods banned from export to the Soviet Union. In the Administration's view, this could be done by broadening the criteria for analysis from "direct military" to "strategically relevant" or "defense-priority" in order to focus the licensing process on critical high technologies as well as broadly military-related products.

While Europeans do not oppose U.S. calls for new CoCom restrictions on selected high technologies of direct military relevance, they are generally against putting additional controls on older—less than state of the art—technologies which they see as readily available in the world market. Some Americans argue that substantive discussions have and can continue to lead to agreement within CoCom on the licensing of specific military-related products sold to the U.S.S.R. But European acceptance of broadened strategic categories of processes as well as products may not be forthcoming, especially if the Europeans continue to perceive those broadly stated categories as unnecessary, ineffective, and unilaterally imposed by Washington.

The West European perspective on the relationship between the economic health of the Soviet economy and Western security is quite different from some American approaches. Limiting Soviet industrial as well as military growth by multilateral controls is not considered an appropriate or effective policy by most CoCom members. A healthy Soviet economy is considered not only acceptable, but in their view preferable to a weak one.

Many Europeans also question American assertions that advances in the Soviet military would have been almost negligible without access—legal and illegal—to Western technology. They instead attribute more achievements of the Soviet military to efforts by their own domestic and CMEA R & D establishments.

The imposition of U.S. export controls in the West-West context remains a highly controversial issue in the Western alliance. The U.S. now requires as many as 13 Western countries to apply for individual validated licenses for seven product categories. Although the lists of countries and categories are classified, one source reports that Austria, Sweden, Finland, Hong Kong, Singapore, South Africa, India, Liechtenstein and Switzerland are among the 13 Western countries controlled. The product categories controlled include: computers, silicon parts, microcircuits, electronic and semiconductor manufacturing equipment, carbon technology and precision measuring devices. These regulations, together with policies permitting extraterritorial reach, retroactivity in contract revocation (breach of contract sanctity), and import sanctions that unilaterally deny the U.S. market to those Western companies violating unilateral U.S. security controls, are likely to remain sources of contention between the United States and its allies in Western Europe and Japan.

Some Western commercial actors also maintain that the explicit use of foreign policy criteria in commercial relations is inappropriate; others feel that trade is a normal instrument of diplomacy. U.S. economic policy toward the Soviet Union has shifted from a balanced policy of rewards and penalties as practiced in the 1960s and 1970s to a policy that is primarily based on penalties to punish the Soviets for: treatment of dissidents, the Afghanistan invasion, Polish martial law, arms buildup, and adventurism in Africa, Central America, and other regions. Meanwhile, the Europeans have continued to see trade with the East as important for economic as well as political reasons. When trade is used politically, the Europeans tend to consider incentives as more effective than sanctions and embargoes, i.e., "carrots" over "sticks," viewing the withholding of benefits as negative incentives.

The U.S. Export Administration Act Amendments of 1985 deal with the issues of contract sanctity and extraterritoriality but do not settle them. American business critics argue that continued uncertainty about contract sanctity will reduce U.S.competitiveness world-wide and will weaken the effectiveness of necessary controls. Moreover, they argue that further extension of extraterritoriality will weaken alliance unity and the competitiveness of U.S.-based multinationals. Others believe, however, that the Western countries will close ranks in self-interest, to retain access to U.S.technology, and out of common concern about Soviet military and economic advances.

The United States has been in the forefront in using the explicit withholding of commercial relations as a means to influence Soviet foreign behavior. The U.S. Congress has facilitated the use of embargoes and sanctions by including "foreign policy criteria" in trade legislation (i.e., the revised Export Administration Acts (EAA) of 1985 and the 1974 Trade Act), thus permitting the withholding of trade benefits as a response to human rights violations, as well as foreign policy infractions. The broad support of South African and Libyan sanctions illustrates the desire expressed across a wide political spectrum to give the President a formal, restrictive, economic club to use in foreign affairs. The South African sanctions are also widely supported in Europe.

Under the EAA, export licensing to communist countries is regulated in accordance with U.S. national security interests, American foreign policy objectives, and, to a lesser extent, limitations on domestic supplies. It was the EAA that empowered Presidents Carter and Reagan to restrict U.S. commercial relations with the Soviet Union in 1980 and 1981–1982. In the latter case, the "pipeline dispute," European commercial relations with the U.S.S.R. were also affected. In the second stage of U.S. reaction to the imposition of Polish martial law, the foreign policy criteria for restricting the exportation of domestically produced U.S. energy equipment were extended to include foreign affiliates and foreign companies with U.S. licensing—the extraterritorial principle.

According to the Europeans, contract sanctity was breached by that U.S. action, and extraterritoriality was applied retroactively. U.S. law was brought into direct conflict with some European laws, e.g., Prime Minister Thatcher directed John Brown Ltd. under British law to give precedence to the laws of the United Kingdom rather than acknowledge U.S. extraterritorial jurisdiction. After settlement of the pipeline dispute, FRG Economic Minister Bangeman threatened German blocking legislation similar to that of the British in response to a controversial restriction of a German sale of telecommunication equipment to East Europe. In defense of extraterritorial reach, the U.S. maintained that American technology had been obtained under certain policy and contractual understandings and these contracted obligations were violated by European exports to the U.S.S.R. and East European countries.

These continued disputes seem to illustrate the lack of a consensus policy on the objectives of controls, especially those applying to industrial improvement in the U.S.S.R. Without a policy consensus among Western leaders, it is difficult to see how the technicians at CoCom can agree on coordinated implementation of control policy.

D. Multilateral Economic Relations and International Forums: United Nations, IMF, World Bank

Traditionally, the Soviet Union considered the world market and the multinational institutions set up after World War II as U.S.-dominated and inimical to Soviet interests. Growth and stability of the world market, and the international monetary system were all Western objectives. In contrast, political instability and unsettled economic conditions that would further political change beneficial to Soviet interests were considered central to Soviet objectives. However, in recent years, as the Soviet Union became a major creditor country, it became more interested in the health of the world economic community in general and more interested in price stability in particular, especially, high level oil price stability, low inflation for goods they were likely to purchase, growth to increase their markets in the West, and a traditional debt payment regimen. Some of the senior Soviet officials seem to have developed a stake in the stability and health of the international monetary system.

Illustrating the new "establishment" strain in Soviet policy is a new degree of acceptance by the U.S.S.R. of the international foundation institutions.[6] Members of the CMEA—namely, Hungary and Poland—applied for membership in the IMF and World Bank with tacit Soviet approval. Other members, such as Romania, by meeting their international debt obligations, illustrate not only self-interest in retaining credit-worthiness but conformance to the international rules of financial behavior. While some influential Soviet editorial writers have favored the Cuban and Peruvian position on the Third World debt crises and supported the "debtors club," Soviet official action has been more traditional than its occasionally radical rhetoric. The Shevardnadze memorandum on "International Security of States: An Important Condition for Improvement of International Relations," submitted to the United Nations Secretary General on January 27, 1986, on balance seems to call for coordinated action to ensure financial, monetary and commercial stability in the global market.

The East and West have mutually accepted in theory and policy statements the norms of international economic behavior based on shared goals of enhanced global interdependence and heightened global responsibility, though in the practical and more far-reaching geopolitics of global interdependence, differences are substantial. In the U.S.-Soviet context, developments in the conduct of agricultural trade (e.g., the introduction of the Long-Term Grain Agreement mechanism) have been the most illustrative of this common system-bridging mechanism. Such precedents in the area of long-term agreements may be replicated in other areas of East-West trade. Until very recently neither the United States nor the U.S.S.R. seemed to have violated either the spirit or the letter of the LTA. The failure of the Soviets to meet their minimum wheat imports in the 1984–1985 purchasing year is the singular exception.

In the East, the emphasis on national economic objectives has shifted from quantitative growth, which characterized the economic strategies

---

[6]Ivan D. Ivanov. USSR, Academy of Sciences, Oleg Bogomolov (consulting editor), *The World Socialist Economy*, Social Sciences Today: Moscow: 1986. Ivan D. Ivanov, *The Soviet Union in a Changing Global Economic Setting: The Prospects for Trade-Oriented Growth*, UNCTAD/ST/TSC/4, Apr. 1986.

of the past, to growth with efficiency. The Stalinist policy of extensive growth has given way to the qualitative, intensive strategy in
Eastern centrally planned economies. The Western economies are,
likewise, increasingly concerned with the changing quality of economic
performance and less preoccupied with quantitative growth rates.

Global interdependence in economic development has been adopted
in lieu of the concept of independence or two markets, which
characterized the policies of the past in both East and West. Eastern
economic isolation and self-sufficiency have ceased being ends in
themselves. Similarly, Western denial of Eastern commercial relations
on *both* economic health and military enhancement grounds has been
dropped in law and practice as a unified Western policy.

III. SOVIET MODERNIZATION PLANS AND THE ROLE OF WESTERN TECHNOLOGY [7]

General Secretary Gorbachev faced the 27th Soviet Party Congress
in February 1986, less than a year after taking power, with a clear
emphasis on domestic and economic improvement. His first priority
in the 12th Five-Year Plan (1986–1990) is to energize and mobilize
his economic resources to get the economy moving. With adoption
of the draft plan for the remainder of the century and also of a new
Party Program—only the third in Soviet history—Gorbachev established the policy basis for the restructuring and reform of the economy.
This two-staged process is not without contradictions. Many feel that
the reform step will prove too costly when Gorbachev faces up to its
full political costs and risks.

Gorbachev's five-year economic plan projects a growth rate of about
4.0 percent, in U.S. national accounting terms, which would
dramatically reverse the downward trend in Soviet economic performance and provide more resources for investment, consumption, and
defense. How much will be allocated for each seems to be in question.

A. Gorbachev and Economic Reform

Mikhail Gorbachev represents the post-World War II generation in
the U.S.S.R. Yet, invoking the style of Lenin, he is attempting to rekin-
dle the perceived revolutionary élan that had previously imbued many
Soviet citizens and leaders alike with enthusiasm, discipline and optimism. He may also be preparing the ideological and political grounds
for significant changes in the economic system. Gorbachev's strategy
may be summarized in the following way:

---

[7]John P. Hardt, *Gorbachev's Domestic Economic Strategy and East-West
Commercial Connections*, Edited by Charles M. Perry & Robert L. Pfaltzgraff,
Jr. *Selling the Rope to Hang Capitalism? The Debate on West-East Trade and
Technology Transfer*, Pergamon-Brassey's Press, 1987.

- Ideologically, Gorbachev's new strategy resembles that of Lenin during the New Economic Policy of the early 1920s, which emphasized a withdrawal of central planning to the "commanding heights" of a more decentralized system based on increased top leadership guidance and oversight.

- The current Gorbachev strategy appears to emphasize short-term gains over long-term improvements; priority to Western regions with pre-existing but aging capital; plants and infrastructure over developing eastern and southern regions with abundant material and human resources; renovation of existing facilities over new, modern complexes. Sectors such as machine building are to be strengthened, while other sectors important to modernization are to be given lessened priority. Moreover, the short-term strategy seems to center on energizing and potentially strengthening the ministerial system and local Party role in the economy which in the long term must be changed to bring about the reforms Gorbachev has been calling for.

- Gorbachev is relying heavily on the "human factor"—better trained and motivated managers, workers and peasants. His purge of the economic bureaucracy continues and an improved incentive system for workers and peasants is being actively explored.

- In order to approach Western levels of efficiency in a market-stimulating economy, changes would need to be introduced within the Marxist-Leninist political system which guides and controls the Soviet economy. The twin objectives of improved economic efficiency and maintenance of the political system may prove to be mutually exclusive in the future, as they have seemed to be in the past. Devolution of ministerial and regional Party responsibility and authority to economic enterprises appears to be essential to this change in management.

- Such an economic formula of the new leadership would require a new environment conducive to technological dynamism, an information revolution, and increased efficiency in the manner in which imported Western technology is absorbed, adapted, and integrated into the Soviet economic system. This would be facilitated by a heightened emphasis on economic modernization rather than on continued, rapid military growth—i.e., a change in the classic guns-growth-or-butter choice.

- Gorbachev's rule may usher in a new stage or epoch for the Soviet economy: a shift from Stalinist extensive development of economic resources in place toward intensive more efficient growth. The adoption of modernization and efficiency as economic criteria may result in increases in quality as well as increases in quantity. If economic modernization is the principal aim of the Gorbachev leadership, the U.S.S.R. might, in time, join the Western industrial nations as an economic and technological superpower.

While the first stage of Gorbachev's economic strategy involving energizing and mobilizing the economy was initiated straight away and may show signs of success, the second—the reform stage—is much more problematic and is largely underway in rhetoric. If, indeed, a politically acceptable growth rate and qualitative improvement in performance are to be achieved in the future, based on fundamental reform in the economic system, hard choices must be made involving a shakeup of the major political-economic underpinnings of the Stalinist system and the structure of the planning and management mechanism. If accomplished, and if one man's will can do so, the Soviet economy might then begin to enter what may be called the "economic modernization stage of Leninist development." In a comparative sense this might approach a Soviet version of *laissez faire*, i.e., initiating a process of removing central authority interference through control or subsidy of day to day management of the factory and farm.

Gorbachev's domestic economic strategy is important in terms of both style and substance. The style is designed to project the Leninist image of intellectualism and to revive the Soviet spirit; in effect, to create a new "efficient technocrat," a professional who upholds a work ethic, a competent manager who is accessible to subordinates, demanding, but fair.

The substance of the Gorbachev strategy is more complex. For each proposed economic change there appear to be offsetting political costs, institutional and personal. Style is not easily translated into substance; words to deeds; overcoming inertia and deep-seated skepticism is extremely difficult. However, if Gorbachev appears to be successful—if he is lucky—he could conceivably develop what early Soviet leaders referred to as the "smell of success," which would enable him to command support in the Party, government, and among the populace. Success may facilitate a translation of style into substance and may assist Gorbachev in establishing himself firmly enough in power to risk significant systemic changes. *But*, the "ifs" are formidable.

In the near future, perhaps through most of the next Five-Year Plan (1986–90), Gorbachev's short-term strategy may or may not show the positive results he promises. By putting professionally efficient and motivated people in charge and generating a work ethic in the Soviet society based on an increasing appearance of reward by accomplishment, the current system, unwieldy and monolithic as it is, may be energized: "workaholics" may replace "alcoholics" at the work place. Through a shortrun strategy of centralizing economic policy and planning in the control of handpicked Gorbachevian lieutenants, of selectively pruning the overgrown ministerial system, and of devolving managerial authority and responsibility to enterprises and collective farms, the performance of the system may be improved in terms of

the growth of output and productivity.[8]
Rising growth rates may give the impression of enhanced quality of performance. Continued scientific centralization with enhanced computerization may give an impression of movement within the scientific and technical community and provide some results. Moreover, Soviet society may accept the idea that the system has been moving toward a more just and responsive society.

Any short-term improvements, however, must be considered against the exceptionally low levels of performance of recent years, the comparatively low level of Soviet productivity by international standards, and the low morale of Soviet society. Weather has at times had an especially negative effect on harvests and construction; industrial growth has been at a post-World War II low. And the popular spirit, the way of life, has been as depressed as the Kremlin's uninspiring, aged leaders that preceded Gorbachev.

Short-term economic success may, paradoxically, reduce the likelihood or pressure for beneficial long-term reform and restructuring of the system. Systemic changes require the effective adoption of new success indicators:

- Better allocation of resources requires accurate measures of costs and revenues, simulation of a market place—a price system.
- Rationalization and decentralization of management should be based on profitability criteria that provide the central planning authorities with an effective measure of accountability and oversight.
- A scientific and technical environment that fosters innovation, scientific communication and rewards those responsible for technological advancement requires criteria such as the world market provides Western industrial economies.

Faced with the problems of reforming the economic bureaucracy, especially streamlining the formidable ministerial system and curbing the regional and local Party organs from intervening in the management system, Gorbachev may not stop short of pursuing the fundamental changes necessary for putting the U.S.S.R. in the ranks of modern industrial economies. He just may use the power accumulated by personnel changes and political success to realize a vision of a more efficient, technologically dynamic economy. Or, like Khrushchev, despite early successes, he may squander his political capital in other political-economic changes that do not provide long-term aid to the economy.

In attempting to reform the economic, governmental, and Party bureaucracy, he has one great advantage over most of his predecessors: the institutions he must change will be populated by his chosen cadres. By the time of the 27th Communist Party Congress in February 1986,

---

[8]Joint CIA-DIA paper to Joint Economic Committee of U.S. Congress, March 19, 1987, *Gorbachev's Modernization Program: A Status Report.* Cf. *Soviet Economy Under a New Leader*, a joint CIA-DIA report published by DIA as DDB-1900-122-86, July 1986.

many of the key economic administrators had become Gorbachev's choices. Gorbachevian "efficient technocrats" may be able and willing to accept market-simulating change. They may give Gorbachev the option of reconstituting the roles of government and Party in the Soviet economy, and they may aid him in exercising that option. Gorbachev's appointees may represent a new class of economic bureaucrats not only able to perform in a changed environment but committed to the process of economic change—an interest group for reform.

Ironically, pressure that pushes Gorbachev to make the necessary systemic changes may be generated by the United States. Only by very basic, long-term changes, can the Soviet Union keep up in the scientific and technological race to keep open the prospect of becoming an economic superpower. Gorbachev is known to be concerned about the widening technological gap between the Western industrial nations, especially Japan and West Germany, and the Soviet Union. Moreover, in view of the dynamic character of military technology, falling further behind in the civilian scientific and technological revolution would erode the long-term security of the U.S.S.R. as a military superpower.

There may also be rising pressure from the populace for material improvement. More goods and services for the Soviet citizen, a more just system, and more involvement in the process—were Gorbachev's "human factor" program successful—could generate rising expectations and create broad-based pressure for the qualitative improvements possible only through reform.

B. Gorbachev's Commercial Strategy

If Gorbachev continues to establish and solidify his domestic power, he may be expected to reassert Soviet control over the East European allies, which had been somewhat loosened during the interregnum. In this process he faces policy dilemmas: how should trade advantages of closer East-West interdependence be weighed against the potential diplomatic gains of exploiting political-economic differences within the developed West? How should the economic benefits of closer Western economic relations be weighed against the security problems— resulting from interdependence, Eastern dependency and political vulnerability?

In this context, Gorbachev must reflect as well on the contributions of the CMEA allies. Is Eastern Europe a burden or asset in economic and security terms? What must he do to improve his net East European assessment? The CMEA-Six tend to favor economic detente and limited usage of trade in Eastern diplomacy. The smaller East European countries tend to prefer more East-West economic interrelations and have less concern than the Soviets about vulnerability and dependency in Western trade relations.

Political gains may flow, to be sure, from exploiting a divided Western policy. These gains, however, might in Gorbachev's view be more than offset by the commercial losses generated by a mixed Western policy of restriction and facilitation.

A preferred Gorbachev commercial strategy that complements his domestic strategy would be one that facilitated expanding trade with the United States as well as other Western countries. The Soviet Union, like the United States, can more easily persuade its allies to adhere to a policy of trade facilitation than a policy of trade restriction. As illustrated by his recent statements, Gorbachev has stressed Soviet commitment to interdependence, a more open economy, and more flexible forms of commercial relations with the West. (Comments contained in his speech, December 12, 1985, to the U.S.-U.S.S.R. Trade and Economic Council in the Kremlin, attended by the author.) Movement toward interdependence and openness would enhance the prospects of mutually beneficial economic relations with the developed countries of the West.

A stable trade facilitation policy encouraging both an Eastern and Western consensus might include the following:

- A delineation of Eastern import needs within an acceptable range of Western security concerns that deemphasizes non-commercial transfers, especially industrial espionage;
- Long-term agreements involving assurances of contract sanctity and government-private commercial partnerships; and
- A shift in import policy from materials to machinery and from products to systems.

IV. UNITED STATES AGENDA FOR COMMERCIAL RELATIONS WITH GORBACHEV'S SOVIET UNION

A. Gorbachev's Economic Strategy

Success in the short run may make the Soviet Union appear to be a more formidable competitor. We should guard against confusing short-term results and appearance of change for the necessary systemic changes needed for long-term Soviet economic and technological dynamism. Soviet economic and technological power in the long-term will require more basic systemic changes, which are both less likely and harder to predict. Most of the critical Soviet choices will be determined by domestic political factors, by the weighty agenda of foreign policy problems such as the costly involvement in Afghanistan and other Third World commitments that increase the burden of empire, and by the burden of maintaining a formidable military establishment. The United States will remain a challenger and competitor to the Soviet Union. If Soviet modernization occurs and results in part from a choice of "growth" over "guns," there may be a moderation of the competition as measured in our military balance. On the other hand, if the Soviet Union is able to join the technological competition, this might be translated into more formidable Soviet military power in the longer run or more competition in the political and economic arenas. Were systemic changes that give a larger role to the Soviet manager and citizen to develop in the Soviet Union, we might find a reformed Soviet establishment a more compatible system.

B. U.S. Response to Likely Soviet Commercial Strategy

If successful, Gorbachev's domestic strategy in the short and long term could benefit from enhanced commercial relations with the West. Thus, Gorbachev's preferred strategy for commercial relations with the West would likely be one of Eastern consensus and Western trade facilitation. The United States can limit that option by trade restriction and by selective use of trade in diplomacy. In that case, the Soviet Union would likely direct its import policy to other OECD countries and restrict economic ties that appear to involve unacceptable dependency and vulnerability. Development of a restrictive Western commercial policy along such lines might provide useful political gains to the U.S.S.R. but would be less attractive economically, i.e., less supportive of their articulated domestic economic strategy. The United States could in this way presumably retard somewhat Soviet progress in effecting a more dynamic program of technological improvement. However, in the past, the major restraints to Soviet attainment of a Scientific and Technological Revolution or information revolution have been the U.S.S.R.'s own overcentralized, innovation-unfriendly system and its inability to effectively utilize the Western technology available. The widely available technology in the West would be of substantive benefit to them only if they were able to effectively use it as other industrial nations have in recent years.

With his ascendancy to the pinnacle of Soviet power, Mikhail Gorbachev brought a new look to Soviet foreign as well as domestic economic policy. His general political-economic policy is important because it will affect not only the East-West agenda but even the details of commercial policy changes, i.e. the determination of contracts for imports, exports and credits. Gorbachev may directly initiate and consummate foreign economic transactions. His Western leadership counterparts in Washington and elsewhere may influence—facilitate or restrict—trade, but are usually not directly involved in the negotiation of commercial contracts involving transfers of technology. In contrast, the Soviet leadership, following its own perceived interests, decides whether to put oil or other commodities or products on the world market. It also makes the decisions that determine which part of the domestic programs will be supplied by foreign imports and by whom.

If Gorbachev decides not to buy from or sell to the United States, there will not be a Soviet market for American goods. To paraphrase Ronald Reagan, "It takes two to trade." Therefore, any assessment of U.S. commercial policy with the U.S.S.R. should give major consideration to the premises and parameters of the Soviet commercial policy and to the presumptions strongly supported by the General Secretary.

Because of large domestic and CMEA production and wide foreign availability of supplies, the Soviet leadership has a wide range of choice for the Twelfth Five-Year Plan [1986-90] and the Fifteen-Year Plan [1986-2000]. There is usually some source in the West to supply non-military imports. As the major Soviet exports—oil, gas, arms and gold—are not purchased by the United States, the pattern of Soviet sales to the West is, by and large, not directly influenced by the United States. Soviet exports and imports are tradeable with many other Western countries. If the United States follows a restrictive policy, the Soviet Union may try to use trade policy as tool to divide the Western Alliance. American policy would be most effective if there were a Western consensus and coordinated action. Consensus in the West on Eastern commercial policy may thus be our key to effective trade policy with the U.S.S.R. and effective response to the new Gorbachevian Soviet economic strategy.

C. Agenda for Future U.S.-Soviet Economic and Technological Interaction

The first U.S.-U.S.S.R. Commercial Commission meeting since Afghanistan was held in Moscow in May 1985. The U.S.-U.S.S.R. Trade and Economic Council (USTEC) meeting in Moscow in December 1985 included 23 heads of companies (CEOs) and more than 300 American executives. Malcolm Baldrige, U.S. Secretary of Commerce, was the senior administration official present at the Moscow meetings and made major trade facilitation statements on contract sanctity and licensing. In their dinner addresses in the St. George Room of the Kremlin, General Secretary Gorbachev and Secretary Baldrige reviewed policy problems and prospects. It should be noted that the Gorbachev dinner reflected a high level of protocol, thus signaling a very favorable political climate for trade facilitation. Specifically, Gorbachev called for reductions in trade restraints and increased interdependence—a word only used by Western leaders prior to Gorbachev's accession to power—and new forms of industrial cooperation. Secretary Baldridge referred to the meeting as a first step toward full normalization and reported a very narrow definition of "breach of peace," accepted by President Reagan, severely limiting the basis for abrogating contracts for foreign policy purposes. While this meeting created a positive environment, the potentiality and putative desirability of further restrictions on commercial relations exist under current policies and regulations. It should be acknowledged that even with trade expansion rhetoric by both sides, bilateral trade is very small and unbalanced and projected increases would still leave bilateral commercial relations very modest for the two superpowers.

Status of U.S.-U.S.S.R. Trade and Projections:

• U.S. exports to the U.S.S.R. less than 5 percent of all nonsocialist country exports to the U.S.S.R. ($1.25 billion).

• Agricultural exports, especially corn, dominate U.S. exports ($2.8 of $3.3 billion). In 1985, the Soviets for the first time failed to meet minimum wheat import commitments under the 1984-85 Long-Term Grain Agreement, but U.S. corn exports to the U.S.S.R. continued.

• U.S. machinery exports to the Soviet Union are very low, currently less than $0.1 billion—a level exceeded by U.S. trade with many LDCs.

• U.S. imports from U.S.S.R. comprise 2 percent of nonsocialist nation imports from U.S.S.R. ($0.6 of 33 billion). General Secretary Gorbachev likened this to our trade with the Ivory Coast.

• Government credits are barred by U.S. legislation and private credit is minimal. The first U.S.-led credit syndication since Afghanistan was subscribed in November 1985 at favorable market terms.

• Major current examples of Soviet-American industrial cooperation are the early 1970s ammonia-urea for superphosphate deal with Occidental and vodka for Pepsi contract with Pepsico. This trade is subject to antidumping action.

• As a result of decreases in hardcurrency earnings due to low energy and merchandise goods sales, the U.S.S.R.'s trade with non-socialist nations moved from surplus to deficit in 1984-85.

• Leading trade partner with the U.S.S.R. remains the Federal Republic of Germany with oil and gas equipment and pipelines representing the dominant exports; oil and gas the major imports.

• Estimates by Wharton Associates project substantial trade expansion between the U.S.S.R. and nonsocialist nations during the Twelfth Five-Year Plan (1985–90): with exports to the U.S.S.R. moving from $37 to $52 billion, while imports from the U.S.S.R. are expected to increase from $33 to $43 billion. The increase in exports to the U.S.S.R. is expected to be focused on plant and equipment, while Western import expansion will center on oil and gas sales.

• Increases in Soviet grain imports will be concentrated in feed grains, such as corn and soybean concentrates. Prospects for increased U.S. sales of grain and soybean concentrate will be determined by the value of the dollar, competition from subsidized foreign exports, and legislative and policy restraints on exports, imports, and credit.

The Summit rhetoric and actions of the principals on both sides raise the potentiality for modest expansion in bilateral commercial relations, and future possibility for full normalization under the most favorable circumstances for centrally planned, communist countries dealing with

Western trading partners. However, many uncertainties remain that may lead to a retrogression to an even lower level of economic interchange. To capture the essence of those alternatives, three alternate U.S.-U.S.S.R. commercial scenarios are outlined below:

1. Current Projections with Adoption of Trade Restrictive Measures: *Restricted Commercial Policy*
If currently proposed and potential limitations on exports, imports and credit are implemented, U.S.-Soviet trade will be further reduced by 1990. If the Long-Term Grain Agreement (LTA) is not renewed, Soviet grain imports might fall to an insignificant level.

2. Modest Improvements Based on Summits and Currently Proposed Trade Facilitation Measures: *Facilitated Commercial Policy*
With expectations of renewal and expansion of the LTA, effective assurance of contract sanctity and more openness in the Soviet economy, significant increases in certain U.S. export areas seem prospective, e.g., agricultural and energy technology. Moreover, reducing import restrictions for Soviet goods entering the U.S. market would increase Soviet hardcurrency earnings needed to pay for increased American imports and expanded cooperative ventures would reduce hard currency constraint. A shift in orders from West European to the United States is a likely short-term approach to increased bilateral machinery trade. Opening up the U.S. government and private credit facilities would substantially improve the competitiveness of U.S. exporters vis-á-vis other Western suppliers.

3. Improvements Consistent with Policies of the Most Favored of the Non-Market Economies (NME) and Socialist Commercial Relations (PRC, GDR, Hungary, and Yugoslavia): *Fully Normalized Commerce*
Fully normalized commercial relations with the Soviet Union presuppose the eventual granting of Most-Favored-Nation (MFN) tariff treatment and opening of the government credit window by the United States to the U.S.S.R. Such a step by Washington would move Moscow closer to the more "normalized" status presently occupied by Hungary and the People's Republic of China in U.S. commercial relations. Extending the other means by which exports, imports, and credit expansion are currently facilitated for trade with the most open of the communist countries would provide an opportunity for American and Soviet commercial interests to substantially expand trade turnover. A major role in this regard could be played by U.S. multinational corporations in promoting transfers of nonstrategic technology and agricultural sales.

Fully normalized commerce would necessarily be in a context of normalized political-military relations. Therefore, the process of normalizing military relations through negotiations on arms control, regional disputes and human rights begun through the Reagan/Gorbachev Summits, is an essential environment for commercial normalization.

Optimistic summit prospects notwithstanding, the political-military relations between the United States and the Soviet Union may retrogress from moderate expectations of cooperation to confrontation. In that environment a contraction of commercial exchange would be likely.

1. Restricted Commercial Policy

Scenario one—*Restricted Commercial Policy*—could lead to a very small, even non-trade United States relationship with the Soviet Union. Without a favorable political environment, grain trade, likely to be the only commercial exchange of substance, could be reduced largely to corn and soybean concentrates exports as the U.S.S.R. seeks other markets for wheat. The Long-Term Grain Agreement need not be extended after 1988 for economic reasons, as the Soviet Union may find domestic supplies of wheat adequate and new markets for corn and soybeans in the People's Republic of China, Brazil and elsewhere.

Court action on countervailing duties and dumping and enforcement of "forced labor" provisions of the Smoot-Hawley tariff bill would effectively wipe out modest imports to the United States from the U.S.S.R. Restraints on private lending may close the commercial bank credit windows to the U.S.S.R. With reduced income from declining oil and gas revenue, withdrawals from the U.S. cash market, largely financed by surpluses in European sales, would be decreased.

Adoption of a more restrictive policy by the United States is not likely to be followed by other Western industrial countries. European nations and Japan may still find the Soviet and East European markets very attractive for both imports and exports and facilitate more trade with mixed credits. As there are limited prospects for members of OECD to extradite themselves from involvement with U.S. technology and credit through multinational and multilateral ties, these Western developed country policies might be frictional or acrimonious. If all U.S. restrictions were accepted, the economic losses could likewise be even greater sources of tension and friction in alliance policy.

2. Facilitated Commercial Policy

More likely, (assuming the Washington and Moscow Summits lead toward substantive broad agreements) and more desirable (considering the common East-West and West-West interests) would be Scenario two—*Facilitated Commercial Policy*. The Soviet General Secretary associated himself with the advantages of interdependence and new commercial forms, such as joint ventures and re-involvement of the United States in large Soviet projects. President Reagan and Secretary of Commerce Baldrige indicated desires to expand commercial relations with more stability of commercial relations and access to U.S. markets and credit. Specifically, the key variables determining the future level of U.S.-U.S.S.R. trade include the following:

(a) Relaxation of U.S. Export Restrictions, Soviet Import Constraints

• **Foreign policy controls** on licensing of oilfield exploration and production equipment and advanced computer technology may be eased by correlating U.S. with CoCom policy; the U.S.S.R. may place substantive orders with U.S. companies to meet priority aims in improving energy sector performance.

A number of foreign policy export controls related to oilfield exploration and advanced computer technology, enacted in the late 1970s and early 1980s against the Soviet Union were removed in January 1987. The controls were set in place in protest to the Soviet trial of Anatoly B. Shcharansky in 1978. The most well-known application of foreign policy controls came in response to the disbanding of Solidarity in Poland in June 1982; their enactment was followed by the "pipeline dispute." Controls on the export of oil and gas equipment and technology are perceived by some in American business as the most onerous of the foreign policy controls enacted over the last seven years and least useful in terms of U.S. national interest. The desire of American business to bring about some change in this area has grown, particularly given the enhanced foreign availability provisions in the new Export Administration Act (EAA) Amendments and the strengthened interest within some quarters of the Administration and Congress in expanding U.S.-Soviet trade. As the EAA contains a sunset provision requiring annual renewal of foreign policy controls, the business community lobbied for removal of these controls.

The rationale of energy security from overdependence on Soviet gas in Western Europe that gave rise to the pipeline dispute has been eased in the short run by the oil and gas glut in the world market. It has also been eased in the long run by plans to develop offshore Norwegian gas, including the massive Troll field, as a means of providing secure energy sources in the 1990s.

The Soviet Union is especially keen about developing new oil fields in the Caspian, Sakhalin, and Barents Sea areas; improving oil field management with improved recovery of residual oil, and improved petroleum refining; production of more energy efficient equipment; and improved gas transmission technology. Each of these priority areas finds U.S. energy equipment suppliers in competitive positions.

• Ambiguous U.S. statutes and agreements designed to promote **contract sanctity** in capital goods exports may be clarified and their impact delimited.

In the view of American businessmen, the contract sanctity question raises uncertainty over the application of foreign policy criteria to U.S. manufacturing exports, e.g., "the light switch problem." Discussions in Moscow in December 1985 centered on the problem of contract sanctity for agricultural technology complexes and energy system exports from the United States to the U.S.S.R.

A major new approach to assure contract sanctity or reliability of supply would be acceptance of the narrower definition of "breach of peace," articulated by Senator Garn in the EAA colloquy as a "serious and direct threat to the strategic interest of the United States." This language and interpretation was specifically attributed to President Reagan by Secretary Baldrige in his Kremlin speech. Another approach would be adoption of the Senate Resolution introduced by Senator Simon which would extend the contract sanctity provisions of the Long-Term Grain Agreement to agricultural technology and equipment (S.R. 103), e.g., the extension of the Executive agreement assurance of the Long-Term Grain Agreement to other contracts.

• Reduced uncertainty over the applicability of U.S. **extra-territorial laws** which inhibit involvement of U.S. multinationals in the Soviet market.

The Secretary of Commerce may grant multiple export licenses under the current EAA to facilitate multiple shipments to noncontrolled countries. However, these distribution licenses require detailed reports from Western suppliers to the United States that prove cumbersome to many and, when audited by U.S. officials, raise again the issue of extraterritoriality. Some American businessmen suggest that the detailed reporting requirements has led many Western suppliers to cut their ties with U.S. firms. Thus, a new form of extraterritorial reach may reduce further U.S. involvement in manufactured goods trade with the U.S.S.R. and cause acrimony in the Western alliance; some foresee a "new pipeline dispute environment." This restraint may be modified.

The Soviets realize that tying into U.S. multinational corporations for supply, distribution and marketing is important for effective Western commercial relations. Healthy competition is likewise beneficial to the U.S.S.R., but unilateral restrictions may limit economic benefits. Political gains may flow from direct Western involvement in the Soviet economy. New Soviet organizational forms in Western trade, such as joint ventures, could provide more access to Soviet end-users and facilitate effective transfer of technology.

(b) U.S. Import Restrictions, Soviet Export Constraints May Be Eased

Absence of tariff privileges, and import restrictions applying specifically to Soviet and centrally planned economy exports constrain levels of Eastern exports. Even with removal of U.S. import restrictions, the Soviet Union would need to develop a more export-oriented policy for manufactured goods to shift away from primary reliance on oil and gas hard currency earnings. OECD countries that extend MFN to the USSR do not have significant levels of manufactured goods imports from the Soviet Union.

A number of issues are being addressed and considered:

• **Jackson-Vanik Amendment Waiver.** Repeal of Jackson-Vanik amendment is politically unlikely and economically unnecessary. There is some sentiment in Congress and the business community to relax import restraints through a "waiver" of the Jackson-Vanik Amendment in return for some improvement in emigration. Also, in this context, some support further discretion in Executive authority using an interpretation of the Supreme Court *Chadha* decision that restricts the right of Congress to override an Executive waiver determination. Multiyear waivers have been suggested from time to time by several members of Congress for the PRC and Hungary. Secretary Shultz discussed the multiyear waiver in Hungary in December 1985. Increased consideration of emigration in the context of resumed Soviet-Israeli relations may be another part of the quid pro quo in these discussions.

• **Fur Embargo, "Seven Deadly Skins".** Section 5 of the Trade Agreements Extension Act, signed into law on June 16, 1951, required the President to suspend as soon as practicable the most-favored-nation (MFN) status of the Soviet Union and all countries controlled by "the foreign government or foreign organization controlling the world Communist movement," i.e., all then-communist countries except Yugoslavia. Suspensions were carried out over a period of time in accordance with the terms of any trade agreements then in force with the affected countries. This action subjected imports from these countries to much higher tariff rates and thus substantially reduced their price-competitiveness in the U.S. market. Furthermore, Section 11 of the Act prohibited the importation of seven types of furskins from the Soviet Union and China, the so-called "Seven Deadly Skins." On January 27, 1983 the ban on imports of furskins from the People's Republic of China was revoked by Section 103 of P.L. 97-446. In return for an offer by Secretary Baldrige to remove this fur embargo in the May 1985 meeting, the Soviet Union agreed to resume direct U.S. business access to Soviet Foreign Trade Organizations.

• **Forced Labor Provisions of Smoot-Hawley Bill.** At the same time, there is Congressional sentiment for tightening restrictions on imports of goods produced by "forced labor." Pending legislation would enforce the provisions of the 1930 Smoot-Hawley Tariff Act, halting millions of dollars worth of imports from the Soviet Union that are considered to have been made with "forced" or "convict" labor. The measure, which was introduced by Representative Frank Wolf (R-VA), would ban certain imports, including petroleum products, gold ore, agricultural machinery, tractor generators and tea. The Reagan administration now apparently opposes this action.

• **Countervailing Duties and Anti-Dumping.** On July 30, 1985, the U.S. Court of International Trade ruled that the U.S. countervailing duty law does apply to imports from nonmarket economy countries, a decision that would have a chilling effect on bilateral trade prospects by opening up the potential for significantly wider import restraints. The ruling overturns a May 1984 Commerce Department determination that the law is not applicable to nonmarket economy imports. The Commerce Department determination was issued in response to a petition filed by U.S. producers of carbon wire steel rod who charged that imports from Poland and Czechoslovakia were subsidized. In making its preliminary finding on the petition, Commerce ruled that while Congress did not exempt nonmarket economy countries from the countervailing duty law *per se*, there was no basis on which to determine that such programs as multiple exchange rates or currency retention schemes constituted a subsidy under Section 303 of the Tariff Act of 1930. On May 1, 1984, in its final determination, Commerce ruled that bounties or grants cannot be found in non-market economies. The Department reemphasized its earlier contention that, even if subsidies existed in nonmarket economies, they could not be reasonably calculated.

Following the negative determination, Commerce dismissed another petition that had been brought against potassium chloride imports from the German Democratic Republic. Since then, Commerce has not accepted countervailing duty petitions brought against non-market economy producers.

If the U.S. Court of International Trade ruling stands, one can expect a number of subsidy petitions against non-market economy imports. Such a recourse would be appealing to domestic producers since, in contrast to the requirements of U.S. antidumping duty law, the petitioners would not have to prove domestic injury. Injury determinations apply only to countries that are signatories to the Subsidies Code of the General Agreement on Tariffs and Trade. As none of the non-market economies have signed the code, subsidy petitions involving nonmarket economy imports would be far easier to win and much less costly to argue. The Administration has appealed the ruling to the Court of Appeals of the Federal Circuit.

In addition to the court ruling, the countervailing duty issue has been raised in the new "artificial pricing" bill introduced by Senator Heinz, (R-PA) which would revise current antidumping/countervailing duty regulations on nonmarket economy imports. The bill is part of a trade package, the Trade Enhancement Act of 1985 (S. 1860)[9], that the Senate may adopt before adjournment. The House is expected to consider parallel action.

The new Heinz bill parallels the "artificial pricing" legislation approved by the Senate during the final months of the last Congress. That bill established a minimum allowable import price, which was defined as "the trade-weighted average price" of foreign market economy producers in arms-length sales to customers in the United States. Those non-market economy producers exporting to the United States below this average free market price would be assessed a penalty in accordance with the price differential.

---

[9]See *Congressional Record*, November 20, 1985. S. 15959-16048.

The Department of Commerce is examining alternatives to the Heinz approach. One such alternative reportedly would base cost comparisons on the U.S. producers price list and provide for establishing a percentage below which non-market economy imports could not undercut U.S. prices. If such imports entered the United States below this price and the International Trade Commission (ITC) determined the existence of injury, Commerce would be empowered to impose a tariff on the non-market economy imports to the extent of the price differential.

(c) U.S. Credit Controls, Soviet Credit Policy May Be Relaxed

Soviet access to Western private and government credit markets may now be favored by Reagan Administration and conservative Soviet credit and debt policy may be changing.

 • **Financial Control Authority.** On March 28, 1985 Senators Garn and Proxmire introduced legislation authorizing the President "to control the transfer of money and other financial resources from the United States to countries against which we (the United States) maintain national security export controls." In introducing the bill, Senator Garn maintained that "the Soviet ability to obtain the sensitive goods and technology from the West that are turned against us in Soviet weapon systems is directly related to their ability to obtain hard currency, Western currencies."

On September 26, 1985 the Senate Banking Committee began hearings on the Financial Export Control Act, S. 812. The sponsors of the bill called for the Administration to put greater pressure upon America's allies to restrict lending to the Soviet bloc. U.S. commercial banks, however, note that U.S. bank exposure in the Soviet Union and East Europe is but a small fraction of CMEA debt to the Western private sector. Thus, they argue that the likely effectiveness of unilateral U.S. control on credits and other financial transactions is limited and that U.S. interests can best be served through a free flow of private capital and trade among nations.

On December 4, 1985, during Senate Banking Committee hearings on S. 812, David C. Mulford, Assistant Treasury Secretary for International Affairs, voiced the Administration's strong opposition to the bill. First, on a practical level, he argued that the bill would never achieve its desired effect because of the fungibility of credit and the impossibility of securing Western support for a credit embargo against the U.S.S.R. On a policy level, the Administration opposes the bill because "capricious political decisions" may damage the international image of U.S. credit markets, create disputes within the Western alliance, and "run counter to the spirit of Geneva." Mulford supported his arguments on the fungibility issue with statistical evidence of the relatively minor role U.S. banks play in meeting the Soviet Union's credit demands.

Stevenson and Byrd Amendments and Jackson-Vanik Act Waiver, as they relate to government credit control. In late 1974, Senator Stevenson amended the Eximbank bill by placing a limit on credits to Moscow at $300 million. A second limit [the Chuch amendment] established a ceiling of $40 million for projects involving oil and gas exploration, and allowed no credits for actual energy production. Should the Soviets request above-ceiling credits, they could be granted only by a presidential statement of national interest, subject to congressional approval. The Stevenson amendment limit of $300 million is not tied to four-year periods, but rather to the extension of the Eximbank bill which comes up for renewal in 1986. The Soviets could get up to $300 million in U.S. government credits if the other impediments were removed, namely, a waiver of the Jackson-Vanik and Byrd amendments to the Trade Act (see above).

The Byrd amendment (Section 613) of the Trade Act generally adds the Stevenson amendment effect to the Trade Bill. Part of the concern of U.S. policy makers over "uncontrolled" or "preferential" use of U.S. government and private credit is that the funds available could be channeled to other purposes possibly adverse to our national interest and be supported by tax funds at less than market rates. Financing intended for a pipeline, such as the Orenburg gas line, was said to be used for supplying hard currency to other Soviet global projects, some of which may have been contrary to the U.S. interests. To deal with these concerns voiced by some of the Garn-Proxmire bill supporters, project financing or other forms of more controlled funding might be more regularly considered by U.S. bankers, with conditions on use of funds as well as payment.

On the other hand, some argue that if the United States is to be competitive in the world market for Soviet, as well as other developed or developing Communist country trade, some mixed credits are deemed desirable. Thesse arguments are especially heard in reference to large projects in the PRC. However, whenever government credits are used, there is additional concern that greater risks are being borne than would be appropriate on economic or national interest criteria, i.e., that the U.S. taxpayer needs protection against credit subsidization that benefits foreign rather than U.S. national interests.

Soviet bankers for their part have argued for balanced trade, minimum debt, and the most favorable credit terms. Their calculations of necessary credit-worthiness conditions are even limited to gross debt, not considering their other hard currency assets or claims. Soviet political leadership must give consideration to the different choices between expanding debt and vulnerability and the costs of holding down imports.

(d) Non-Commercial Transfers May Be Reassessed And A Narrow, Consensus Control Policy Adopted

Western concerns about uncontrolled transfers may be proceeding toward consensus and resumed Eastern exchanges and other non-trade links. Beyond commercial relations—controllable by either contract or legislation—technology transfer of U.S. origin may be expanded through people-related transfers, scientific communication, espionage, and more restricted industrial, but relaxed unilateral U.S. control of West-West trade. The resolution of the issues in those trade related areas may provide a basis of trade facilitation.

The imposition of U.S. export controls in the West-West context remains a highly controversial issue among the U.S. allies. The United States now requires 13 Western countries to apply for individual validated licenses for seven product categories. (See above).

The Europeans do not oppose U.S. calls for new CoCom restrictions on some selected high—"top"—technologies, but rather are against putting additional controls on older—even obsolete—technologies which they see as readily available.

French and U.S. intelligence disclosures have revealed an upsurge in Soviet espionage efforts to obtain key military products to fill critical bottlenecks rather than broad technology transfers. The disclosures reveal a greater importance of products than technology, ". . . batch acquisitions and samples which are reverse-engineered outstrips the acquisition of technology and use of more immediate value to the Soviets." Moreover, other analyses stress the Soviet desire for independence of deniable technology in such critical areas of military development. In the classic case of the defection of Alfred Sarant-Filipp Stavos in the 1950s to become the "father of Soviet microelectronics," the technology transfer was embodied. The series of expulsions of Soviet espionage specialists with diplomatic status throughout the West indicated a broad Western consensus on reducing this form of illegal transfer. As it is very expensive for the Soviet Union to deploy on a wide front for technological knowledge that can only be ineffectively transferred through intermediaries, e.g., the KGB, some more cost-effective approach may be sought by the Soviet Union. Interruptible transfers would make the Soviet Union subject to "technological blockades." Thus, a Western, CoCom-wide, consensus approach, is for more control over Soviet in-country diplomatic-industrial espionage, and as the Gorbachev leadership may accept our assessment of the ineffectiveness of broadnet Soviet industrial espionage, an accommodation on security and technology transfers seems possible. The narrowing of the Soviet priorities for their espionage might now be negotiable with a narrower Soviet focus on high tech military acquisition. A basis for an effective Western control program seems to be available and may be more effectively pursued. This more stable approach would involve a sharp separation of technology transfer through industrial cooperation for civilian programs and military espionage; which would be more effective from a Soviet perspective. This delineation would be a basis for a more effective CoCom policy of control and a narrower more effective Soviet program of acquisition.

A preferred policy for Gorbachev for economic effectiveness would be greater stress on industrial cooperation through open links between Western multinational enterprises and Soviet end-users. More freedom for Soviet enterprises by industrial sector and region to arrange Western deals, including financing and cooperation at the operating level would likewise improve the effectiveness of technology transfer in commercial relations. Industrial connections between energy producers, such as Caspian offshore developers, Western energy equipment suppliers and global energy purchasers would be improved. More independence for the enterprises in the East Siberian-Far Eastern, BAM region to deal directly with Pacific Rim trading countries would be more effective for both Soviet and Western partners.

Non-trade technology transfers are not easy to stop. Measures to restrict the modest transfers that take place through scientific communication have been discussed within the U.S. scientific, academic, and governmental communities. The Corson report recommendation of a strategy of building "tall fences around narrow areas," without restricting the free flow of scientific information seems reasonable as well as a policy of "security through accomplishments," fostered by our traditional scientific methods rather than security by control. The broad scientific communication control policy would tend to substitute the stultifying restraints of the Soviet authoritarian system for our more flexible, dynamic and productive system. Such a restrictive policy might be ineffective in limiting Soviet espionage for core military programs and injurious to the effectiveness of the U.S. scientific and technological community.

The issue of scientific communication is raised again by proposed revival of the entire panoply of agreements, including the "umbrella" S & T agreement. The umbrella agreement encompassed eleven U.S.-Soviet S & T bilateral agreements, covering projects or cooperation in areas such as physics, chemistry, oceans, space, public health and medicine, environment and energy (see above). At their peak, the bilateral activities under these agreements involved up to 10,000 scientists on both sides. From evaluating the academic exchanges agreed to and being discussed in the summit process, the new, formal scientific communication through bilateral exchanges could substantially exceed the earlier high-water mark.

Judging from previous experience, requirements for effective exchange require that they be properly arranged, well administered and implemented, closely monitored, and periodically professionally assessed. If these conditions of proper management obtain, the United States may gain specific net benefits. According to an earlier participant in supervising these programs, we would expect the United States to obtain net benefit on the following conditions:

1) The United States draw on very advanced Soviet work in some S & T areas which they have not achieved (e.g., theoretical physics and mathematics, selective energy, medical and industrial processes);

2) The United States tap into work not undertaken here and utilize Soviet facilities, saving time, resources and money; and

3) The United States can get access to extensive research data and records (medical, environmental, oceanic) that are otherwise unavailable in or to the United States.

The Soviets would likewise benefit from access to a number of specific areas of research. In negotiating the exchange, the Soviets and the U.S. would try to include areas in which each could respectively benefit most. In a broader sense, access to the technologically dynamic communications system of the U.S. science and technology environment would benefit the Soviets most, in general terms. Their compartmentalized bureaucratized system has little of the flexibility of the United States system with its "invisible college" or peer group relations. While this raises again the U.S. intelligence community question on needed control of unintended transfer, the logic of the Corson report—carefully monitoring of sensitive data ("tall fences") and "security by accomplishment" still obtains.

The general benefit to the United States of formal exchanges is from unavailable access to closely monitored Soviet programs in exchange for more effective access by other means to U.S. programs largely in the public domain. For example, some Soviet programs may be only 10 percent accessible from public sources, while the United States counterpart may be 90 percent in the public domain. A larger aim of understanding and influencing the Soviet development may likewise be relevant.

3. Fully Normalized Commerce

Were the summits from Geneva to Washington to Moscow to develop a momentum of change for commercial facilitation, we might explore the parameters of Scenario Three—the potential development and necessary conditions for what Secretary Baldrige referred to as the steps toward full normalization. All the issues addressed in Section 2 above, *Facilitated Commercial Policy,* are relevant and would be carried fully forward for maximum facilitation.

Fully normalized commerce between the United States and the Soviet Union might entail consideration of trade facilitation measures consistent with policies of the most favored and most open of the Non Market Economies (NME) and socialist country commercial relations with the West (PRC, GDR, Hungary, and Yugoslavia). Fully normalized commercial relations with the Soviet Union presuppose the eventual granting of Most Favored Nation (MFN) tariff treatment by the United States to the U.S.S.R., as well as the granting of status in other aspects of our import, export and credit policy comparable to the most favored of the centrally planned or socialist countries having trade agreements with the United States, but also the most normalized of Eastern countries with other Western partners. The Soviet Union, in turn, might be expected to open its economy as do the most open Eastern countries to normal economic relations approaching the practices of the Western market system. Of course, these are parameters of change unlikely to be easily reached, but they would provide a useful framework for assessing change in the context of a full normalization process. Such steps by Washington would not only elevate Moscow to the status presently occupied by Hungary and Yugoslavia and the People's Republic of China in U.S. trade policy, but raise consideration of a relationship like that of the closest East-West commercial relations involving Austria and Hungary, the two Germanies, Italy and Yugoslavia, Japan, Hong Kong and the PRC.

In economic terms, the Gorbachev goal of reform and restructuring the economy—a modest Soviet form of *laissez-faire*—might be reinforced by an effective opening of the Soviet economy to the world market. Reform would be further facilitated by participation of the Soviet Union in the foundation institutions in the international economic community—a return to the early Soviet position of involvement in the Bretton Woods process.

President Reagan articulated three major objectives for normalizing U.S.-Soviet relations in 1983, which were reiterated by Secretary Baldrige in Moscow in December 1985 as the necessary context for commercial change:

1) To reduce, and eventually eliminate, the threat and use of force in solving international disputes;

2) To reduce arms stockpiles; and

3) To establish a better working relationship between our countries.

In order to attain those preconditions to full normalization of commercial relations a process of improvement would involve:

• A system of arms control agreements to stabilize the bilateral relationships;

• An acceptable code of conduct for the global superpowers for dealing with affairs endangering our vital interests in the various regions of the world; and

• An acceptable conduct in the human rights area based on norms laid down in the Helsinki and United Nations agreements.

Progress on the political-military agenda, so central to U.S.-Soviet relations, would provide a foundation for improvement in commercial relations. The interdependence found in expanded commercial relations would thus reinforce these broader, more central areas of contention in superpower relations, making normalization of the overall relations a cyclical pattern.

V. CONCLUDING REMARKS

The pattern of interrelations between superpowers has broadened and deepened. Trade relations are becoming a part of a pattern of commercial, financial, scientific, political and security intercourse with some longer term commitments built in. This new pattern might be reversed if the Reagan-Gorbachev summit process were aborted. But if continued to its projected resolution a qualitative change in the relationship may be in store.

The increasing importance of allies and other power centers has diminished the prospects for unilateral reversal and the continuation of global cycles in East-West relations led by the two superpowers. The East and West countries of Europe and Asia all have favored a trend of normalization over cycles of confrontation and cooperation and now have more power to bring this about. The traditional strengths of the United States in technology, credit and competitiveness have seriously eroded leaving other Western nations with an edge in the third technological-information revolution; U.S. debt and trade deficits have increased the influence of Japan and the European Community in controlling credit policy. The Soviet shift under Gorbachev toward more reliance on political and economic factors in international relations and increased needs for interdependence is moving the Soviet Union toward a stabilizing posture in the global economic arena.

With the broadening, normalizing, and stabilizing of East-West relations, openness may lead the Soviet Union toward more reliance on effective commercial technology transfer and exchanges and less on their traditional reliance on espionage. The American thrust toward competitiveness in the world market and normalization with the Soviet Union would have the effect of reducing the U.S. unilateral use of controls and sanctions. While competitiveness in the global market may sharpen due to imbalances of supply and balance of payments, the divisive force of unilateral U.S. trade policy seems likely to ameliorate.

As interdependence increases the economic costs of reversal are likely to mount reducing the prospects of renewed grain, pipeline and credit embargoes. While economics remains a small part of the broad power balance of the superpowers, the fact that it represents the major area of mutual benefit makes commercial relations a uniquely positive force in bilateral relations. Buyers and sellers mutually profit from expanding economic intercourse.

Chapter VI

THE U.S.S.R. IN THE 1980s AND BEYOND

Robert F. Byrnes

INTRODUCTION

Determining accurately what has happened in another culture, especially the Soviet Union, is difficult. Analyzing today's developments is even more puzzling, and making judgments concerning the next ten or fifteen years in the Soviet Union is hazardous in the extreme. This is especially so because none of us is objective concerning that rival. Our knowledge of the society as a whole is new, rests largely on study from afar, and suffers from sharply restricted access to information. We also lack confident understanding of the relationships among the leaders of the Soviet Union and above all of the ways their minds work. Moreover, we live in a world that is changing rapidly in every way. No one can anticipate the impact of social and intellectual developments, or of economic or scientific transformations, even within his own society: no forecasters in 1945 even mentioned the computer. Finally, of course, no one can foresee catastrophes or events as influential as the escalation of oil prices in 1973 or the overthrow of the Shah in 1979.

Nevertheless, observers benefit from a vastly expanded range of knowledge and an international research base that has examined practically every aspect of Soviet society. In addition, while changes will continue to occur in the Soviet Union, the USSR is a remarkably stable and conservative system, one that not only lacks a mechanism for change but is conditioned to resist innovation.

THE GORBACHEV LEADERSHIP

The accession to leadership of Gorbachev in February 1985 and his bringing into positions of authority men from his generation does raise the possibility of changes in policy and, perhaps, ultimately in the system itself. These may sharply affect Soviet power and even more the perceptions foreigners have of the Soviet Union and its policies.

It is difficult to define Gorbachev's goals and his ability to achieve them. He and those who rule with him share the values and qualities of those who selected them, embrace and benefit from the communist system, and view the world in much the same way as their predecessors did. However, they entered political life after Stalin's death, they have had different experiences and have acquired different knowledge and ideas, and they have gradually set aside the stable, aged, oligarchy who ruled such a long time. They are more aware of the acute character of Soviet problems and more eager "to get the country going" than their elders have been. Debates among them over particular issues and the rate of change do occur, and those jostling for place and power may advocate particular changes they believe necessary to advance the interests of their bureaucratic or territorial constituencies or simply to increase their personal power. Our knowledge of relations among those in the central circle of power is limited, but the leadership has been fundamentally collective for so long and the general agreement on policy has been so great that we must assume decisions will be reached within the Kremlin walls and that any increases, diminutions, or transfers of authority will be orderly and peaceful.

Gorbachev apparently seeks to create a flexible, dynamic, technologically advanced socialist state capable of competing effectively in political, economic, and military power with the Western democracies. At the same time, he expects to maintain the Communist system in which he grew up and in which he has reached the leading position.

He has also given (the correct word) intellectuals and the media more freedom, he has released Sakharov and some other political prisoners, he has "pardoned" some dissenters, and he has emphasized the role of *glasnost'* throughout society. In foreign policy, he has accepted some Western arms control offers he had previously denounced, and the Soviets have made some attractive proposals of their own. But he has not concluded any arms control agreements, or made any significant revisions on Afghanistan, support of Vietnam in Kampuchea, or his relations with the People's Republic of China, although he has created the impression he seeks changes. In short, in more than two years he has introduced only corrections or modifications, not major modifications in structure or policy. He has promised more than he has delivered, as do most statesmen and politicians.

Moreover, Gorbachev has encountered increasingly visible resistance to his domestic policies, from within the Politburo and the Central Committee and from provincial party officials, planners, managers, workers, intellectuals, subsidized groups, and others who have benefited from the system. He has also collided with the passivity and inertia that the system has long encouraged and that it now seeks somehow to energize. He rules peoples very different from those of China, and even more different from those of Portugal, Spain, or the Republic of Korea. Resistance to change is institutionalized throughout the party, the government, the main institutions, the economy, and the country as a whole. Any leader who seeks to innovate would need several years to consolidate his position, to remove those reluctant to change from their responsibilities, and to create a lasting coalition throughout the party, the government, and the vast country in order to overcome inertia and resistance and to enforce new ideas and approaches.

Some observers believe Gorbachev has firm control of power, that the Soviet Union has no alternative or rival leader, and that he is moving slowly because the opposition has deep roots and because the encouraged appearance of opposition increases Western sympathy for him and his policies. Others agree, but conclude that he is not certain of his long-range goals. Others surmise that he has not yet consolidated his authority and that he and those who support him are balancing between groups who oppose change, who seek slow and gradual change, and who seek a thorough restructuring of the economy and even of the political system. Some conclude that this dilemma will lead to the failure of any attempt at modernizing the system and the replacement of Gorbachev by someone less ambitious for change. Still others believe that this will persuade Gorbachev (perhaps already has) to concentrate power in his hands and then force through the changes he seeks, as Peter the Great and Stalin did. In this, he would seek especially the support of the intellectuals and approval of the outside world that Peter and Stalin received.

In short, no foreign observer, and perhaps even Gorbachev himself, can be certain of the extent of Gorbachev's authority, his goals, and the means he will use to achieve those aims. The nature of the system and the number and complexity of the problems suggest that Gorbachev or someone like him will acquire full authority and then seek to make the Soviet Union a technologically modern state. The nature of the scientific and technical revolution and of the shrinking world suggest that no authoritarian system can create the modern economy Gorbachev seeks.

In any case, the basic question is: can Gorbachev and the narrowly constituted elite, comfortable in its achievements and power, aware of the serious problems the USSR faces, but reluctant to face the hazards of change, generate the will to move innovatively to overcome stagnation, decline, and ever more serious future instabilities? Can they persuade the bureaucracy, the factory and farm managers, and the passive population to demonstrate the initiative and entrepreneurship that effective modern industrialization requires? Can they choose between the disagreeable and the intolerable? What will be the consequences of their decisions upon Soviet foreign policy? And what can the United States and its allies do to influence developments within the Soviet Union?

One can conclude with some confidence that the Soviet Union in the next decade or two will remain an authoritarian state controlled by a small group in the Communist Party and a powerful military state with an economy less able to compete with that of other advanced countries than now; that it will confront a set of fundamental, long-term, inter-related, and complicated economic, social and cultural problems even more critical than those its rivals face; and that these issues will require very demanding choices by the leaders, decisions for fundamental structural change that these men will remain reluctant to reach and would find difficult to put into effect. Throughout these years, the USSR is likely to muddle through or muddle down, but will not decline sharply or collapse. Its internal difficulties are such that the leaders, whoever they may be, will almost certainly devote more energy and resources to trying to resolve these problems and less to the empire beyond Eastern Europe, some of which may slip away. The Soviet Union will not become a congenial member of the international community, but will remain a destabilizing element in world politics.

IDEOLOGY

Pragmatists and reasonable men and women find it difficult to understand others who hold fixed ideas or dogmas. Marxism is irrelevant for the great majority of Soviet citizens, including many party members, but some elements of Marxism and of Leninism deeply affect those who rule and their advisers. These ideas create the framework and the atmosphere, or "the political culture," in which these men view the world and the vocabulary in which they think and express themselves. The Soviet leaders believe firmly that Communist Party rule as "the vanguard of the proletariat" is essential within the Soviet Union and that their government must use all resources necessary to sustain rule of those they consider communists elsewhere in the world.

They perceive the world as one in which two rival systems engage in a permanent, implacable struggle for domination, a conflict in which they will inevitably triumph, if only after long and cruel conflict. They have successfully blended these Marxist and Leninist doctrines with Russian nationalism in a way that unites most Soviet peoples emotionally behind them. However, they lack the fervor and messianism of Lenin's generation.

THE POLITICAL SYSTEM

The Communist Party will retain control over the Soviet Union, with no likelihood of significant change, especially such as those Spain and Portugal have enjoyed since 1975. The Soviet peoples will remain fundamentally patriotic, loyal, satisfied, and submissive. Dissidences will survive, as will disaffections. In fact, both may increase within a framework the leaders consider manageable, if the current Soviet policy toward openness remains in effect. Disaffections will grow among the workers should living standards remain stagnant, as seems likely.

Debates over policies and disagreements on details will continue among the elites and no doubt among those few who exercise authority, but agreement upon coherent principles and above all on the primary need to maintain control will prevail. These debates occur within a group that combines political, military, economic, and social power. There are no significant institutional rivalries; the Soviet military forces are an inherent and fully enmeshed part of the political system.

Soviet policy will devote special interest to ensuring domestic controls and to maintaining Soviet military power in a world the rulers consider unstable and threatening. The military forces, as the foundation of the system's legitimacy and pride and of the Soviet Union's status as a world power, will retain their high priority in the assignment of economic and intellectual resources. The Soviet Union is an isolated state, supported only by clients, surrounded by hostile peoples and states (some ruled by communists), and facing the likelihood that Japan and China will enlarge and improve their military forces, in part because of fears Soviet policy has helped increase. The armed forces will almost certainly continue to improve in quality and strength, whether or not some arms control agreements on specific categories and numbers of weapons are concluded and whether or not some relaxation of world tensions occurs. They have powerful political and popular support; they represent an unquestioned military-industrial complex; they constitute the principal source of Soviet political influence in the world; and they will continue to reflect the Soviet rulers' fear of Western, especially American, science and technology, as weapons become ever more powerful and accurate.

The system's controls over the Soviet peoples will almost certainly remain complete, whether or not the government relaxes its controls over intellectual life in order to engage the support of Soviet intellectuals and to persuade the outside world the political system is changing drastically, because of the rulers' insistence upon complete authority, especially in uncertain times.

The Soviet rulers, whoever they may be, are likely to direct increased energy and resources inward over this period. This will reflect the acute character of long-neglected domestic problems; the instability of Eastern Europe, which the Soviet leaders consider an essential part of the Soviet empire; and the high costs of empire. The total costs of empire in the early 1980s (excluding defense outlays, but including export credits, military and economic assistance, covert activities, and implicit trade subsidies) was between thirty and forty billion dollars annually, compared to five or eight billion in 1971.[1] Moreover, these ventures abroad have produced deep frustrations and disappointments, beginning of course with China. The likelihood is high that the Angolan and Mozambique governments, and perhaps that of Ethiopia, will turn against communism and the Soviet Union, strengthening the Soviet tendency to turning inward, continuing the break-up of any international communist organization, and profoundly shaking the faith of communists and non-communists everywhere in the inevitable triumph of communism.

THE ECONOMY

The Soviet economy, in a splendid burst of growth from the mid-1960s until the early 1980s helped double the standard of living, transform the Soviet Union from a state that had to retreat embarrassingly in 1962 to one that today possesses military strength approximately equal that of the United States, and at the same time greatly expand the Soviet empire in southeast Asia, the Middle East, Africa, and now Central America.

However, as Gorbachev and many of his associates appreciate, this economy faces acute, fundamental problems so interrelated that resolution appears almost impossible. Paradoxically, some problems are the consequence of the progress achieved and of the means adopted. Above all, they reflect the shortcomings inherent in the Soviet political system as well as the explosions of energy and of new scientific-technical developments in the advanced industrial states, especially the United States.

The central problem is the continuation of a long process of decelerating economic growth: most observers anticipate annual rates of growth of approximately two percent and perhaps basic stagnation. The fundamental cause of this is systemic, over-centralized control, planning, and management of an increasingly complex economic system for which centralization is now counter-productive. The labor supply will increase at only one third the rate at which it grew in the 1970s, and most of the increase will come from Muslim Turks, far removed from the traditional industrial centers, reluctant to move, and likely to become increasingly restive whether or not industrial growth increases greatly in their areas, close to restless fundamentalist Muslim countries. Productivity is only about forty percent that of the United States; the increases in investment goods and consumer supplies necessary to raise this would greatly reduce resources available for the military forces. Agriculture remains a comedy and a tragedy, burdened by the dead hand of the "city boys" and their system, the absence of incentives, and a price system that contributes eight or nine percent

---

[1]Charles Wolf, Jr., K. C. Yeh, Edmund Brunner, Jr., Aaron Gurwitz, and Marilee Lawrence, *The Costs of the Soviet Empire* (Santa Monica: RAND, 1983).

of the gross national product to subsidies. These destroy rural initiative and spoil urban residents in the same way as in Poland. The high cost of empire constitutes another essential part of the problem.

The decline of economic growth at a time when most other advanced economies are growing rapidly and changing in character weakens the Soviet Union's attraction as a model and its ability to compete with the United States in international politics. Above all, the resource stringency created by this basically fixed economic pie provides delicate and complicated problems of determining priorities in resource allocation. The international situation and their ideology together persuade the rulers that they must continue to devote thirteen or fourteen percent of the annual product to the military forces, perhaps even a higher percentage, especially of scarce scientific and technical resources. However, the economy can resume growth only if the government can allot increased resources to investment and to consumer goods.

In addition, the West does not stand still. Soviet progress in the old "smoke-stack" industries has slowed just when another wave of the industrial revolution, based on discoveries in science and on improved technology, has created a series of new industries for which the Soviet Union lacks human and material resources. Moreover, the shortened life-cycles of the new technologies that rely heavily on the role of innovative individuals and small firms in the rapid race for new products make it ever more difficult for a centralized economy to catch up. Paradoxically, the pressures of these rapidly-changing advances persuade the Soviets to cling tenaciously to centralized control in order to channel resources to high priority sectors. Finally, a central element of this new wave, called the age of information or telematics, has made knowledge more than ever the world's most important product, one transforming life in the advanced countries and causing a significant change in relations among peoples throughout the world. This revolution rests above all on open access to information, which constitutes a most serious challenge to authoritarian control. In short, the Soviet Union must somehow obtain the resources necessary to enter this new world of international telecommunications or fall behind, as it would have if it had rejected jet engines or nuclear power. But an age in which every micro computer connected to a printer becomes a potential printing plant is far more hazardous for the system than unjammed radio broadcasts.

The slower rate of economic growth, deferred economic modernization, and the new era in science and technology, its products, and its potential therefore constitute fundamental problems. They are not immediately life-threatening, but they will become ever more acute the longer their resolution is delayed.

Gorbachev's program for the economy, as for Soviet life in general, has thus far provided more encouragement to innovate, promises of a better life under dynamic innovation, and cheer-leading rather than policies. The June 1987 session of the Central Committee may provide a clear description of specific policies, or may instead indicate that Gorbachev's reluctance to announce specific policies or rooted opposition are going to restrict changes to increased social discipline and rhetoric.

A number of Soviet economists for several years have appreciated the problems the economy faces, and their proposals resemble those Western economists have suggested and that Gorbachev publicly proclaims. However, Gorbachev in a feverish national and international publicity campaign first emphasized increased labor discipline and set out to destroy the cancers of corruption and alcoholism. He then transferred his talents to encouraging openness or publicity concerning the shortcomings of the economy, the sterility of cultural life, and the need for dynamism. This was designed to encourage attacks upon the "cake of custom" that encrusts the economy and to win the support of intellectuals for the "restructuring" essential. This has produced some effects that may spill over into the economy: even men such as Sakharov, whom Gorbachev released from exile in Gorki, support him as "the last best hope."

Basically, Gorbachev appears to seek to transform Gosplan and central planning institutions into "think tanks," the ministries into planning organizations, and enterprises into relatively independent concerns. Selected enterprises are allowed to decide the use of their earnings. However, he remains opposed to "market socialism," and the ability of "independent" enterprises to innovate effectively when they lack direct access to raw materials and markets and when prices remain fixed seems low. He has encouraged small family business in service industries, where rapid improvements are likely and popular approval sure to follow. Perhaps his most sensational decision was that to end the vast and expensive river diversion project, the planned investments in which he can now divert to more productive uses. If the draft decree now under consideration for allowing "joint ventures" in the Soviet Union with foreign enterprises should become law and should be sufficiently attractive to foreign corporations, that too might have a dramatic effect, especially upon foreign opinion.

In agriculture, where the People's Republic of China began its remarkable economic advance ten years ago, Gorbachev has increased state procurement prices and encouraged contract brigades, which decentralized authority and introduce incentives through piece work and a bonus system. In Kursk, an experiment plows profits back into a cooperative and ties earnings directly to productivity. Above all, Gorbachev has been discussing *prodnalog*, a tax in kind for collective and state farms. This might have the same effect as a similar tax with which Lenin introduced the NEP. Indeed, many foreign observers remain surprised that Gorbachev has not adopted the NEP policies, retaining control of "the commanding heights" of the political and economic system and allowing the released energies to resolve the economic issues. Gorbachev could also weaken opposition to such economic policies by wrapping the mantle of the Great Lenin around himself and this approach.

Thus far, Gorbachev has retained the political and economic system without significant change and has only introduced more discipline, enthusiasm, and efficiencies. These small changes may have significant temporary influence upon production and may even lead Gorbachev further toward restructuring than he plans to go. However, the Central Committee meeting in June 1987 on economic reform and the special Party conference in 1988 on democratizing the Party, but only the Party and only up to the regional level, are critical for Gorbachev and significant progress toward "restructuring."

SOCIAL AND DEMOGRAPHIC ISSUES

The loyal and passive Soviet peoples have always rallied to their government and state when these have been in hazard, and they have demonstrated enormous recuperative abilities in the most grueling circumstances. They will continue to show these qualities. However, they are increasingly dissatisfied. This is because Soviet achievements have created a differentiated social structure and rising expectations, because of increased knowledge of the benefits people in the advanced industrial states enjoy and of the special advantages their privileged exploiters possess, and because of the increasing strains and shortages of recent years. As a great historian wrote of an earlier critical period, the Soviet Union is "a swollen state, a spent society." It must now replenish the strengths of society or face drastic decline.

Thus social and demographic issues are becoming increasingly obvious and grave. The state in its obsession with economic and military growth has paid inadequate attention to the visible and invisible infrastructures which underlay all modern societies, so that neglected housing, transportation, and health care have created serious social problems and undermine the bases of Soviet power. Alcoholism is a social disease in both sexes and even among the young, one against which even a forceful and dramatic campaign will make little progress.

Demographic trends show a very low rate of population growth among the Russians and the others who live in European Russia, but a rate two and a half times higher among the Muslim Turkic peoples of Central Asia. Indeed, the Soviet Union is already the largest Muslim power in the world, and one of every five Soviet citizens will be a Muslim in 2000. The rise of dissident nationalisms and the revival of Islam and other religions create very delicate issues, especially because the national and religious minorities tend to live along sensitive boundaries and have excitable and interested friends abroad. These problems are manageable for the next ten or fifteen years, but constitute a visible strain and will become ever more crucial and complicated. The rising rate of infant mortality and the declining rate of male longevity foreshadow basic issues the deferral of which will raise ever more grave consequences.

Lethargy and passivity among the workers and peasants constitute another serious issue. The unsatisfied thirst for consumer goods hampers efforts to increase productivity, and the pessimism and nostalgia evident throughout Soviet life sap the confidence supposedly characteristic of communism. In short, a corrosive crisis of morale is becoming ever more dangerous. This is especially visible among "the heroes' children," unappreciative of their elders' achievements, deeply infected by Western culture, and cynical because of the gap between what they see and what they are taught.

CULTURAL AND INTELLECTUAL LIFE

The "silence in Russian culture" that Sir Isaiah Berlin noted three decades ago and that Gorbachev has identified more recently has become more pronounced.

Basically, the Soviet Union is a formal, rigid, intolerant, and cynical society. Marxism-Leninism has little impact upon most Soviet citizens, in spite of the constant hammering and perhaps in part because of it. Evidence abounds, especially in the relentless drives against religion, that many, perhaps most, reject official values and that old and new faiths are growing, especially among the young. Signs of intellectual vigor stir beneath the surface, particularly among scientists, other intellectuals, and the media, but these flowers rarely break through the cracks. The current campaign of openness in the arts has led to a kind of flowering of literature and the theatre in particular and has won Gorbachev enthusiastic support of most Soviet intellectuals, even Sakharov and some dissidents, and many foreign observers. However, Soviet, East European, and Chinese experience all suggest that the government may find the surge of ideas it has unleased difficult to manage and that it will again restrict this thaw or blooming.

Dissidents are few—perhaps 500,000 in a population of 275,000,000 —but Lunacharsky noted that the harder one hits a nail on the head, the deeper it goes into the wood. The disaffected may represent the tip of an iceberg that is growing beneath the surface and that will become increasingly visible as time passes and as *glasnost* spreads.

Western culture, high and low, has swamped Soviet urban society, and seeps throughout the country. This and the character of Soviet intellectual resources indicate that the USSR is not well equipped to compete in an international competition in which culture at every level plays an increasingly important political role.

EASTERN EUROPE

The Soviet leaders consider control over Eastern Europe vital to Soviet survival. The six states and their peoples add military bases and great human and economic strengths to the Soviet Union and to communism. Their leaders, military and security as well as political, are loyal to the Soviet Union. They share most Soviet goals and policies and realize that their existence and survival depend upon the Soviet Union. These states' economies are substantially bound to that of the Soviet Union. The rulers and their people also appreciate that the Soviet leaders will not hesitate to use "raw force" to ensure control.

However, while the Soviet Union exercises hegemony in Eastern Europe, it cannot ensure security or stability. Eastern Europe resembles "the sick man of Europe" of the nineteenth century or an organism trying to reject an alien system grafted upon it in time of weakness. Eruptions of one kind or another similar to those that have broken out on occasion since 1953 are quite likely. Indeed, the NATO states should prepare policies now for the kinds of crises likely to arise in the unstable area in the next two decades.

Poland, led by a military junta, is a cancer, at the moment in remission. The Polish people have simply rejected communism, root and branch: no regime in the world faces a people and their church so united in rejection.

All these countries' rulers are handicapped by a double illegitimacy: they are communists, and they are considered agents of an alien government. Nationalisms as they have revived have turned from hostility to Germans to antagonism against the Soviets. The economic problems, except in Hungary and Eastern Germany, are like those of the Soviet Union, but are more grave, as are their social and cultural tensions and popular awareness of political incompetence and corruption.

The East European states at one time contributed economically to the Soviet Union, but they are an increasingly expensive economic liability, draining perhaps as much as twenty billion dollars a year from their Soviet neighbor. They desperately require access to Western science, technology, and energy to renovate their economies. The magnet of the West, from jazz and jeans and colas to information and computer technology, attracts them as powerfully as the sun does a sunflower.

The transfer of authority and the changes in policy and style under Gorbachev are introducing disruptions into Soviet policy for Eastern Europe, as it has every time since 1953. Finally, of course, each ruling party in each East European country must transfer authority from one set of aged leaders to another generation, an issue even more delicate than in the Soviet Union because of the nature of the economic and social strains, Western influence, the role the Soviet Union plays, and, above all, the absence of the kind of collective agreement among the ruling group that prevails within the Soviet Union.

Thus, Eastern Europe constitutes an intractable problem, one which paradoxically has grown more serious as the fruits of the economic and social changes the communists have produced have grown. The Soviet Union has no attractive options: allowing the Polish government to honor the 1980 agreements, for example, would lead to changes unacceptable to the Soviet government, even if those changes could be controlled within Poland and could somehow be restricted to Poland. Increasing the subsidies is difficult, if not impossible. So tighter controls, ideally unobtrusive, seem increasingly likely, as do efforts to strengthen CEMA and the Warsaw Pact and to make them somehow reliable Soviet instruments.

THE WORLD OUTSIDE

The Soviet Union is becoming ever more an integral part of a shrinking world community, in spite of its rulers' efforts to isolate their peoples. The elite's level of knowledge and understanding of the world, and that of the ordinary Soviet citizen, both continue to grow. Diplomatic relations bring states together at the top, infecting all those who travel or deal with foreigners. Foreign trade, the acquisition of Western science and technologies, cultural exchanges, communists from other lands, radio broadcasts, even and perhaps especially *glasnost*—all contacts sap the control over access to information central to the system. The Soviet rulers recognize that ignorance loses wars, but that education foments revolution—but expanded education is central for survival and progress in the twentieth century.

At another level, international politics center upon competition between two great powers for influence and power. In this test, the Soviets' main strength, indeed almost its only resource, is military power. This has won respect and created a fear useful for Soviet political purposes, and it has helped establish communist states controlled by or loyal to the Soviet Union. However, Soviet inability to compete in economic power, cultural and intellectual vitality, and scientific and technical advance handicaps the Soviet Union in the basic competition with Western states. The poor performance of Communist states in the past decade or two has reduced the attractions of that faith almost everywhere, especially in the power centers of the world. The end of the Soviet myth and the declining attractiveness of the model have affected performance and faith within the Soviet Union as well. If the People's Republic of China should prove able to maintain successfully its efforts "to achieve socialism with capitalist methods," it would produce a number of significant consequences for the Soviet Union. Thus, it would not only create a sparkling rival communist model, weakening Soviet influence throughout the world, but it would also transform this vast backward neighbor into one more prosperous, advanced, and powerful.

Of course, sudden successes abroad—in the Philippines, Central America, or South Africa, would revive Soviet power and enthusiasm. But the renewed education the expansion of Soviet power since 1975 has provided the world, especially the invasion of Afghanistan, suggest that opportunities abroad will continue to decline and will provide Soviet leaders another reason to turn inward.

CONCLUSIONS

All societies at all times face problems or challenges. Indeed, the United States at home and abroad faces a set of issues that in some ways resemble those of the Soviet Union and that may be as grave. American difficulties do not constitute an emergency nor threaten overthrow of the system, nor do those of the Soviet Union, but the Soviet dilemmas are so numerous and complicated that they may reflect a systemic crisis. The Soviet situation is as acute as in the 1920s. Then a great leader defined an inspired reversal of policy called the New Economic Policy, instilled dedication and enthusiasm, and obtained some foreign assistance in order to reconstruct the economy and create the foundations for a "new society."

The problems of the last part of this century are just as grave, but they are also cumulative, interrelated, and intricate, and they involve the Soviet Union's role in international politics. The system established in the decade before the Second World War may have outlived itself. In any case its heroic age ended some time ago. However, it is not going to collapse or change greatly. It retains great reserves of power and resources, uncontested control over society, powerful traditions of patriotism and loyalty, a sense of discipline many societies lack, and a "cake of custom" as powerful as in other established systems.

The likelihood of significant political change seems low, even under Gorbachev, and sharp economic innovations remain unlikely because drastic economic shifts would so directly affect the political system, which seems incapable of readjusting to new problems.

One of the most forceful impediments to transformation is the primacy Soviet leaders grant the military forces and foreign policy. These together provide the system its legitimacy and constitute the main instruments of Soviet power and prestige. Ideological restrictions are also important. Soviet leaders are convinced that the party alone has the right and capacity to define policy and to direct society. A third limitation is the character of the issues the system faces and the way in which they are so interrelated, as they are in all complex societies, that any action to affect one would deeply influence the others and reverberates throughout the entire system. The Soviet Union in effect resembles a delicate mobile more than a monolithic bloc.

Another limitation is the character of Soviet society, ironically one of the principal goals and achievements of more than sixty years of communist rule. No authoritarian government can expect to overcome years of encouraged inertia and passive acceptance of authority when it urges its people to respond quickly to permission or even to an order to innovate. In fact, encouraging initiative and enterprise in an authoritarian system is a contradiction in terms. Moreover, the Soviet government could hardly expect its thousands of officials suddenly to abandon their beloved authority.

But the principal supporter of present arrangements and the abiding opponent of innovation is the system itself. The party bureaucrats and the economic managers see innovation as a challenge to ideology and control, and *control* remains the basic word in the communist vocabulary, for the leaders as well as for the "grey barons" throughout the country. Those in authority are committed by their concern for personal security and power, their ideology, and their view of the world to defend their preceptorial role and to resist any change that might challenge their position. In addition, all the other millions who benefit from communist rule are not only reluctant to accept new policies but are positioned to hamper even the most skilled and resolute rulers who seek change.

Increased Soviet participation in the world economy, welcome though that might be to all who see fruitful consequences from such an action, could not provide much assistance toward resolving the deep-seated troubles, and would in fact raise the temperature of political issues. The reluctance of the advanced industrial states to advance large credits will remain great, unless Soviet behavior is quite different from that since 1975 and unless a depression strikes the Western world. Even so, the rigidity of the Soviet planning system, its price structure, the quality of its manufactured products, and Soviet inability to produce goods other than oil and gold, both of which have internal and external limitations, to pay for imports, reduce the likelihood that greater participation in the world economy could be a *deus ex machina*.

The likelihood is therefore great that the Soviet leaders will continue to talk a great deal about change, but will emphasize labor discipline, law and order, Soviet and Russian nationalism, small economic relaxations and efficiencies, patching, tinkering, and increasing Soviet military power. They will probably reduce their costly overseas commitments, and at the same time acquire whatever foreign economic-technical assistance they can, without the infections that accompany. Small changes can of course lead gradually to large ones, but the high likelihood on domestic problems is muddling through and a slow decline or erosion of Soviet power, rather than any dramatic transformation.

Soviet foreign policy will depend as much upon the policies of the United States and its allies and upon the appearance of opportunities as it will upon the domestic sources of Soviet strengths and weaknesses. In any case, Soviet leaders will surely be as alert as they will be prudent. The Soviet Union, like most societies in apparent decline, is also likely to sharpen and improve its diplomatic and political warfare skills. Soviet sophistication in traditional political warfare, as well as in disinformation, aid to "liberation" groups, the use of proxies, and terrorism, is likely to improve as some of its other more fundamental strengths decline.

Gorbachev and those around him no doubt recognize the gravity of the Soviet plight and may reiterate Lenin's policy of the 1920s, which maintained political controls and ideological purity, allowed some freedoms in the arts, and encouraged some innovations (that proved temporary) in the economy, especially in agriculture. Such a policy, which seems sensible and even absolutely necessary to Western observers, would win the support of intellectuals and wrap the mantle of Lenin around the changes. They might weaken the barriers throughout the Soviet system that thwart innovation and release energies that would enliven the Soviet economy. Such a program would promise enormous benefits, but would also put the established system, and those who rule and benefit, at risk.

Under such a program, the party would retain full control of the commanding heights of political monopoly, the military and security forces, information, heavy industry, and foreign trade. It would also encourage family units and the expansion of private plots in agriculture, with some freedom in trade for those peasants; broadened autonomy for industrial units; some small-scale private enterprise or genuine cooperatives in the production and distribution of consumer goods; increased importation of foreign capital and technology through some of the devices Lenin adopted or that the People's Republic of China encourages; and a stance and slogans in foreign policy that appear peaceable. Under such a program, the willingness to believe the Soviet Union a pacific state would burgeon in Western Europe and among credulous and fearful people throughout the world. Foreign businessmen would rush to assist, and some governments would provide easy credits. The Soviets could play with increasing skill upon the varieties of anti-Americanism that flourish around the world, launch new "peace" offensives, encourage the drift of Western Europe and the United States away from each other as their interests and policies in much of the world collide, and capitalize upon the opportunities for meddling and scavenging that will inevitably arise.

But all this is unlikely, sensible and necessary though it may seem to outsiders and perhaps even to Gorbachev himself.

Throughout the next ten or fifteen years, whatever the Soviet leaders choose to do, the principal policies upon which the United States should concentrate upon include:

1. Strengthening the American economy and resolving its basic social problems.
2. Maintaining strong and resolute military forces, including revitalized mobile conventional forces, based upon a national service act.
3. Working closely with its European, Japanese and other allies to reach an agreed definition of Soviet policies and consistent allied goals, concepts, strategies, and policies. The United States should coordinate allied defense, trade, cultural, and human rights actions toward the Soviet Union and Eastern Europe. The absence of mutual confidence, general understanding, and agreement constitutes one of the West's major handicaps.
4. Encouraging the Western European states to become self-

confident, to move toward further political, economic, and military unity, and to increase their ability to defend themselves.

5. Widening the Atlantic community area and encouraging other countries to benefit from increased trade with the advanced industrialized countries and the free flow of men, information, and goods in conditions that encourage them to develop and control their own economic resources.

6. Cooperating with the Soviet Union and all other states in efforts to reduce the basic problems that affect all the world, such as pollution.

7. Encouraging the Soviet Union to reform its political and economic system and to participate actively in the world economy.

8. Defining carefully with its allies that information and those technologies and equipment that all should deny to the Soviet Union because they would directly increase Soviet military capabilities, which is clearly not in the West's best interest.

9. Devising joint actions to respond to outrageous Soviet domestic and foreign policies, other than trade restrictions, which are inefficient and divisive.

10. Encouraging slow, gradual change in Eastern Europe, differentiating among the six countries and making economic assistance conditional upon continuing progress toward greater independence and more open and pluralistic political, economic, and social arrangements.

11. Raising the quantity and quality of the flow of information into Eastern Europe and the Soviet Union by expanding cultural and educational exchange and broadcasts from satellites, and pressing for fulfillment of the Helsinki agreement. Raising the level of knowledge and understanding and intensifying the Western orientation are among the most important and least expensive actions we can undertake to assist these peoples, and ourselves.

12. Recognizing that the contest with the Soviet Union will be a long one, that it will remain at heart a political struggle, that American capacity to change the Soviet system or to reduce its authority is very limited, and that no quick solutions or early answers are likely.

13. Increasing greatly popular knowledge and understanding of the Soviet Union and of the world. In a democratic society, policy necessarily and properly requires public support: the most sensible policies will be effective only when the public understands and endorses them.

Chapter VII

SINO-SOVIET RELATIONS TO THE YEAR 2000: IMPLICATIONS FOR U.S. INTERESTS

*Guocang Huan**

I. INTRODUCTION

On July 28, 1986, Mikhail Gorbachev gave an important speech on Moscow's Asian policy in Vladivostok. The Soviet Union's China policy since then has undergone many important changes. It has been reported that "the atmosphere of Sino-Soviet governmental consultations has improved dramatically." For the first time, the Soviets showed willingness to discuss seriously with the Chinese the Kampuchea issue and the Soviet occupation of Afghanistan. The two sides have begun referring to each other as "comrades," a word suggesting that no serious ideological difficulty exists between them. Moscow has pulled out a few thousand troops from Afghanistan and expressed the willingness to withdraw the rest if "other foreign countries" would stop their military aid to the Afghan resistance movement. Moscow has sponsored the negotiations between the Pakistani and Afghan governments about the possibility of ending the war in Afghanistan.[1] In March 1987, shortly before the tenth round of the Sino-Soviet talks, the Soviet Union withdrew one of its six divisions from Mongolia.[2]

For its part, Beijing has welcomed Moscow's new initiative yet is waiting for Moscow to make more genuine concessions in security affairs. Deng Xiaoping's personal comment on Gorbachev's speech was that the Soviet Union had to push Hanoi to get out of Kampuchea,

---

*Dr. Guocang Huan, a scholar from the People's Republic of China, was a Visiting Senior Fellow of the Atlantic Council of the United States.
[1]*Far East Economic Review,* Mar. 5, 1987, p. 42; *Beijing Review,* Vol. 30, No. 11, Mar. 16, 1987, p. 11.
[2]*Beijing Review,* Vol. 30, No. 15, Apr. 13, 1987, pp. 11–13.

the most difficult issue among China's "three preconditions for the improvement of Sino-Soviet relations.[3] Beijing has also indicated that Moscow's withdrawal of a few thousand troops from Afghanistan was "not enough," and the division of the Soviet Army that left Mongolia "had been stationed in the northern part of Mongolia, not on the Chinese border."[4] Meanwhile, Beijing has improved its ties with most Eastern European states and reestablished relationships with most communist parties in Western Europe.

Economically, Sino-Soviet trade has doubled during the past two years and reached US$1.9 billion in 1985 and 2.6 billion in 1986.[5] Moscow and Beijing have signed a number of longterm trade agreements. Soviet and Eastern European technicians have begun to provide technical assistance to help Beijing replace 156 industrial projects imported from the Soviet Bloc during the 1950s, which played the key role in China's process of industrialization.[6]

Cultural ties between Beijing and Moscow have also expanded. After a twenty-year break, the two countries have begun again to exchange students and scholars. Academicians in both countries have rapidly expanded their research and study programs about each other's economic development, politics, foreign policies, and other fields. More importantly, while Chinese scholars have been optimistic about Gorbachev's reform program, Soviet scholars have recently expressed more favorable views on Chinese economic reform and the "Open Door" policy in over one hundred articles.[7]

On the other hand, the strategic relationship between the two communist powers has not undergone significant change. Moscow has not reduced its military and political pressure on China, nor has it met Beijing's three preconditions for further improvement of Sino-Soviet relations: reduce substantially Soviet troops deployed along the Sino-Soviet and Sino-Mongolian borders; cut back its support for Hanoi's occupation of Kampuchea; and pull its troops out of Afghanistan completely. Rather, the Soviet Union has continued to enlarge its Pacific

---

[3]*Asian Survey,* Vol. XXVII, No. 1., Jan. 1987, pp. 49–50; *The Far East Economic Review,* Mar. 19, 1987, pp. 15–16.

[4]See, *Beijing Review,* Vol. 30, No. 15, Apr. 13, 1987, pp. 11–13.

[5]*Shijie Jingji Daobao (The World Economy Herald,* Shanghai, China), Aug. 18, 1986, p. 2 and Aug. 25, 1986, pp. 1–3.

[6]During the recent Sino-Soviet talks, the Soviets proposed to help China to update these 156 projects free of cost to China. Also see "Sino-East European Ties Furthered," *Beijing Review,* June 10, 1985, Vol. 28, No. 23, p. 7; Chen Muhua, "On Trade with Eastern Europe," *Beijing Review,* Sept. 3, 1984, Vol. 27, No. 36, pp. 16–17.

[7]Wang Chongjie, "The Progress of Reform in the Soviet Union," *Liaowang,* Mar. 3, 1987, pp. 26–28; Wang Jinqing, "Why the Sino-Soviet Strains?" *Beijing Review,* Jul. 9, 1984, Vol. 27, No. 28, pp. 31–32; G. Rozman, "Moscow's China-Watchers in the Post-Mao Era: the Response to a Changing China," *China Quarterly,* June 1983, No. 94, pp. 215–241.

Fleet, strengthened its air force in the Far East, increased its military aid to Hanoi, and expanded its military presence in Cam Ranh and Da Nang Bays.[8] Moscow has also deepened its involvement in subregional political and security affairs, as in the Korean peninsula and South Asia, where Beijing and Moscow do not share many common interests. In sum, the limited relaxation of tensions between China and the Soviet Union has not yet changed Moscow's long-term strategic objectives, to contain China strategically through increased military power around China's periphery and push Beijing away from Washington and Tokyo.

For its part, Beijing continues to view the Soviet Union as the primary threat to its national security. Though Beijing has modified the "three preconditions" by not demanding that Moscow solve all three issues at once,[9] its basic security and strategic interests have not changed: these are to reduce Moscow's political and military leverage over China and to break down Moscow's strategic encirclement around China. In May 1987, Beijing suddenly decided not to send Li Peng, a Soviet-trained Vice Prime Minister and the most likely successor as Premier, to visit Moscow. At the same time, Yang Shangkun, the Standing Vice Chairman of the Central Military Commission and the second most powerful person in the Chinese Army, made a very successful trip to the United States. During his trip, Mr. Yang told his American hosts that "the development of Sino-American relations is the historical tendency; it benefits both countries, and contributes to the peace of the world."[10] Beijing continues its efforts to develop political and military cooperation with the United States, especially with regard to the security of the Asia-Pacific region. Beijing also plays the major role in supplying weapons to the resistance forces in Kampuchea and in maintaining military pressure on Vietnam. In addition, Beijing continues its efforts for greater cooperation with ASEAN, especially Thailand. Beijing has repeatedly expressed its interest in maintaining the stability of Northeast Asia. In Southwest Asia, the Chinese government has continued its full support for both Pakistan and the rebels in Afghanistan, while making efforts to improve relations with India. All in all, the sharp conflicts in security and strategic interests between Moscow and Beijing have not been significantly reduced and will continue to influence strongly the dynamics of Sino-Soviet relations in general in the years ahead.

The development of Sino-Soviet relations has had and will continue to have strong impact on the further dynamics of the struggle between Moscow, Beijing and Washington. It will also affect the balance of

---

[8]E.L. Rowny, "Arms Control: The East Asian & Pacific Focus," *The State Department Bulletin,* Vol. 87, No. 2120, pp. 37–39.

[9]*The People's Daily,* April 23, 1987, p. 1; *Meizhou Huaqiao Rebao (China News Daily,* New York) April 12, 1984.

[10]*The People's Daily,* May 22, 1987, p. 1; May 23, 1987, pp. 1 and 4.

power and stability in the Asia-Pacific region. Furthermore, it will continue to be a major factor in reshaping Chinese foreign policy in general.

Three related factors will determine the dynamics of Sino-Soviet relations in the next decade: China's Soviet policy, the Soviet Union's China policy, and the dynamics of the international environment. This chapter will examine each of these factors, then discuss the possible developments of Sino-Soviet relations in the next decade, and finally suggest basic policy options that Beijing may choose in dealing with the Soviet Union.

II. CHINA'S DOMESTIC DEVELOPMENT AND SINO-SOVIET RELATIONS

In general, China's policy towards the Soviet Union is determined by three interrelated factors: China's domestic development, the international environment, and Moscow's policy towards China. During the past few years, each of these factors has undergone significant changes, and the degree to which each of them affects China's policy towards the Soviet Union has also changed.

Domestically, the most important changes which have taken place during the past decade are the post-Mao political, economic, and cultural reforms. These developments have had strong effects on Beijing's foreign policy, including its policy towards Moscow.

The Reform Group, led by Deng Xiaoping, has pursued a political reform program. This program, together with the government's economic reform and "Open Door" policy, has changed the following aspects of China's political life and political institutions:

—The personality cult and personal dictatorship, which were one of the key factors leading to the Sino-Soviet split during the 1960s and the first half of the 1970s, have been banned in China. The decision-making process has been made less personal, more consultative and rational. A multipolar power structure has been established among the party-government institutions. The political struggle within the party no longer resorts to violent methods.

—The relationship between the State and society has changed significantly. Mass political terror has ended. Most victims of the previous political struggle have been rehabilitated. A certain degree of personal freedom, though not political freedom, has been allowed. While the society has become increasingly alienated and independent of the State and there has been an increased tendency toward "non-cooperatism," the credibility, authority and capacity of the government to control and mobilize the society have been weakened. Through non-institutionalized channels, various interest groups have begun to pressure the decision-makers indirectly. While the society has begun a process of "de-politicization," individualism and personal interests have become the core principle guiding social behavior in general.

—Various political institutions have been reformed. The decision-making process has been decentralized. There has been a process of professionalization of both civilian and military bureaucrats. A large number of younger, well-educated and more pragmatic technocrats, many of whom have had experience of either studying or visiting in the West, has replaced old and conservative political bureaucrats.

—The official ideology, which was another important factor leading to the Sino-Soviet split during the 1960s and the first half of 1970s, has changed significantly. The Chinese have already largely accepted the Soviet view on many important theoretical issues regarding international relations which were seriously debated between Beijing and Moscow during the 1960s, such as war and peace, nuclear weapons and nuclear war, the nature of international politics, and the possibility of peaceful coexistence between capitalist and socialist states.[11] Furthermore, the Chinese have studied and introduced many aspects of the culture and the successful experience of economic and political development of the Western countries (including Japan) and Asia's newly industrialized nations.

The economic reforms have gone even further, although they have experienced some serious difficulties during the past few years.

—The most successful policy is the decollectivization of the People's Commune system. This policy allows eight hundred million peasants the freedom to decide what, how, and how much to produce. It also allows them to develop free markets and private ownership. This policy has undercut the party organizations in rural areas and created a new generation of a peasant elite.

—In both rural and urban areas, the government has encouraged the development of the private sector. As a result, millions of "Nepmen," a term used in the 1920s to refer to private entrepreneurs in the Soviet Union during the New Economic Policy period, are now operating their own businesses in China.[12]

—The government has altered its developmental strategy; it has put strong emphasis on the production of consumer goods and encouraged a "consumer revolution." While slowing down the development of the heavy and military industries, the government has transferred more resources into light industry.

—The central planning system has been reformed. The government has permitted local authorities greater flexibility to make their own decisions. It has introduced a price reform aimed at developing the market mechanism and creating a "mixed economy." Further, the managerial institution has been professionalized; enterprises have been granted greater autonomy; and the Communist Party's control over enterprises has been weakened.[13]

---

[11]See, for instance, *Liaowang* (*The Outlook Weekly,* Beijing, China, the North American Edition), 1985, No. 42, pp. 13–15.

[12]T.B. Gold, "China's Private Entrepreneurs—Small-Scale Private Business Prospers Under Socialism," *The China Business Review,* Nov.-Dec. 1985, pp. 46–50.

[13]*The People's Daily,* April 13, 1987, pp. 1–2.

Third, the Chinese government has adopted the "Open Door" policy.

—It has altered the Maoist policy of self-isolation and self-sufficiency and actively expanded China's economic ties with the outside world, notably with industrial nations. China's foreign trade has doubled during the last ten years and now amounts roughly to 20 percent of GNP.[14] The government has put high priority on importing technology from industrial nations.[15]

—China has become more active in the world market and in international economic institutions, such as the World Bank and the International Monetary Fund (IMF). It has begun to sell bonds and export labor abroad.[16]

—The Chinese government has made great efforts to attract direct foreign investment. It has set up four Special Economic Zones and allowed the district of Hainan Island and fourteen coastal cities to enjoy similar rights to attract direct foreign investment. By the end of 1986, over seven thousand foreign-involved enterprises operated in China.[17] The degree of interdependence between the Chinese economy and the world market has increased. The economic interest in gaining more technology, industrial equipment, and capital investment, and expanding foreign trade has become increasingly important to the foreign policymakers in Beijing.

—The government has sent over fifty thousand students to Western countries, including Japan, for study and training.[18] Thousands of scholars have been invited to China to give lectures and seminars on various subjects—the sciences, technology, business management, law, and the humanities. The Beijing government has significantly reduced its restrictions on the information flow into China. Western cultural influence has spread rapidly and widely.

On the other hand, there have been a number of problems and difficulties presenting serious challenges to the government. These problems have already made the reform process painful and difficult and will create uncertainties for China's future development and its foreign policy.

In the first place, the forthcoming succession remains uncertain. It is uncertain because the reformers have not been able to institutionalize and legitimize their policies fully. The conservatives, who want China to return to the so-called "golden age from 1949 to 1956," and aim at a Soviet-type system with Chinese characteristics, still retain their strong influence within the top leadership circle. More importantly,

---

[14]*Liaowang,* Aug. 11, 1986, 12–13.
[15]*The People's Daily,* Nov. 4, 1985, p. 1.
[16]See, Guocang Huan, "China's Opening to the World," *Problems of Communism,* Nov.-Dec. 1986, pp. 59–77.
[17]*The People's Daily,* Dec. 6, 1986, p. 1; *Liaowang,* Apr. 21, 1986, p. 1.
[18]*The Peoples' Daily,* May 14, 1986, p. 1; Jun 6 1986, p. 4; Jun 19, 1986, p. 1.

conservatives have appeared capable of challenging not only the reformers' policies but also their political power. In December 1986, under the strong pressure of the conservatives, General Secretary Hu Yaobang, one of the leading reformers and Deng Xiaoping's successor, was ousted. A repressive political campaign against intellectual freedom has been launched. The conservatives have thus strengthened their position within the party, notably in the ideological and cultural fields. These political changes have weakened the reformers' position, damaged their credibility, deepened tensions between the State and society, and increased political uncertainties.[19]

In the second place, the reformers themselves have imposed certain restrictions on their program. Politically, they are not prepared to reform the society in a pluralized direction, nor are they in a position to create a new generation of technocrats to support their policies in the near future. They have not had much control over the party's ideological affairs, nor have they created a new ideology to justify their policies. Instead, under strong pressure from the conservatives, they have periodically vacillated in one or another direction.

Thirdly, although the agricultural reform has been quite successful, the urban industrial reform and the "Open Door" policy have appeared to encounter increasing difficulties. During the past two or three years, inflation rates have remained high[20] and the central government has had difficulties in managing the scale of national investment and the money flow.[21] There has been neither a mechanism nor policies to coordinate the reform programs in different economic sectors. Nor has the central government been able to carry out an effective political reform to moderate the conflicts between the ongoing economic reforms and the existing political institutions. Besides bureaucratic politics and ideological restrictions, the major reason for such problems is the lack of knowledge "how" to reform.

Fourthly, the "Open Door" policy is also facing political challenges. The conservatives have launched strong attacks on the "Open Door" policy, referred as "Westernization." Culturally, the conflicts between traditional Chinese values and the conservative views of the Party on the one hand and the newly imported Western culture, and the problem of coping with the materialistic youth and alienated intelligentsia, have already increased tensions between the state and society. In addition, the adoption of the "Open Door" policy has created new tensions between those who have benefited by the policy and those who have not. Economically, the lack of knowledge and experience in in-

---

[19]Guocang Huan, "Social Changes and Political Development," *The Ninetieth* (Hong Kong), March 1987.

[20]Yuan Mu, "On Price Reform," *Liaowang*, 1985, No. 43, pp. 18–20; *The People's Daily*, April 13, 1987, p. 1.

[21]*Shijie Jingji Daobao*, Oct. 21, 1985, p. 2; *The People's Daily*, Nov. 24, 1985, p. 1.

ternational business and management of macroeconomic and financial policies have been the major factors in the loss of control of the country's balance of payments.[22] In addition, the existing institutional gap between the Chinese economy and market economies abroad, the continual political disagreements within the leadership, the frequent policy swings, severe bureaucratism, and the shortcomings of legal institutions have continued to be a barrier to attracting more foreign investment and advanced technology. Finally, the continued world recession, the decline in prices of raw materials and oil in the international market, and increased international protectionism in the industrial world against developing or underdeveloped nations have continued to restrict China's performance in the international market.[23] These economic difficulties have seriously affected Chinese politics and challenged the reform group, which has been generally in charge of economic policy-making, and will continue to have an impact.

Two directions of future development are basically possible in China in the next few years. The degree to which each of them would affect China's policy towards the Soviet Union is different. In the first and more likely case, the reform program will continue. Following the succession to Deng Xiaoping, the reform group will further pursue its policy of political liberalization and institutional reform. It will also continue its economic strategy and "Open Door" policy. As a result, China will enjoy greater political stability; the policy-making process will be further rationalized; the present political system may continue to move in a more pluralistic direction; and the participation of the society in public life will increase while economic and cultural life will be further depoliticized. Economically, the country will enjoy stable growth and expanded cooperation with industrial market economies. While the institutional gap between the Chinese economy and market economies will be narrowed, the degree of interdependence between the Chinese economy and the world economy will increase further.

In this situation, China will not have strong domestic incentives to develop an equidistant relationship with the United States and the Soviet Union. Instead, strong economic interests will allow policymakers in Beijing to move closer to the West, especially the United States. In political and security affairs, Beijing will continue to seek relaxation of tensions with Moscow and the reduction of the latter's military pressure, but not at the cost of jeopardizing its ties with the United States.

In the second case, the reform programs will be reversed, notably in urban industrial sectors, either by the conservatives taking over or by a change in the reform strategy by the reformers themselves. In this case, the course of political development in China will move in a similar

---

[22]Ibid., also J. Stuemer, "The Foreign Exchange Situation," *China Business Review,* Jan.-Feb. 1986, pp. 14–17.
[23]*Liaowang,* Mar. 10, 1986, p. 1; *China Daily* (Beijing), May 28, 1986, p. 1.

direction to that of the Soviet Union in the post-Khrushchev period. The present efforts to reform the political and economic system will be reversed. The political system will be more repressive and less liberal. The government's political control over public life will be strengthened. China may alter its "Open Door" policy and instead look for increased economic and technological assistance from the Soviet bloc. China's economic development will slow down. Given the increased degree of political independence of the society from the state, this development is likely to jeopardize the country's political stability.

If the second possibility occurs, the conservative government will have strong domestic reasons to change its foreign policy, i.e., to cut back its ties with the West, especially the United States and Japan. It will certainly have political and ideological incentives to move closer to Moscow. Nevertheless, whether such a move will alter China's security strategy towards the Soviet Union may largely depend on the further dynamics of China's security environment, and especially on whether Moscow substantially reduces its military and strategic pressure on Beijing and whether the Taiwan issue gets out of control in Beijing-Washington relations.

III. CHINA'S INTERNATIONAL ENVIRONMENT AND ITS POLICY TOWARDS THE SOVIET UNION

China is an Asia-Pacific power of global strategic importance. Its security interests concern primarily the Asia-Pacific region. Two factors in particular—the triangular relationship among the United States, the Soviet Union and China on the one hand and the dynamics of the Asia-Pacific region on the other—have appeared to be increasingly significant in determining China's foreign policy, notably its security strategy. During the past few years, both factors have undergone important changes, which have strongly affected China's foreign policy, including its policy towards the Soviet Union.

One of China's leading experts on international relations, Huan Xiang, writes, "Contemporary world politics is largely determined by the dynamics of the 'triangle' between the United States, China and the Soviet Union. The politics of the Asia-Pacific region is largely determined by the relations between four powers: the United States, the Soviet Union, China and Japan."[24] This statement expresses well China's perspective on contemporary international politics and China's role in the international system.

During the past few years, the "big" triangle between Washington, Beijing and Moscow has undergone the following important changes. These changes are likely to continue in the years ahead:

—The triangular relations have tended to be more stable than before. This is because China, the weakest power of the three, has chosen a

---

[24]*Shijie Jingji Daobao,* Oct. 13, 1984, pp. 1–2.

more realistic approach to dealing with both superpowers and adapted its foreign policy in a much less general and simplistic way. In addition, all three powers have more clearly defined the balance of power among them, their specific interests in dealing with each other, and their capability to pursue these interests. There is less room than before for any of the three powers to shift its position dramatically within the triangle.

—The competition between the two superpowers has become the center of conflict within the triangle. Gorbachev's reform program has improved the image of the Soviet Union in the West. Moscow's concessions in the area of human rights have also reduced political tensions between the two superpowers. The internal political needs of both Washington and Moscow have generated incentives on both sides for improving further their relations and making efforts to constrain the nuclear arms race.[25] Moscow has recently initiated a proposal to reduce intermediate-range nuclear missiles deployed in both Europe and Asia. So far, Washington has responded to this proposal favorably. Nevertheless, even if the two superpowers were able to reach an agreement on this issue, whether or not it would be implemented effectively is still an open question, as there have been serious debates about the issue in the United States and Western European countries. The reduction of intermediate-range missiles in Europe is directly related to the balance of short-range missiles and conventional forces, where most European and American strategists believe that the Warsaw Pact has superiority over NATO. Together with potential shifts in Washington's policy, these debates may either delay the process of reaching the agreement or block its actual implementation. More importantly, neither Moscow nor Washington are likely to make further significant compromises to each other in other areas. Such an agreement, if it is signed, thus may not slow down the arms race in general.[26]

The ongoing political difficulties within the Reagan Administration have weakened Washington's capacity to formulate a consistent policy towards the Soviet Union, not to mention the fact that the forthcoming presidential election will likely increase this uncertainty. Washington will continue to speed up its research program for the Strategic Defense Initiative (SDI) and plans to deploy the system in the near future.[27] Moscow, in turn, has not appeared ready to slow down its military

---

[25]D.B. Fascell, "Congress and Arms Control, *Foreign Affairs,* Vol. 65, No. 4, Spring, 1987, pp. 730–749; L. Zuckerman, pp. 35–41; Highest Folly," *The New York Review of Books,* Apr. 9, 1987, pp. 35–41; and T. Hasegawa, "Soviets on Nuclear War-Fighting," *The Problems of Communism,* Jul-Aug. 1986, pp. 68–79.

[26]*The Economist,* Mar. 3, 1987, pp. 11–13; and D. Healey, "A Labor Britain: NATO & the Bomb," *Foreign Affairs,* Vol, 65, No. 4, Spring 1987, pp. 721–729.

[27]P.H. Nitze, "The Nuclear and Space Negotiations: Translating Promise to Progress," *The State Department Bulletin,* Vol. 87, No. 2120, pp. 29–33.

buildup and alter its expansionist global strategy.[28] The superpowers' competition in Europe seems likely to continue. Further, neither side has appeared willing to moderate its competition in the Middle East and Asia-Pacific region, nor have they reached an agreement to resolve other regional conflicts such as in Southern Africa and Central America. In sum, recent developments in the U.S.-Soviet arms negotiations have not significantly changed the strategic and security relationship between the two superpowers. In most areas of international politics, their competition is likely to continue and intensify. In the foreseeable future, chances for a new detente between them seem slim.

—In Eastern Europe, Moscow has already experienced and will continue to face serious political challenges from domestic popular forces. Gorbachev's reform program in the Soviet Union, if it continues, will certainly encourage most Eastern European states to pursue their economic and political reforms. Yet the reform process in these countries is likely to increase their independence from Moscow, thereby challenging the latter's political authority and jeopardizing political stability in Eastern Europe. Political stability there will continue to provoke political conflicts between East and West, notably between Moscow and Washington.

—In a number of Third World countries which have strategic significance, such as South Africa, Pakistan, and the Philippines, conflicts between authoritarian regimes and the political opposition continue to provide opportunities to Moscow to expand its political and even military influence. Such developments would reinforce the competition between Washington and Moscow.

—In contrast, relations between China and the two superpowers have appeared less tense, more manageable and flexible. Besides making efforts to improve its relationship with Moscow, Beijing has played down the need for security cooperation with Washington, especially since the second half of 1982, when the Second Sino-American Shanghai Communique was signed. Yet the military exchange program between them has advanced.[29]The cultural and economic ties between the two countries have expanded rapidly; the United States is now China's third largest trade partner.[30] The Taiwan issue seems to be more manageable than before. As a result, the foundation of Sino-American ties is no longer based only upon mutual security

---

[28]D. R. Simes, "Gorbachev: A New Foreign Policy?" *Foreign Affairs,* Vol. 65, No. 3, Winter 1987, pp. 477–500; M. M. May, "The U.S.-Soviet Approach to Nuclear Weapons," *International Security,* Spring, 1985, Vol. 9, No. 4, pp. 140–153; and Ibid.

[29]G.J. Sigur, "China Policy Today: Consensus, Consistence and Stability," *The State Department Bulletin,* Vol. 87, No. 2119, pp. 48–51; *Asian Survey,* Vol. XXVII, No. 1, Jan. 1987, pp. 15–16 and pp. 51–52; M. Oksenberg, *Foreign Affairs,* "China's Confident Nationalism," *Foreign Affairs,* Vol. 65, No. 3, pp. 505–513.

[30]Ibid.

interests, but rather on a combination of political, economic, and strategic interests. The working relationship between Washington and Beijing has improved.

During the past few years, the Asia-Pacific region has also experienced many important changes. Economically it continues to be the region with the highest growth rate in the world. It has become more competitive in the international market, and its share of world trade has continued to increase. Its intra-regional economic transactions have expanded rapidly as well. Although increased protectionism in industrial nations has hurt the Newly Industrialized Nations (NICs) in Asia, they have made strong efforts to adjust and upgrade their economic structure. The recent appreciation of the Japanese Yen has weakened Japan's position in the international market; and Japan's trade war with other industrial market economies is likely to intensify, thereby slowing down its economic growth. Yet Tokyo's recent policy of deregulating control over capital flow between Japan and other nations has allowed Japan to play an increasingly important role in the international financial market. This policy in turn is likely to restructure the international financial market and speed up the process of the integration of the economy of East Asia into the world economy.[31]

Politically, however, the region has presented a more complicated picture. During the past decade, the Soviet Union and its allies, notably Vietnam, have made greater efforts than the United States and its allies to develop their military capability in the region. The trends in the regional military balance have favored the Soviet Union and its allies and semi-allies, not the United States and its allies. While maintaining land forces of roughly fifty divisions along the Chinese border, Moscow has doubled the size of its Pacific Fleet—its largest fleet—significantly strengthened its tactical and strategic air forces, and deployed about 200 SS-20 missiles in the Far East. Moscow has also built up strong transportation, communication, and supply facilities. Thus it is not an exaggeration to say that the Soviet Union has already built up its military capability for fighting a two-front (Europe and Pacific) war.[32]

More importantly, Moscow's strategic position in the region is stronger than ever. In Northeast Asia, it maintains strong military and political pressure on both Beijing and Tokyo. Recently, it has appeared

---

[31]See, L. Silk, "The United States and the World Economy," *Foreign Affairs,* Vol. 65, No.3, pp. 459–476; K. G. Van Wolferen, "The Japan Problem," *Foreign Affairs,* Vol. 65, No. 2, pp. 237–249; *The Far East Economic Review,* Mar. 17, 1987, pp. 111–113.

[32]See: G. T. E. Bok, *The USSR in East Asia,* The Atlantic Institute for International Affairs, Paris, Mar. 1986, pp. 12–26 and 40–60; D. S. Zagoria, "The Strategic Environment in East Asia," *Soviet Policy in East Asia,* ed. by D. S. Zagoria, Yale University Press, 1982, pp. 1–28; P. F. Langer, "Soviet Military Power in Asia," *Soviet Policy in East Asia,* pp. 266–280; D. S. Zagoria, "The USSR and Asia in 1984," *Asian Survey,* Jan. 1985, pp. 21–32; *The Military Balance* (1986–1987), pp. 29–30.

to want to play a greater role on the Korean peninsula. In comparison with Beijing, Moscow is able to provide more and better weapons to Pyongyang. In Southeast Asia, the Soviet Pacific Fleet has been allowed to use bases in Cam Ranh and Da Nang Bays, where it has also deployed long distance bombers. If the United States loses its bases in the Philippines in the next few years, the Soviet Union's presence in Vietnam could be even more challenging to the stability and security of the region. While ASEAN has been weakened by divergences in security interests among its member nations, especially between Thailand and Indonesia, and internal political difficulties, Hanoi has become more aggressive due to Moscow's increased political support and military aid.

In Southwest Asia, the dynamics of the strategic balance have continued to favor the Soviet Union and its strategic partner, India. Rajiv Gandhi's succession has given some hope that he might alter his mother's pro-Soviet position. The overlap of political and strategic interests between the Soviet Union and India is unlikely to change in the near future, as it is deeply rooted in the balance of power in the region and India's domestic politics as well as its culture. Strategically, the Soviet-Indian security partnership serves their interests in pressuring both Pakistan and China and deterring further U. S. involvement in the region's security affairs. India's dependence on Soviet weaponry supply and political support in order to be the dominant power in the region is unlikely to decline. Domestically, India's increased conflicts between different ethnic groups and political instability have been and will continue to be the major political obstacle to the relaxation of tensions with Pakistan. In 1986, Moscow proposed to offer India MiG-29 fighters. Shortly before and after Gorbachev's trip to India in spring 1987 Delhi revived the issue of territorial disputes with Beijing. This event indicated Delhi's uneasiness about Moscow's efforts to improve Sino-Soviet relations and its political dependence on Moscow.[33]

For Beijing, the key country serving its security interests in the region is Pakistan, a country with which Beijing has had a close relationship over three decades. Yet domestic political and economic difficulties have continued to jeopardize the authoritarian regime's capacity to manage its internal affairs and its popularity abroad. The military and political pressure by the Soviet Union from the north and India from the south will continue to threaten Pakistan's security and its relations with both China and the United States.[34]

Such a security environment has worried Beijing's policymakers. China's basic security interest is to create a relatively peaceful and stable international environment for its ongoing modernization program. This interest includes reducing Moscow's political and military pressure on Beijing and breaking down Moscow's strategic encirclement of China.

---

[33]*Liaowang,* Mar. 30, 1987, p. 29; *The People's Daily,* April 16, 1987, p. 1.
[34]E. Van Hollen, "Pakistan in 1986,: Trials of Transition," *Asian Survey,* Vol. XXVII, No. 2, pp. 148–150 and 152–154.

It is also in China's interest to prevent increased confrontation and maintain the political stability of the Korean Peninsula; to reduce the possibility of a consolidated, militant "united Indochina" under Hanoi's dominance and with Moscow's backing; and to prevent Pakistan from coming under Moscow's shadow. In addition, Beijing is interested in a peaceful resolution of the Taiwan issue. Finally, Japan's great potential to transform its economic power into commensurate political or even military power is a serious issue that Beijing has to face up to in the long run.

In pursuance of its strategic interests, Beijing has given Moscow three preconditions for the normalization of their relations: substantial withdrawal of the Soviet Army from the Sino-Soviet and Sino-Mongolian borders; the elimination of Moscow's political support and military aid for Vietnam's occupation of Kampuchea; and a pull out of Soviet troops from Afghanistan. Together with Tokyo, Beijing has also been calling for the removal of Soviet SS-20 missiles from the Far East.

Although Moscow has recently expressed its willingness to "solve" these issues, Beijing is still facing a number of difficulties in furthering its security interests. The military balance between China and the Soviet Union favors the latter; and this situation is not likely to change in the foreseeable future. The key issue here is that while facing a well-armed Soviet Army with a strong offensive capability, the Chinese army is only in a defensive position. The efforts that China has made to improve ties with the Soviet Union have reduced border tensions between the two countries and reopened border trade on both China's northeast and northwest borders. Moscow has not appeared, however, willing to make serious efforts to slow down its military buildup in the Far East, nor does China have much leverage to force it to do so. The withdrawal of one division of Soviet ground forces from the People's Republic of Mongolia was well received in Beijing. Nevertheless, a further reduction of Soviet armed forces along the Chinese border seemingly will be a long and difficult process, as Moscow expects Beijing to make similar moves. Such a reduction in Chinese forces would further weaken China's position vis-à-vis the Soviet Union, as the Chinese Army has far less mobility and depends more on predeployment. In addition, any significant withdrawal of forces along the Sino-Mongolian and Sino-Soviet borders will naturally cause strong reactions from the U.S. and its allies, notably Japan, thereby jeopardizing China's relations with the West and Japan as well as the power structure in the Far East.

In Southeast Asia, Hanoi is unlikely to be willing to pull out its troops from Kampuchea, nor is Moscow likely to cut back its support to the Vietnamese. Hanoi does derive advantages from the Sino-Soviet conflict. Its strong nationalism, which aims to establish a "united Indochina" under its own dominance, contributes to its relative independence of action from Moscow. Its experience of war over four decades has created a militant and ambitious regime. Finally, both Hanoi and Moscow acknowledge the strategic significance of the Cam Ranh and Da Nang Bays to the security of Southeast Asia, if not the whole Asia Pacific region.

In Southwest Asia, the present trends in the dynamics of the security environment and the balance of power are likely to continue. The Soviet Union's military operation in Afghanistan will probably not destroy the resistance movement completely, as long as the latter continues to receive sufficient weapons from Washington and Beijing. The resistance movement, on the other hand, will probably be unable to drive the Soviet troops out completely, especially since its supply line is increasingly threatened by Moscow's political and military pressure on Pakistan.[35] Neither Beijing nor Washington can do much to help stabilize the domestic situation in Pakistan. The existing balance of power between India and Pakistan restricts both Beijing and Washington's efforts to secure Pakistan, nor can they expect any significant shift in India's pro-Soviet position in the near future. In sum, it is unlikely that China's security environment would improve significantly by expanding economic, cultural, or even limited political ties with the Soviet Union.

In the Asia-Pacific region as a whole, the United States' military presence is essential to counter Soviet military expansion. Sino-American security cooperation and military exchange will continue to serve China's interests of deterring any attack or military threat by the Soviet Union. Without equilibrium there will be no peace. To leave open the option of upgrading such cooperation would also strengthen Beijing's bargaining position vis-à-vis Moscow. On the Korean peninsula, Sino-American cooperation provides the most feasible way to maintain stability and open North Korea gradually to the international community. In the long run, the process of Japan's rearmament and the development of its strategic role would shift the balance of power in the region and the world, thereby changing the nature of regional and world politics. For China, a strengthened U.S.-Japanese security relationship and U.S. military presence in the region would be a safeguard against Japan becoming an independent regional military power.

In Southeast Asia, China has made major efforts to cooperate with ASEAN, especially Thailand, to contain Vietnamese regional expansionism. Such efforts have not been institutionalized, however. Besides the historical tensions still existing between China and some of the ASEAN states, the low-key policy that Washington has taken towards

---

[35]*The Economist,* Mar. 28-Apr. 3, 1987, p. 40; *Far East Economic Review,* Jan. 29, 1987, pp. 25–16; A. E. Rubinstein, "Afghanistan and the USSR," ORBIS, Vol. 3, No. 4, Winter 1987, pp. 589–608; *The Problems of Communism,* Jan.-Feb. 1986, pp. 1–20.

Southeast Asia is the major reason.[36] In the long run, Washington and Beijing may find it necessary to further their cooperation to restrain the continuation of Soviet and Vietnamese expansion in the region and to prevent the Philippines from becoming a second Vietnam.

In Afghanistan there is an increased need for Washington and Beijing to coordinate their efforts to support the resistance movement and the security of Pakistan. Without an effective coordination between China, Pakistan, and the United States, it would be difficult for any of them to improve their ties with India. More important, strong political support from *both* Washington and Beijing is the key to preventing Pakistan from falling under Moscow's shadow. Such coordination would of course begin with high level but informal strategic consultation.

During the past few years, the United States has not been a threat to China's national security, but rather its principal potential strategic partner against the Soviet Union and its allies and semi-allies, which have presented the primary and direct threat to China's national security. Developing political and security cooperation with Washington has increased Beijing's capacity to cope with regional security issues on China's periphery. Taken together, the dynamics of China's security environment will continue to constrain its incentive to improve significantly its ties with the Soviet Union. To reduce tensions with Moscow, while continuing to develop its economic, cultural, political and security relations with Washington and its allies would serve China's best interests.

IV. MOSCOW'S CHINA POLICY

Moscow's China policy has the following distinct characteristics. Unlike Beijing's policy towards the Soviet Union, Moscow's attitude towards Beijing is much less influenced by the Soviet Union's domestic politics and economic development. This is due primarily to the Soviet Union's relatively greater political stability and its institutionalization of decision-making in foreign policy. Its policy towards China has not been a serious issue in Soviet party politics since the middle of the 1960s. Secondly, Moscow's China policy is more consistent than Beijing's policy towards the Soviet Union. This consistency entails a certain rigidity which explains why Moscow has been unable to respond effectively to Beijing's more flexible approach to Moscow.

Finally, unlike China, the Soviet Union is a superpower with broad global political and security interests. Moscow's China policy is only a part of its global strategy, although it is viewed as central to Moscow's strategy towards the Asia-Pacific region. Given the fact that the Soviet Union's capacity and global interests have rapidly expanded during

---

[36]C. Johnson and K. Um, "The United States and Asia in 1986," Asian Survey, Vol. No. 1, Jan. 1987, pp. 20–23.

the past decade, its China policy has been less determined by specific interactions with Beijing and has increasingly become a function of its global and Asia-Pacific strategy.

Generally speaking, three basic factors now determine Moscow's China policy: ideological divergence and convergence between Beijing and Moscow, economic and cultural ties between the two countries, and international politics, including the dynamics of the triangle between Beijing, Moscow and Washington.

The post-Mao reform in China has removed most of the previous ideological barriers between Beijing and Moscow. Gorbachev and his associates have expressed strong interest in China's experience of economic reform and the "Open Door" policy and begun to carry out their own reform program.[37] Since the second half of 1986, the Soviet press has ceased its criticism of China's domestic development. Instead, many Soviet scholars and journalists have begun to discuss China's experience of reforming its economic system and expanding its economic ties with industrial nations. Beijing has restored ties with most communist and socialist parties, both in and out of power, around the world. As a result, previous ideological conflicts which had prevented Beijing and Moscow from re-establishing party-to-party relations have been overcome, though Beijing has repeatedly announced that it has no incentive to do so in the near future.

Despite this development, a number of new ideological and political problems have appeared between Beijing and Moscow. Like reforms in most East European countries, China's economic reform and "Open Door" policy have strong foreign policy implications. Conservative Soviet China scholars and policymakers, who have strong influence within the bureaucratic establishment, have appeared to be increasingly worried about whether Chinese reforms "have gone too far." In particular, they have been anxious about the rapid expansion of Western influence in China and the danger that it may undercut China's official ideology. The increasingly expanded economic and cultural ties between China and industrial market economies will, the Soviets fear, make China even more dependent on the West, especially the United States, leading thereby to a harsher Chinese approach towards Moscow.[38]

China's ongoing economic reforms have already had a strong impact on Eastern Europe. Eastern European states are particularly interested in China's experiences in introducing the market mechanism, the development of a private sector, the rapid expansion of economic

---

[37]*Shijie Jingji Daobao,* Jun. 17, 1985, pp. 1–2.

[38]Ibid.; I. Alexayev & F. Nikolayev, "Some Trends in PRC Policy," *International Affairs* (Moscow), 1984, No. 12, pp. 38–39; G. Rozman, *A Mirror for Socialism: Soviet Criticism of China*, Princeton University Press, 1985, pp. 82–84 and 226–241; and my interviews with Soviet scholars who were visiting the United States in 1985 and 1986.

cooperation with the West, and China's independent foreign policy vis-à-vis the Soviet Union. In the long run, if China's reform process continues, it will likely become a significant inducement to East European states to look for alternatives to the Soviet model and to seek to escape Moscow's political dominance. This potential development is probably viewed by Moscow as a possible political challenge to its authority in Eastern Europe, as economic reform in East European states is usually accompanied by attempts at political independence from Moscow.

The deep distrust between Beijing and Moscow still exists. This distrust has been exacerbated in Moscow by Beijing's active efforts to cooperate with the West, notably the United States, in security issues. Soviet scholars and policy makers remain critical in their views of Beijing's foreign policy and security strategy. Such distrust is unlikely to be easily overcome by the limited relaxation of tensions between the two countries, unless the balance of power in the Asia-Pacific region and both countries' basic security interests shift dramatically.

China has signed agreements with the Soviet Union and East European countries for technical assistance. Thousands of Chinese cadres and technicians who studied in the Soviet Union during the 1950s and 1960s now play key roles in various governmental and nongovernmental institutions in China. They are particularly influential in the party's ideological establishment and among technocrats. Trade between China and the Soviet Bloc is compatible: China can provide the Soviet Bloc with agricultural and consumer goods; the Soviet Bloc can supply China industrial equipment. More importantly, neither China nor the Soviet Bloc has to pay hard currency in their trade. Such trade is guided by both sides' central planning systems, thereby involving limited risk and instability. Prices of Chinese consumer goods are relatively cheaper than those of Western countries and NICs, thus they are competitive in the markets of the Soviet Bloc. Finally, it is unlikely that in the near future the Soviet Bloc will launch a war of protectionism against Chinese goods. For these reasons, the trade between China and the Soviet Bloc is likely to increase in the years ahead.

There are, however, some important limitations on a potential increase in Sino-Soviet trade. China's ability to export agricultural goods to the Soviet Bloc is not unlimited. Although the successful agricultural reform has increased China's agricultural output significantly during the past decade, the increase appears to be slowing down. This is happening because the increase was due primarily to substantial institutional reform, but a further increase in agricultural production will largely depend upon the amount of capital investment and technological development.[39] Meanwhile, the Chinese rural

---

[39]A. D. Barnett, *China's Economy in Global Perspective,* The Brookings Institution, 1981, pp. 270–275; the World Bank, *China: Long-Term Issues and Options, Annex B: Agriculture to the Year 2000: Perspectives 7 Options,* 1985, pp. 93–100.

economy is experiencing an important transition: peasants are putting more and more capital and labor into the development of rural industry and trade between rural and urban areas, not into agricultural production.

Trade with the Soviet Bloc amounted to about 5 percent of China's total foreign trade during the last two years.[40] Since the Sino-Soviet split of the 1960s, trade between China and the Soviet Bloc declined significantly and the latter stopped providing technology to China. Meanwhile, China imported a large amount of industrial equipment and technology from Western nations and Japan. As a result, the Chinese economy has become far less dependent on Soviet technology than it was fifteen years ago. On the contrary, it has become increasingly dependent upon Western and Japanese technology. Further, the Soviet Union does not seem capable and willing to supply the high technology that China needs (notably in computers and telecommunications) in its modernization drive. In sum, while Sino-Soviet trade will continue its smooth growth in the years ahead, its growth will not be faster than China's trade with industrial market economies. Nor will it play a significant role in influencing the political and security relationship between Beijing and Moscow.

In the area of international politics, Sino-Soviet relations have experienced some important changes during the past few years. Beijing and Moscow have appeared less antagonistic outside the Asia-Pacific region. They have been less critical towards each other's policies in the Third World. Beijing has taken a "neutral" position over U.S.-Soviet rivalry over various issues outside the Asia-Pacific region, such as the arms race between the two superpowers, and recent developments in Southern Africa, the Middle East, and Central America.[41] Moscow, in turn, has avoided talking about Beijing's policy outside the Asia-Pacific region. Moscow has also encouraged Eastern European states and communist parties in Western Europe to develop ties with Beijing.

Within the Asia-Pacific region, however, the Sino-Soviet relaxation has been a limited process. The two communist powers are still in sharp conflict, especially with regard to regional security issues. For Moscow, the China factor is important to both its global strategy and its strategy towards the Asia-Pacific region. Globally, Moscow is in a relatively un-

---

[40]The International Monetary Fund, *Direction of Trade Statistics Yearbook,* 1986, pp. 104–105 and 137–138.
[41]See, for instance, Jin Junhui, "Reagan's Diplomacy: An Overall View," *Beijing Review,* Jun. 17, 1985, Vol. 28, No. 24, p. 21; Zhang Liang, "U.S. Facing Middle-East Choices," *Beijing Review,* April 1, 1985, Vol. 28, N. 15, pp. 11–12; Huan Xiang, "International Conflicts and Our Choices," *Beijing Review,* Nov. 26, 1984, Vol. 27, No. 48, pp. 16–18; Wu Xueqian, "Chinese Principles on Central America," *Beijing Review,* Jun 3, 1985, Vol.28, No.22, p. 7; and Li Nan, "The Continuous Increase of Defense Spending of the World," *Liaowang,* Mar. 23, 1987, pp. 26–27.

favorable position within the triangle: it is faced with an increasingly stronger challenge from Washington, and the limited process of Sino-Soviet relaxation has not altered the strategic conflict between Beijing and Moscow. Thus, the potential possibility of an anti-Soviet partnership between Beijing and Washington (perhaps one should add Japan and Western Europe) still exists. In the long run, Moscow has to face the possibility that the world's most populous nation may be armed by American and Japanese technology and backed by Washington and Tokyo in a challenge to its entire eastern border. This possibility is the basic reason why Moscow has not ceased its efforts to continue its military buildup in the Far East, to encircle China strategically, and to maintain its military and political pressure on Beijing. In addition, building its capability to fight a "two-front war"—in Europe and the Asia-Pacific region—is Moscow's major deterrent to Washington, Tokyo, and Beijing.

The strategic importance of the Asia-Pacific region to both superpowers seems likely to increase. It is a region which has a very complicated political structure: two superpowers, two regional powers (China and Japan), and other states with many regional confrontations. In addition, many states in the region face serious political challenges, both domestically and internationally. In the next few years, many countries in the region will undergo political successions. Political institutions in many of these countries may undergo important transformations, thereby creating certain political instability. The Soviet Union does not have much political and cultural access in support of its expansionism in this region, nor does it enjoy strong economic influence. The only capital that Moscow and its allies can exploit is their increased military power. The potential political instability in the region will provide opportunities for Moscow to exercise its military power to undermine the current political structure of the region.

In Northeast Asia, Beijing and Moscow share certain common interests: to reduce border tensions between them, maintain stability in the Korean peninsula, and *in the long run,* to prevent Japan from becoming an independent military power. Nevertheless, in each of these areas, Beijing and Moscow are either in competition or conflict with each other.

Will Moscow substantially cut back its troops stationed along the Chinese border in the years ahead? The answer seems to be "No." To maintain strong military pressure on Beijing is the key to Moscow's strategy of forcing Beijing to move away from its pro-Western foreign policy. Unless Beijing moves against the United States and returns to the "communist camp," the remaining deep distrust between the two communist powers will likely continue to make it difficult for Moscow to alter its strategy towards Beijing and cut back dramatically its forces deployed along the Chinese border.

Strategically, Soviet forces (especially the Soviet air force, navy, and nuclear weapons) stationed in the Far East also threaten the security

of Japan and the United States presence in the Pacific. They defend
the Soviet Union's eastern border (the Trans-Siberian Railway is close
to the Sino-Soviet border). This deployment supports the Soviet
military presence in the South China Sea. These military missions are
a part of Soviet long-term global strategy. It is hard to imagine that
a limited process of Sino-Soviet relaxation would lead Moscow to alter
its global strategy, to weaken its own capacity to compete with the
United States and its allies in the Asia-Pacific region, or to reduce
significantly its armed forces in the Far East.

In terms of the military balance, Soviet troops in the Far East have
the upper hand vis-à-vis China's People's Liberation Army, not to mention the Soviet Union's superiority in nuclear weapons. The fifty Soviet
army divisions deployed in the Far East are far better equipped and
trained, with greater mobility and firepower, a better supply system,
and stronger support from air and sea power. During the past two
decades, Moscow has built a strong infrastructure in the Far East,
including military bases, airports, roads, and railways. These facilities
enable the Soviet Army to receive easily supplies and necessary support
from the Western Military Regions. The Soviet Pacific Fleet has already
developed the capacity to blockade and land on the northern Chinese
coast. To pull back a few divisions from the Chinese border, if it
occurred, would not weaken militarily Moscow's position vis-à-vis
Beijing.[42] The Soviet Union will continue to enjoy a great superiority
over China in air force, navy, and nuclear offensive forces. As a result
of Moscow's developing a strong offensive capability in the Far East,
Beijing will continue to be under a serious military threat from Moscow,
which places the latter in a strong bargaining position with Beijing.
From both the strategic and military perspectives, Moscow therefore
does not have a strong incentive to reduce substantially its military
pressure on Beijing and to cut back its forces in the Far East. Thus the
current military imbalance between the two countries is likely to remain in the years ahead.

At present, both Beijing and Moscow have an interest in maintaining stability on the Korean peninsula, as any serious military confrontation between the two Koreas could possibly lead to a regional or even
global war. It might no longer be possible to control such a war at the
conventional level. Nevertheless, the dynamics of the peninsula are
largely determined by its internal developments. Pyongyang will
undergo a succession in the next few years. The process or outcome
of the succession may heighten tensions and confrontations between
North and South. It may also intensify the Sino-Soviet competition in
the North. In the South, the intensified struggle between the
authoritarian regime and the democratic movement may jeopardize
South Korea's political stability. This in turn might provoke a preemptive attack fron the North because of the fear that Seoul would seek

---

[42]*The Military Balance* (1986-1987), pp. 29–30 and 113–115.

to escape domestic turmoil. The deepened Japanese involvement in the peninsular's security affairs may push Pyongyang to move closer to Moscow in an attempt to gain greater political support and military aid.

Moscow is now better situated than Beijing to compete for influence in Pyongyang. It is better able to provide more economic and military aid to Pyongyang and capable of taking a strong anti-American line to support Pyongyang's demands for reunification. If the ongoing U.S.-South Korea-Japan security cooperation continues to develop, it is likely that Pyongyang will lean toward Moscow for political support and a security guarantee. Recently, Moscow and Pyongyang have increased their security cooperation. Moscow has provided Pyongyang with MiG-23 fighters; Pyongyang, in turn, has invited Soviet fleets to visit its harbors and allowed Soviet military planes to fly over its territory. These moves have clearly shown the new Soviet leadership's strong interest in the Korean peninsula.[43]

During the past few years, Beijing has modified its previous policy towards the Korean peninsula. It has announced that it will not support an attack by Pyongyang on the South, although it would help Pyongyang if the latter were attacked by the South.[44] Beijing has encouraged Pyongyang to open its doors and to increase its contacts with the West. Beijing has in fact warmly received Kim Il Song's son, while at the same time developing its informal ties with Seoul. All these moves have helped to reduce tensions between the North and the South, but they do not necessarily strengthen Beijing's capability to compete with Moscow.

Beijing and Moscow have different views about Japanese rearmament and U.S.-Japanese security cooperation, although neither of them wants to see Japan become an independent military power in the future. Beijing would not strongly oppose Japanese moves if they neither alter Japan's security strategy vis-à-vis the Soviet Union nor make Japan an independent military power with an offensive capability. U.S.-Japanese security cooperation is therefore essential, as such cooperation can guide Tokyo's strategic intentions.[45] For its part, Moscow opposes any attempt at Japanese rearmament. Close security ties between Washington and Tokyo would certainly provoke a strong reaction from Moscow. Finally, *in the long run,* if U.S.-Japanese security ties failed to prevent Tokyo from becoming an independent military power and altering its military strategy, Beijing may have little alternative but to turn to Moscow.

---

[43]D. S. Suh, " North Korea in 1986: Strengthening the Soviet Connection," *Asian survey,* Vol. XXVVII, No.1, pp. 57–59; *The Far East Economic Review,* Jun 20, 1985, vol. 128, No. 24, pp. 26–31.

[44]*The Wall Street Journal,* Nov. 25, 1983; *Meizhou huaqiao Rebao,* Jun. 27, 1984.

[45]*The New York Times,* Jul. 11, 1984.

With respect to the Sino-Soviet conflict, the central issue in Southeast Asia is whether Moscow will cut back its support to Hanoi. Since 1979, when China "taught Vietnam a lesson," Moscow has made a huge capital investment in Indochina, notably Vietnam. Since 1978, Hanoi has received over US$5 billion from Moscow. Moscow's aid to Hanoi has amounted roughly to over US$3 million per day, three times the amount of its aid to Cuba.[46] Hanoi has received large amounts of advanced weapons and built up the world's fourth largest military power and fifth largest air force.[47] Over 20,000 Soviet advisors and technicians are now working in various Vietnamese military and civilian institutions and thousands of Vietnamese are receiving training in the Soviet Union. In return, Hanoi serves Moscow's strategic interests by challenging China's southern border, threatening the ASEAN states' security especially Thailand's, and providing military bases for the Soviet Pacific Fleet and its air attack force to compete with U.S. Pacific forces. The Soviet-Vietnamese strategic alliance has been solidified.

Both globally and regionally, Soviet-Vietnamese security cooperation has great strategic significance. Globally, to have access to military bases in Cam Ranh and Da Nang Bays strengthens the Soviet Pacific Fleet's strategic position vis-à-vis the U.S. Seventh Fleet, threatens Japan's supply lines, and supports the Soviet military presence in the Indian Ocean.

Within the region, Soviet-Vietnamese security cooperation is an important part of Moscow's strategic encirclement of China, threatening China's southern sea line. It also serves Moscow's strategy in Southeast Asia. During the next few years, the political transformation in the Philippines will likely have an important impact on the region. If the Aquino government fails to create a stable political situation, the United States may lose its military bases in the Philippines, the ASEAN alliance will face a real challenge, and the strategic map of Southeast Asia will look more favorable to the Soviet Union. If this situation arises, the Soviet navy and air force operating from military bases in Cam Ranh and Da Nang Bays, together with well-trained and fully equipped Vietnamese troops, could be quickly sent to the Philippines, if required.

Moreover, the relationship between Hanoi and Moscow is an interdependent one. Hanoi knows well its strategic value to Moscow and takes appropriate advantage of the Sino-Soviet conflict. It is also a relatively independent regime able to mobilize strong, militant nationalist sentiment. It has been fighting for decades for the goal of a "unified Indochina" under its own dominion. Since 1985, with Moscow's support, the Vietnamese troops have made some progress in the war with the Kampuchean resistance movement.[48] This war, however, does not seem likely to end in the near future. The serious

---

[46]*The Economist,* Jan. 10–16, 1987, pp. 86–90.
[47]*The Military Balance* (1986-1987), pp. 136–137.

economic crisis and the recent restructuring of the leadership in Hanoi may reduce the degree of Vietnamese militancy. It is unlikely, however, that Hanoi would be willing to pull its troops out of Kampuchea. As China is viewed as the principal obstacle to its ambitions, Hanoi is unlikely to soften its anti-Chinese attitude.

In sum, in Moscow's calculations the strategic importance of Soviet-Vietnamese security cooperation outweighs any possible gain Moscow might obtain by cutting back its support to Hanoi. Beijing might take a more "neutral" position than at present between Moscow and Washington, but this shift would count for less, in Moscow's eyes, than its current relations with Vietnam. In the foreseeable future, therefore, there is little incentive for Moscow to pursue a policy of rapprochement with China at Vietnam's expense, nor will Hanoi be either passive or cooperative with such a prospect.

Although the war in Afghanistan still continues, the key security issue in Southwest Asia in the years ahead for both Beijing and Washington is the security of Pakistan. The Soviet Union has expressed a willingness to pull out more of its troops from Afghanistan if other powers would stop their support to the resistance movement in the country. While the Pakistani and Afghan governments are holding difficult negotiations about the withdrawal of Soviet troops from Afghanistan, the Afghan air force has continued to raid Pakistani territory.[49] The occupation and control of Afghanistan has strengthened Moscow's strategic position in the region, whose dynamics affect the security and stability of the Gulf, the Indian Ocean and the entire Middle East. Both Iran and Pakistan may experience significant political changes in the next few years. The continuation of the Soviet operation in Afghanistan, though costly, will strengthen Moscow's capability to cope with such changes. Through Afghanistan the Soviet Union can put direct political and military pressure on Pakistan. A withdrawal of troops from Afghanistan would both weaken Moscow's strategic position and damage the credibility of its willingness and capacity to exercise power abroad. Given the geopolitical situation of the region and the political and military restraints on both Washington and Beijing, Pakistan has been increasingly worried about its security. Thus in the mid-term it is unlikely that Moscow will meet Beijing's demand to withdraw its troops completely from Afghanistan.

Will Moscow reduce its political support and economic and military aid to India, the key country in the region? The answer seems to be "No." The Soviet-Indian security partnership serves a number of Moscow's central interests: it is an important part of Moscow's strategic encirclement of China; it allows the Soviet Fleet access to a harbor in the Indian Ocean, which is essential to Soviet competition with the U.S. Sixth fleet; and it enables Moscow further to pressure Pakistan.

---

[48]*Asian Survey,* Vol.XXVII, No.2, Feb. 1987, pp. 97–102 and 115118.
[49]Ibid.

The Indian-Soviet strategic partnership, moreover, has a long history going back to the 1960s. During the Sino-Indian border war of 1961-1962, Moscow provided New Delhi with a great deal of military aid and strong political support. Since then a large part of the weapons that India imported has come from the Soviet Union. Moscow has helped Delhi build up its own defense industry; and a large number of Indian military personnel have been trained in the Soviet Union. In both Indian-Pakistan wars (1965 and 1971), the Soviet Union strongly supported India both politically and militarily, while Washington and Beijing backed Pakistan. In the Soviet-Indian Friendship Treaty, signed in 1971 soon before the Second Indian-Pakistan War broke out, Moscow and Delhi declared that the two powers will consult in time of crisis and refrain from conflict with the other.[50] This is similar to the tone used in the Soviet-Vietnamese Friendship Treaty signed in 1978, a few weeks before Vietnam's invasion of Kampuchea.[51] At present Moscow still supplies over 70 percent of the weapons that India imports.[52] Without Moscow's support India cannot realize its ambition to be the dominant power in the region. As long as Sino-Indian rivalry and the Indian-Pakistani conflict continue, India will likely continue its dependence on Soviet military and political support and maintain the Soviet-Indian strategic partnership.

Finally, in the near future Pakistan is likely to be the next theater in which an intensification of the conflict between Moscow on the one hand and Washington and Beijing on the other will unfold. The ongoing conflict between the military authoritarian regime and the opposition movement in Pakistan is likely to intensify, partially because of the country's economic difficulties and partially because of the regime's decreasing popularity in broad sections of Pakistani society.[53] Such political instability may be exploited by Moscow as an opportunity to undermine the regime or to force it to alter its pro-Washington and Beijing foreign policy.

In the years ahead, the relationship between Pakistan and India will likely continue to be tense. Domestic political and racial tensions in India will continue to be an important motivation for Delhi to seek external conflict to deflect domestic disarray. Its ambition to be the dominant power in South Asia and the Indian Ocean, and the cultural and religious stress between the two countries, will continue to accen-

---

[50]See,D.H.Bayley, "India: War and Political Assertion," *Asian Survey,* Feb, 1972, Vol.XII, No. 2, p. 93.

[51]See *Asian Survey,* Jan. 1979, Vol. XIX, No. 1, p. 89.

[52]See, J. Banerjee, "Moscow's Indian Alliance," *Problems of Communism,* Jan.-Feb. 1987, pp. 3–5; R. Menon, "Soviet Arms Assistance to the Third World," *Journal of International Affairs,* Vol. 40, No.1, Summer 1986, pp. 59–76; P. S. Kreisberg, "India After Indira," *Foreign Affairs,* Spring, 1985, pp. 881–883; and *The New York Times,* Mar. 10 and 16, 1985.

[53]See, *The Economist,* "Survey on Pakistan," Jan. 17–23, 1987, after page 50.

tuate the conflicts between them. Pakistan's close ties with both Beijing and Washington will continue to sustain India's strategic posture as a partner of the Soviet Union and to increase its motives to put strong political and military pressure on Pakistan.

Furthermore, the Soviet Union will also continue to exert its own political and military pressure on Pakistan. Moscow's strategic objective is either to "Finlandize" Pakistan or to put Pakistan under its own control. Should Pakistan come under Moscow's control, China's two politically sensitive provinces, Xinjiang and Xizang (Tibet), bordering the Soviet Union, Afghanistan, India, and Pakistan, will feel much more insecure. Lack of capacity to help Pakistan to preserve itself would also damage Beijing's and Washington's international credibility.

In sum, Beijing and Moscow have sharp conflicts of interest in Southwest Asia. These conflicts are likely to continue and even intensify in the years ahead. As the political structure of the region continues to be unstable, Moscow will surely take geopolitical advantage of this situation to further weaken Pakistan's security. Beijing would certainly make every effort, including the development of an informal framework of strategic cooperation with both Washington and Islamabad, to support Pakistan.

V. BEIJING'S BASIC POLICY OPTIONS IN DEALING WITH MOSCOW

In the years ahead Beijing seems to have three basic policy options in dealing with Moscow. The first could be to pursue a rapid process of Sino-Soviet reconciliation. Economically, Beijing could continue to increase its trade with the Soviet Bloc and import more technology and industrial equipment from the Soviet Union, thereby increasing the degree of economic dependence on Moscow. Culturally, Beijing can further eliminate its differences with Moscow on ideological issues and rapidly expand exchange programs with Moscow. Beijing can reduce the number of its students studying in the West and Japan, while sending more scholars and students to the Soviet Bloc.

Beijing could also dramatically improve its political relations with Moscow. The two communist parties could restore their ties; and Beijing could continue to strengthen its relations with Eastern European states and communist parties around the world, although a new international communist movement is unlikely to be reestablished. Beijing may even improve its state-to-state relations with Moscow by establishing a regular mechanism for consultations at the summit level, with both sides willing to solve the border issue and to pull back a certain amount of their armed forces along the Sino-Soviet and Sino-Mongolian border. Outside the Asia-Pacific region, Beijing may try harder to avoid contests with Moscow and to take similar strong positions to Moscow's against Washington's Third World policy, although continuing its competition with Moscow for influence in the Third

World. Beijing would further distance itself from Washington and play down its common security interests shared with Washington. The Taiwan issue may once again become a highly emotional political background in Sino-American relations.

This approach will further reduce political tensions and improve state-to-state relations between Beijing and Moscow. It will to a certain extent reduce Moscow's political and military pressure on Beijing. Economically, China will receive more technology and industrial equipment from the Soviet Bloc. More Chinese scholars and students will have the opportunity to study in the Soviet Union, where the political system and official ideology are similar to China's own, thereby presenting far less challenge to the Chinese political system at home. Domestically, this approach will well serve the interests of those conservatives within the party and government and contribute to their efforts to rebuild a post-Khrushchev Soviet-type political and economic system.

This approach will further reduce conflicts between Beijing and Moscow outside the Asia-Pacific region, thereby allowing Beijing to take a more flexible position in the Third World. To a certain extent it may also increase Beijing's bargaining power vis-à-vis Washington. Within the Asia-Pacific region, Sino-Soviet reconciliation will moderate their competition for influence over Pyongyang, thereby reducing the latter's incentive to lean toward Moscow politically. This approach will put Japan in a difficult position, because Moscow will surely continue its political and military pressure on Tokyo while Beijing may become more critical of Japan's rearmament. Given the regional geopolitics and Beijing's influence on Japan's public opinion, such international pressure may affect Tokyo's security planning and foreign policy making. In Southeast Asia, Moscow may convince Hanoi to reduce tension with Beijing and to turn its attention south. In Southwest Asia, Beijing may expect Moscow to reduce its pressure on Pakistan and promise not to threaten China's Western border and to convince India to reduce tension with China.

The costs of taking this approach, however, will be high. Economically, Beijing may have to change its developmental strategy from an "open door" to the West to a dependence on the Soviet Bloc for economic and technological assistance. China's position in the international market will thus be weakened, while Moscow is unlikely to be capable of meeting China's needs to obtain technology to upgrade its industrial bases. Nor will the readoption of the Soviet model improve China's economic efficiency in general and its competitiveness vis-à-vis other nations in particular. Culturally, the younger generation and the intellectual establishment, who have been deeply alienated from the official ideology and strongly influenced by the new information imported into the country during the last few years, are likely to feel increased resentment at a rapid Sino-Soviet reconciliation, as the Soviet model is widely viewed as a symbol of political repression, bureaucratism, and economic inefficiency.

In the international arena, this approach is unlikely to improve China's security environment significantly. Moscow would neither slow down its military buildup in the Far East, nor stop its expansionist activities in the Asia-Pacific region, since Beijing does not have much leverage to force it to do so. More importantly, a limited withdrawal of Soviet ground forces from the Chinese border will not change the existing military imbalance between the two countries. Moscow has already built up an adequate military infrastructure and supply system in these areas; and its deployment of air and naval forces in the Far East will not be affected by the improvement of Sino-Soviet relations.

Moreover, this approach will destabilize the current triangular relationship between Moscow, Beijing, and Washington. It will also reshape the balance of power in the Asia-Pacific region and once again put China at the center of conflicts. This is because Washington and its allies in the Asia-Pacific region will react strongly to a rapid Sino-Soviet reconciliation by restructuring their security strategies. As a result, with the strong encouragement of Washington, Tokyo will further speed up its process of rearmament. Political tensions between Washington and its Asian allies on the one hand and Beijing on the other may revive. Current Sino-American relations may undergo a fundamental change. Washington could become a new security threat which could possibly include South Korea, Japan, and the ASEAN nations. The present relative stability of the region would thus be undermined. Such an international environment might force Beijing to increase its dependence on Moscow, thereby further weakening its bargaining position vis-à-vis the latter.

On the Korean peninsula, a rapid Sino-Soviet reconciliation will not necessarily reduce tensions between the two Koreas, as such a development will reduce Beijing's incentive and capability to cooperate with Washington to prevent a possible military confrontation between North and South. In addition, the forthcoming succession to Kim Il-Song will naturally accentuate the competition between Beijing and Moscow for influence over Pyongyang.

In Southeast Asia, Moscow is unlikely to reduce its military presence, given its ambitious global strategy and the region's unstable political future. Nor will Hanoi alter its position vis-à-vis Beijing, unless Beijing were willing to soften its stance on the Kampuchean issue. China's ties with ASEAN may face increased difficulties, as changed Sino-Soviet relations may force Washington either to increase its direct involvement in the region or to encourage the ASEAN nations to pursue an appeasement policy toward Hanoi.

In Southwest Asia, Pakistan's security might still be endangered because the continuing war in Afghanistan could expand. More importantly, a rapid Sino-Soviet reconciliation would probably not change India's attitude towards China, nor would it reduce Indian-Pakistani tensions. While the common security interests shared by Washington and Beijing will be jeopardized, domestic stability in

Pakistan will remain under challenge. The region's political structure will become more unstable.

To sum up, it would be possible for Beijing to pursue a rapid Sino-Soviet reconciliation, but it would require China to adjust its foreign and security policy significantly. This approach may reduce political tensions between Beijing and Moscow. It will, however, destabilize the balance of power and the international system in the Asia-Pacific region, if not the world as a whole. China's basic security interests will thus continue to be challenged.

Theoretically, Beijing has a second policy option in dealing with Moscow. This is a "cold war" approach. Under this approach, Beijing will once again cut back its cultural and economic ties with Moscow. On the political front, Beijing can freeze both party-to-party and state-to-state relations with Moscow. Instead, it can work more closely with Yugoslavia, Romania, and those Western European communist parties which have kept their distance from Moscow and challenged Moscow's authority. On the global level, Beijing would surely move closer to Washington and actively participate in Washington's containment strategy. In the Third World, as we saw during the 1960s and most of the 1970s, such a development would likely revive serious competition between Beijing and Moscow.

In the Asia-Pacific region, Beijing, by increasing its political support and military aid to Pyongyang, can intensify its competition with Moscow for influence over North Korea. It will also make further efforts to develop strategic cooperation with the United States, Japan and Western Europe in order to counter Moscow's pressure. In Southeast Asia, Beijing will demand that Moscow reduce its military presence. It will also increase military and political pressure on Hanoi, actively support the resistance movement in Kampuchea, and coordinate its policies with the United States and ASEAN, especially Thailand. If the Vietnamese-Thai confrontation intensified, with the encouragement of Washington, Beijing will surely launch another border war against Hanoi. In Southwest Asia, Beijing will continue its support to the rebels in Afghanistan. It may also encourage an increase in the U.S. military presence in the Indian Ocean and work more closely with both the United States and Pakistan against the Soviet-Indian partnership.

Moscow will surely react strongly to this approach. In terms of the military balance, Beijing is still in a much weaker position vis-à-vis Moscow. Moscow might speed up its military buildup along the Chinese border. It may also increase its efforts to encircle China strategically by heightening its political and military pressure on China and destabilizing China's periphery. China would thus once again become the central target of Moscow's security strategy in the region. What and how much support Beijing may receive from Washington in the event of a Sino-Soviet confrontation is still an open question, not to mention that so dependent a relationship on the United States may undercut the Beijing government's domestic legitimacy. More importantly, it is not in Beijing's interests to become once again the central target of Moscow's containment strategy in the Asia-Pacific region. Increased dependence on the political and military support of the United States will also weaken Beijing's bargaining position vis-à-vis Washington.

On the Korean peninsula, a sharp confrontation between Moscow and Beijing will likely destabilize Pyongyang's politics and probably undermine the stability of the peninsula in general. If Pyongyang chose to lean toward Moscow, Beijing would face a second Vietnam, armed by the Soviet Union to challenge its Northeast border. Faced with a strong military threat from Moscow, Beijing may have to support Tokyo's efforts at rapid rearmament, which in the long run may challenge China's own security. In Southeast Asia, while the United States may continue its low-key non-direct-involvement policy and the ASEAN alliance remains weak, both politically and militarily, China may find it increasingly difficult to deal with an increased Soviet military presence and the Soviet-Vietnamese military alliance. Given the nature of the geopolitics of Southwest Asia, an intensified Sino-Soviet confrontation is likely to lead to an upgrading of Soviet-Indian strategic cooperation. In the worst case, such a cooperation may undermine Pakistan's security and threaten China's Western border.

Considering all factors, to pursue a militant approach towards Moscow is not desirable for Beijing, as it will jeopardize China's goal to create the relatively stable and peaceful international environment which is needed for its economic development. This approach will also weaken Beijing's position in the "big" triangle and undermine the stability and peace of the Asia-Pacific region.

The third and clearly the most rational approach that Beijing could take is to pursue a limited detente, while continuing its competition with Moscow in matters of security. It is important for Beijing to prevent any dramatic changes within the Washington-Moscow-China triangle. Consequently, Beijing's fundamental security interests may be defined as reducing Moscow's military and political pressure while creating a relatively stable and peaceful international environment. Under this approach, Beijing will continue to expand its economic and cultural ties with Moscow, but it will not put an end to Beijing's cultural exchange programs and economic cooperation with the Western world. Outside the Asia-Pacific region, Beijing may continue to be less critical of Moscow's foreign policy. It should not, however, pursue an "equal distance" policy between Washington and Moscow, as Moscow still presents the principal threat to China's national security. Beijing will continue to make efforts to reduce border tensions with the Soviet Union and improve state-to-state relations with Moscow. It should not downplay its demand that Moscow withdraw its troops substantially from the Chinese border, remove its SS-20 missiles from the Far East, cut its support for Hanoi's occupation of Kampuchea, and pull out its armed forces from Afghanistan.

With this approach, Beijing can advance its cooperation with Washington in order to maintain stability on the Korean peninsula and encourage Pyongyang to open more to the international community. In the short term, Beijing could take a low-key approach towards Tokyo's rearmament, as long as these efforts do not lead Japan in the direction of becoming an independent military power. Beijing should also advance its low-level security cooperation and military exchange programs with Washington.

In Southeast Asia, while demanding that Moscow reduce its military involvement in the region, Beijing should maintain strong military and political pressure on Hanoi, as long as the latter keeps its troops in Kampuchea and threatens the security of Thailand. With Washington's encouragement, Beijing should continue its efforts to cooperate with the ASEAN nations against the Soviet-Vietnamese alliance.

Beijing should continue its support for Pakistan and the Afghan rebels while trying to improve its ties with India. Should Pakistan's security come under serious challenge from either the Soviet Union or India, Beijing will surely be willing to provide all possible support to Pakistan, including direct joint operations with Washington.

Compared with the first two options, the third option does not require Beijing to readjust significantly its current foreign and security strategy. It will contribute to the stability of the current Washington-Beijing-Moscow triangle, as well as the international system in the Asia-Pacific region. This approach will lead China's policy towards the Soviet Union in a "dual-track" direction, i.e., China will continue to improve its cultural and economic ties with Moscow and to reduce certain political tensions; at the same time, with regard to the security of the Asia-Pacific region, Beijing will continue to make strong efforts to break down Moscow's strategic encirclement of China. It will give Moscow an incentive to moderate its expansionist activities around China and reduce its motivation to advance its strategic cooperation with Hanoi and Delhi against Beijing. Continued Sino-Soviet conflicts will tend to be more manageable and less likely to develop into direct military confrontation between the two countries, unless the international environment changes suddenly and dramatically. Thus, the limited relaxation of Sino-Soviet tensions will contribute to the region's stability.

Finally, to leave open the option of upgrading its security cooperation with Washington and its allies will serve Beijing's interest in deterring Moscow's further expansionism against China. It will not, however, eradicate an increasingly intensified competition and confrontation between the two superpowers. More importantly, developing the working relationship with Washington can strengthen Beijing's capability to cope with sub-regional security issues in the Asia-Pacific region.

VI. CONCLUSION: U.S. INTERESTS AND OPTIONS

The most likely possibility in Sino-Soviet relations until the year 2000 is a limited detente. Rapid improvement in Sino-Soviet relations would strongly affect U.S. interests. Globally, Washington wants to see a stable triangular relationship among the United States, the Soviet Union, and China. Although Washington no longer views China as a global power, but rather as a regional power of global strategic importance, it would not be in the U.S. interest if there were a major reconciliation between Moscow and Beijing, or if Beijing pursued an "equal distance" policy towards the two superpowers. This is primarily because U.S.-Soviet competition and confrontation at the global level is likely to intensify in the years ahead. Any significant move on the part of Beijing, either closer to Moscow or away from Washington, would not only allow Moscow to remove a part of its military forces from the China front, releasing them to concentrate on the United States and its Atlantic and Pacific allies, but would also have a strong political and psychological impact on the strategic and military planning of the United States and its allies, especially Japan and West Germany. Such a change may also lead Beijing to be more critical of Washington's Third World policy, particularly outside the Asia-Pacific region. Given China's political influence in the Third World, such a shift would put the United States in a more difficult position.

Within the Asia-Pacific region, with which the United States now conducts 40 percent of its total trade, the dynamics of Sino-Soviet relations have an even stronger impact on the regional balance of power and political stability. Both countries play a very important political and strategic role in a region where the U.S. military presence and political influence have declined during the past decade. At present, the United States has only limited military forces in the West Pacific, and the Soviet Union and its allies and semi-allies have made efforts to invest greater resources in order to change the military balance of the region. None of the U.S. allies in the region has sufficient military strength to protect itself; all of them continue to depend heavily on the U.S. security umbrella; and many of them face serious political challenges and economic difficulties. This trend is likely to continue in the years ahead. If a rapid Sino-Soviet reconciliation occurred, especially if Beijing and Moscow changed their strategic relationship dramatically, Moscow may be able to increase further its military pressure against the United States and its allies in the region.

On the Korean peninsula, it is in the United States' interests to maintain present stability, reduce the tensions between North and South, and prevent possible Soviet dominance of North Korea. Without a certain degree of political cooperation with China, however, it is difficult for the United States to pursue these interests solely by its efforts to maintain the military balance and to encourage deepening involvement by Japan in the political and security affairs of the peninsula. In addition, the current Japanese rearmament serves U.S. security interests in countering the Soviet Union's military build-up in the Far East. In the long run, however, a rapid process of Japanese rearmament, especially without U.S. guidelines, would destabilize the balance of power in the region and provoke political tensions between Japan and other U.S. allies in the region, notably South Korea and the ASEAN countries, and between Japan and China. This development, if it occurs, will thus challenge U.S. political and security interests in the region.

In Southeast Asia, it is in the United States' interest to prevent a "united Indochina" under Hanoi's dominance, contain the rapidly expanded Soviet military presence, and guarantee the security and political stability of the ASEAN states. Yet, it is unlikely in the near future that the United States would be able to send its troops back to defend Thailand. The ASEAN nations share few common interests with regard to security issues, nor are they able to defend themselves. Furthermore, the ongoing political struggle in the Philippines may still result in an anti-American government that would expel the American military bases. This in turn would undermine the ASEAN alliance and bring about dramatic changes to the region's strategic map.

In Southwest Asia, the United States will continue its support of the Afghan rebels. The United States will also strengthen its ties with Pakistan and make every possible effort to secure the country. Moreover, the United States, in looking to improve its relations with India, will seek to induce the latter to alter its pro-Moscow policy. There are, however, a number of difficulties which confront the United States in pursuing its interests. In the first place, the resources that the United States can invest in the Asia-Pacific region are limited, as the Middle East, Europe, and Central America will continue to be Washington's highest strategic priorities. Secondly, the United States has only limited ability to help Pakistan stabilize its domestic politics. Thirdly, the interdependent relationship between the Soviet Union and India has deep historical and strategic roots, and is unlikely to change significantly.

Finally, it is in the United States' interest to continue its efforts to develop its ties with China. As a regional power, China plays the key role in many subregional security issues. China continues to tie down one-fourth of total Soviet military forces. China shares substantial common interests with the United States in many subregional security issues in the Asia-Pacific region. In the long run, China is also a great potential market for American commerce.

Faced with the dynamics of Sino-Soviet relations until the year 2000, theoretically the United States seems to have the following three options: 1) do everything to prevent a limited detente between China and Soviet Union; 2) do nothing to influence the further development of Sino-Soviet relations; and 3) do something to influence the process of limited Sino-Soviet detente and to further its own interests.

The first approach is based on the assumption that any improvement in Sino-Soviet relations would hurt U.S. interests and that the big "triangle" is the only factor in determining Beijing's policy toward the Soviet Union and Moscow's China policy. Under this assumption, the United States will react strongly to any step that Beijing makes in the process of achieving a limited Sino-Soviet detente. It may tighten restrictions on technology transfers to China, downgrade the military exchange program and security cooperation with China. It may also discourage American investment in China. In addition, Washington might heighten its differences with Beijing regarding Taiwan. Washington will shift its strategy towards the Asia-Pacific region from cooperation with both Japan and China to simple dependence upon Japan. In Southeast Asia, Washington might speed up the process of normalizing its ties with Hanoi and discourage cooperation between the ASEAN nations and China. In Southwest Asia, Washington will pressure Beijing by developing its ties with India. Finally, there is always a theoretical possibility that Washington would try to have a new detente with Moscow.

This approach will put strong political pressure on Beijing, but may even push Beijing away from Washington. Beijing values highly its economic and cultural ties with Washington, but it always has the option of importing technology from other industrial market economies. Instead, Washington's strong and obvious political pressure may intensify domestic political opposition in China and provoke strong Chinese nationalism. It could strengthen the hand of the conservative, anti-Deng forces in China. In the matter of security, a rapid process of Japanese rearmament would not only speed up the process of Sino-Soviet detente, but destabilize the balance of power in the Western Pacific and create conflicts between the United States and other Asian nations. Similarly, Washington's efforts to develop ties with Hanoi may heighten the differences among ASEAN states and reduce Beijing's incentive to maintain strong pressure on Vietnam and support Thailand's defense. Rapid improvement in Indian-American ties may not alter New Delhi's pro-Soviet policy, but further weaken Pakistan's security. In sum, such an oversensitive and overreactive approach does not serve U.S. interests, but would rather prove to be counterproductive, giving Moscow the leverage to play its "China card" with Washington. More importantly, this approach may even push China farther away from the United States. In the worst case, it may result in fundamental change in the balance of power and in the political structure, both regionally and globally.

The second approach is based upon the assumption that the dynamics of Sino-Soviet relations flow exclusively from the interaction between Moscow and Beijing; on this assumption, the triangular and other international players have no ability to influence the process. This assumption ignores the significance of the United States' international capacity to influence both Moscow's and Beijing's foreign policy-making. Furthermore, it does not reflect the fact that the "big triangle" has become increasingly important in its impact on the three powers' policies towards one another. This approach will not serve U.S. interests, as it may strengthen both Moscow's and Beijing's position vis-à-vis Washington. It will also reduce China's incentive to further its economic, political, and security cooperation with Washington and its Asian allies. In addition, without having to consider possible U.S. reactions, Moscow and Beijing may speed up the process of mutual detente. Finally, Washington's weak attitude towards a limited Sino-Soviet detente may also demoralize its Asian allies, thereby further destabilizing the international system in the region and damaging U.S. credibility with its allies in Asia.

The third approach is based on the assumption that the dynamics of the international environment and the behavior of other international players, especially the United States, have an important influence on the development of Sino-Soviet relations. As argued above, the most likely course of Sino-Soviet relations up to the year 2000 is that of limited detente. The policy option here therefore is for the U.S. to do what it can to influence the dynamics of Sino-Soviet relations and further its own interests.

This approach can be characterized as the following:

—To continue the present course of Sino-American relations by expanding cultural and economic ties with China. The United States, for instance, can increase the number of Chinese scholars and students who come to the United States, especially those in the fields of international relations, international law, political science, and economics. The United States should also expand exchange programs between non- or semi-governmental foreign policy research institutions in China and in the United States. Further, Washington should continue to encourage American corporations to invest in China, expand trade with China, and increase technology transfer to China.

—In the area of Asia-Pacific security, Washington and Beijing are generally not in conflict. Both view Moscow as the principal threat. Washington should continue to develop low-level military exchange programs with Beijing, especially personnel exchange and consultations on security issues in the Asia-Pacific region. Such programs should be undertaken without much publicity. Moreover, Washington can develop its political cooperation with Beijing in various sub-regional security issues. A low-key approach, for instance, can be taken by Beijing and Washington (one may add Tokyo) to help North Korea "open its doors" and gradually change its extreme political characteristics. In Southeast Asia, Washington should continue its efforts to encourage the ASEAN countries to cooperate with China and coordinate their support of the resistance forces in Kampuchea. Washington might work together with Beijing, which has political influence and potential in the Philippines, in providing policy options which might reduce Soviet influence in the country. In Southwest Asia, Sino-American political cooperation should focus on the coordination of their support for the Afghan rebels and the security of Pakistan.

—To keep diplomatic channels open in order to express Washington's concern for developments and trends in Sino-Soviet relations.

This approach will expand areas of common interest that the United States and China share and strengthen long-term American influence in China. It can indirectly contribute to the ongoing economic and political reforms in China, thereby consolidating the foundation of Sino-American relations. It will also help create a new generation of policy-makers in China who are more pragmatic and realistic with broad international perspectives, but less ideologically oriented. Moreover, this approach can increase the economic incentives for Beijing to continue its "open door" policy and maintain its present pro-West foreign policy.

Internationally, this approach will increase the common interests that the United States and China share in the area of Asia-Pacific security. It might reduce Beijing's incentive to speed up the process of Sino-Soviet relaxation. It can gradually build up and institutionalize a framework of political cooperation between Washington and Beijing. Moreover, this approach may in the long run create a broad "united front", including China, the United States, and its allies in Asia vis-à-vis Moscow's proposal for a "collective security" program in Asia.

This approach is not intended to undermine the current balance of power in the Asia-Pacific region. Nor will it intensify the ongoing sub-regional conflicts and confrontations in the Asia-Pacific region but rather restrain the possible expansion of these struggles, since Sino-American cooperation, with the support of United States' allies, will become one of the most effective methods of deterring the expansion of Moscow and its allies in the region.

Chapter VIII

WESTERN AND EASTERN ECONOMIC CONSTRAINTS ON DEFENSE: THE MUTUAL SECURITY IMPLICATIONS

Timothy W. Stanley

I. INTRODUCTION

This paper concentrates on the period between now and the year 2000, although more immediate economic and budgetary crises, including the effects of the Gramm-Rudman-Hollings (GRH) legislation, are also considered. It deals primarily with the United States and the Soviet Union and features an analysis of the situation in the USSR contributed by Congressional Research Service Sovietologist John Hardt. (See Section IV and the Appendix.) To a limited extent the analysis also touches the analogous problems of key allies of the superpowers in NATO and the Warsaw Pact.

Relations among three separate but interacting variables complicate the search for strategic stability and affect U.S.-Soviet relations as they influence mutual threat perceptions and the economic consequences of the armaments programs of both sides.

One useful, if admittedly simplified way of illustrating these relationships is shown in the two back-to-back right triangles diagrammed below. Side (a), the altitude, is composed of the mutual threat perceptions, taking the "threat" as military capabilities discounted by inten-

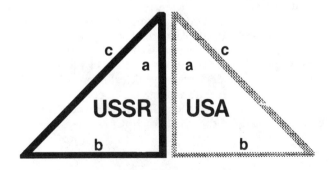

tions, which dominate U.S.-Soviet and, to a lesser extent, NATO-Warsaw Pact relations. The base of the triangle (b) represents the armaments programs in part generated by these mutual threat perceptions and includes the arms control desiderata resulting from the vulnerability of both sides to technologically sophisticated nuclear and conventional weapons of great power, including potential applications in space.

The hypotenuse of the triangle (c) represents the economic costs and consequences and potential economic constraints of both sides' national security programs. The drawing is intended to be illustrative of the elementary principle that strategy (or threat evaluation and response) military programs, and defense budgets (and their limitations) are all interrelated. No quantitative comparisons are intended.

Every math student knows that the square of the hypotenuse is equal to the the the sum of the squares of the other two sides, represented by the formula $a^2 + b^2 = c^2$. However, in the world of politics these relationships may or may not apply. Three basic viewpoints were expressed during the discussions of the Atlantic Council Working Groups on U.S.-Soviet Relations and Strategic Stability.

One view takes the "a", or perceptions of threat to national security as a given; it in turn drives the related armaments programs, limited only by arms control imperatives and possibilities. The hypotenuse is then treated simply as a derivative, representing economic consequences which must simply be accepted, given the high priority both superpowers and their major allies assign to national security as they perceive it.

According to a second view, the mere existence of large military establishments, bureaucracies and interlocking industrial relationships generates its own momentum in the arms race. Thus, quite frequently, the "threat" is cut to fit the desired pattern of the military-industrial complex. Scholars of Soviet affairs note that while economic incentives and constraints may play a somewhat smaller role in the USSR than in the West, the bureaucratic and political power, as well as allocation priorities determined by the armaments elements of Soviet society, are of great importance. They reinforce the ideological "threat" from the West, at once stimulating the military capabilities that the West has developed in response, and justifying still larger Soviet bloc efforts. This interaction may be particularly relevant during the current subterranean struggles as General Secretary Gorbachev seeks to consolidate power and impose his priorities on the Soviet bureaucracy.

A third view is that under present political-economic conditions, the economic hypotenuse of the triangle is becoming an independent variable, which at any shorter length will alter the dimensions of the altitude and the base of the triad for both the Western and Eastern alliance systems. This paper will explore the ramifications of this third viewpoint.

II. THE UNITED STATES

The United States has recently undergone the largest ever peacetime buildup and modernization of its defense establishment, initiated in President Carter's last year of office following the Soviet invasion of Afghanistan, and continued and expanded under President Reagan. In part this development reflects a perceived lag in the U.S. strategic posture vis-à-vis that of the Soviet Union, which continued its own long-term buildup even while the U.S. had unilaterally capped its strategic offensive forces in quantity, if not quality. Moreover, U.S. modernization and readiness were lagging.

It also reflects a disillusionment with the progress and prospects for arms control. Some, including former arms limitation advocates, maintained that the actual effects have been at best neutral, if not indeed harmful, in ratifying (and thus encouraging) ever more and better nuclear weaponry on both sides. Arms control opponents claimed that the process has failed to impede Soviet efforts to gain superiority even as it hindered U.S. efforts to redress a deteriorating military balance.

Also involved, of course, are the Reagan Administration's political-ideological campaign to shrink the role of civilian government activities, its staunch anti-communist, anti-Soviet outlook (though its more extreme rhetoric has now been muted) and its conviction of the need for expanded defense efforts to catch up to a perceived higher level of threat from the Soviet bloc.

Under the Reagan Administration, from FY 1981 through 1991 as projected by OMB, there will have been no real increase in *non*defense government spending because both the FY '81 and '91 figures are $555 billion (in constant FY '82 dollars). But there will have been a 60 percent real increase in defense, which will have grown from 23 percent to 33 percent of total government (including off-budget items) outlays, while nondefense will have fallen from 77 percent to 67 percent. Congress, of course, may or may not act accordingly.

The point of this paper is not to agree or disagree with these viewpoints, but rather to explore their ramifications in defense economics.

Tables I and II below take the Administration's own figures—*before* mandated Gramm-Rudman-Hollings (GRH) cuts—and compare them with alternative U.S. economic growth paths and percentages of GNP allocated to defense.

Table I (in constant 1982 dollars, which factors out inflation) uses as growth alternatives ranges of 4 to 5, 2 to 3, and 1 to 2 percent, which are averaged to 4.5 percent, 2.5 percent and 1.5 percent real annual increases in GNP, respectively. It then applies defense percentages of GNP of 5 and 6 percent to each. Since 1970, except during the Vietnam War, the U.S. GNP share for defense has been either 5 or 6 percent—the latter primarily during the Reagan Administration buildup, which OMB projects to continue through 1991, as does the Pentagon.

It should be noted that the table lists or projects actual outlays, as

TABLE I

ESTIMATES OF REAL GNP GROWTH AND PROJECTED DEFENSE SPENDING AS A PERCENTAGE OF GNP
(billions of 1982 dollars)

	4.5% Real GNP	Percentage of GNP 5%	6%	2.5% Real GNP	Percentage of GNP 5%	6%	1.5% Real GNP	Percentage of GNP 5%	6%	Projected Total Outlays	Defense	Defense as a % of Outlays	GNP
1985	3576	179	215	3576	179	215	3576	179	215	846	227	27	6
1986	3736	187	224	3665	183	220	3629	182	218	856	232	27	6
1987	3905	195	234	3757	188	225	3684	184	221	829	238	28	6
1988	4080	204	245	3850	193	231	3739	187	225	824	243	29	6
1989	4264	213	256	3947	197	237	3795	190	228	830	236	30	6
1990	4456	223	267	4045	202	243	3852	193	231	828	266	32	6
1991	4656	233	279	4147	207	249	3910	196	235	830	275	33	6
1992	4866	243	292	4250	213	255	3968	198	238				
1993	5085	254	305	4356	218	261	4028	201	242				
1994	5314	266	319	4465	223	268	4088	204	245				
1995	5553	278	333	4577	229	275	4150	208	249				
1996	5803	290	348	4691	235	282	4212	211	253				
1997	6064	303	364	4809	240	289	4275	214	257				
1998	6337	317	380	4929	247	296	4339	217	260				
1999	6622	331	397	5052	253	303	4404	220	264				
2000	6920	346	415	5178	259	311	4470	224	268				

TABLE I (continued)

HISTORICAL AND PROJECTED DEFENSE AND NON-DEFENSE OUTLAYS
(billions of 1982 dollars. Numbers may not add up due to rounding)

	Total Outlays	Defense	Non-Defense	Percentage of GNP For Total Outlays	For Defense
1971	509	203	307	38	8
1972	528	191	337	34	7
1973	528	175	352	31	6
1974	529	163	365	30	6
1975	586	160	426	26	6
1976	610	154	456	24	5
1977	623	154	468	24	5
1978	652	155	497	23	5
1979	660	159	501	23	5
1980	699	164	535	23	5
1981	727	171	553	23	5
1982	745	185	560	25	6
1983	777	201	576	26	6
1984	789	210	578	27	6
1985	846	227	619	27	6
1986	856	232	618	27	6
1987	829	238	592	28	6
1988	824	243	582	29	6
1989	830	256	574	30	6
1990	828	266	562	32	6
1991	830	275	555	33	6

Source: Office of Management and Budget, "Historic Tables: Budget of the U.S. Government," Table 6.1

TABLE II

ESTIMATES OF GNP GROWTH AND PROJECTED DEFENSE SPENDING AS A PERCENTAGE OF GNP
(billions of current dollars)

FY	GNP estimates[1]	% Nominal Growth of GNP	Defense Spending[2]	Defense Spending as % of GNP
1987	4,538.1	8.3	311.6	6.9
1988	4,902.9	8.0	332.4	6.8
1989	5,268.9	7.5	353.5	6.7
1990	5,623.4	6.7	374.7	6.7
1991	5,955.2	5.9	395.5	6.6

[1]Office of Management and Budget, "Historic Tables: Budget of the U.S. Government," Table 6.2
[2]Department of Defense, "Annual Report to the Congress—Fiscal 1987, Executive Summary," Table 2

ESTIMATES OF 6% NOMINAL GNP GROWTH AND PROJECTED DEFENSE SPENDING
(billions of current dollars)

FY	GNP Nominal Growth of 6%	Percentage of GNP 5%	Percentage of GNP 6%	Defense Spending[1]	Defense Department Projections minus Defense Spending as % of GNP 5%	Defense Department Projections minus Defense Spending as % of GNP 6%
1987	4,538.1	226.9	272.3	311.6	84.7	39.3
1988	4,810.4	240.5	288.6	332.4	91.9	43.8
1989	5,099.0	255.0	305.9	353.5	98.5	47.6
1990	5,404.9	270.3	324.3	374.7	104.4	50.4
1991	5,729.2	286.5	343.8	395.5	109.0	51.7

[1]Department of Defense, "Annual Report to the Congress—Fiscal 1987, Executive Summary," Table 2

opposed to appropriations or new obligational authority.

The actual and projected calendar year 1985-91 defense expenditures in Table I exceed even six percent of real GNP for all years but one, except under a very high growth scenario of 4.5 percent, which practically no independent forecaster would predict today.[1]

The gaps between the resources thus projected and the stated requirements do appear manageable under the six percent alternative, on the 2.5 percent growth assumption, which appears to reflect current mainstream thinking in the economic community. However, over time it may be more realistic to expect the defense share to run closer to 5 percent of GNP, owing largely to congressional sentiment for deeper defense cuts, the intractable government budget deficit, and the deficit-related GRH mandate, which is complicated for the moment by the Supreme Court ruling on the role of the Comptroller General in the automatic enforcement provisions of the law.

Table I suggests that the gaps will not be manageable (under the medium growth, 5 percent of GNP, scenario) and could average over $50 billion in *annual* shortfall (in constant 1982 dollars) over the six calendar years from 1986-91.

Table II confirms this situation and magnifies it as stated in current dollars, assuming a nominal 6 percent growth in GNP—for example 2.5 percent growth and 3.5 percent inflation—where the gaps might average $98 billion per year from FY 87 to FY 91 under a 5 percent of GNP assumption and nearly $47 billion per year even under the 6 percent assumption.

It is not possible at this writing to factor in the impact of GRH on this picture, given the uncertainties of how both Congress and the Administration will finally respond to the Supreme Court decision. But assuming that the original GRH target of reducing the Federal deficit to $144 billion in FY 1987 is met, the Congressional Budget Office has estimated that under across-the-board cuts, a 15-plus percent cut would have to be made in the Administration's FY 1987 defense budget proposal (not outlays) of $320 billion and that such cuts would likely accelerate in future years.

This $50 billion GRH cut, in addition to any shortfalls projected from the preceding analysis, looms large in a long-range defense program in which Stealth costs may be upward of $80 billion; 100 new attack submarines could cost $100 billion; and 5,000 army light combat helicopters might require around $30 billion. Finally, $20-30 billion would be needed for SDI's R&D phases alone, according to estimates published in *Washington Post* articles. (Total 10-year costs of a

---

[1]Early hopes that lower energy costs and interest rates would stimulate growth at such higher rates have yet to be realized due in part to badly damaged sectors of the U.S. economy such as agriculture, mining, oil and energy and basic manufacturing, and in part to major losses of market share through massive trade deficits during the high dollar era.

deployed population defense system have been projected as high as $770 billion, with more limited, e.g. silo-type defense, estimated at $160 billion.[2]

Shortfalls of such magnitudes would appear to require substantial strategic and program adjustments beyond the tighter management and procurement reforms recommended by the Packard Commission, important as these measures may be in their own right.

The conclusion, starkly stated, is that under the most realistic political assessment of congressional willingness to fund defense priorities[3] and the most realistic economic scenarios, the U.S. cannot get from here to where the Administration wants to go in its national strategy and force posture.

If this conclusion proves correct, there are a number of possible lines of policy response:

(1) The government could simply ignore the budget deficit problem and let it grow as it will. Virtually all economists agree that this attitude could lead to disastrous consequences in the long run as inflation would rise, U.S. interest rates would go up sharply—in part to attract more of the foreign capital which is already financing over half of the deficit. The probable result would be domestic recession or a return to the stagflation of the seventies, even without the two crippling oil shocks that disrupted that decade.

(2) The Pentagon could try to muddle through, deferring some big ticket procurement, reprogramming, attempting to live off already appropriated but unspent funds, and hoping for the emergence of greater national consensus on the defense buildup and an economic growth path closer to the 4.5 percent upper range. Judging from past experience, this is the most likely bureaucratic response, since all the other alternatives are politically painful and bound to meet with objections.

(3) "National security" could be given enough priority to warrant major revenue increases, for example from income and income surtaxes, consumption taxes, oil import levies or energy or other user fees. This response seems out of tune with the current climate of "revenue neutral" tax reform, with the GRH mandate, and with the President's firmly stated opposition to tax increases of any kind.

(4) The government's nonmilitary expenditures could conceivably

---

[2]Various articles in *The Washington Post,* spring 1986; see, for example, March 22, 1986, p. A8. The SDI estimate is based on a study for the Johns Hopkins Foreign Policy Institute, reported in the *Post,* July 23, 1986, p. A12. The Pentagon disputes this or any other cost estimates at the present stage of research.

[3]As described in *The Secretary of Defense Annual Report to the Congress, FY 1987* (Washington: Department of Defense) 1986.

be trimmed even more, although many would argue that they have already been cut to the bone and major additional cuts would encounter fierce congressional opposition. In any case, what could be done in practice would seem far too little to meet defense gaps of the size outlined above.

(5) The entire U.S. approach to strategy and force posture could be revised. The challenge is awesome, to say the least, since among other things, it could reopen the bloody battles over roles and missions of the four services that raged in the late forties, call for assigning greater responsibility for European defense to the other NATO allies, essentially a burden-sharing issue; or require shifting to a reliance on mobilization as opposed to readiness. This last-mentioned adjustment would tacitly accept the risks inherent in reliance on political (as distinguished from strategic or tactical) warning, predicated on the assumption that signs of a more aggressive Soviet policy or buildup would become evident in time to employ mobilization[4] and reserve force assets—and that the U.S. and its allies could muster the consensus and political will to do so. Major cutbacks in defense spending would also entail curtailments and cancellations of major weapons systems, each with its own constituency. It would take a large team of expert defense policy analysts many months to outline such structural alternatives and estimate their costs and risks, and no such effort will be attempted here.[5]

(6) The Administration could actively embrace, rather than struggle against, the possibility of major East-West arms control regimes in a way that could lead to significantly lower military requirements. But, it takes two to tango and past Soviet responses to unilateral U.S. restraints have not been encouraging. Either the Soviets have proceeded with their own buildup out of sheer bureaucratic momentum, or they have calculated that U.S. restraints reveal a weakness that could be exploited to shift the correlation of forces further in their favor.

Whether the present Soviet leaders, given their current problems at

---

[4]There are, however, major questions about the adequacy of the U.S. mobilization base, as more and more capacity in certain vital but endangered industries, such as ferro-alloys, are driven offshore or out of business, leaving the United States dependent on foreign sources for important components and for strategic materials, many of which the United States has stockpiled, but now may sell off over time under the Administration's July 1985 proposal.

[5]One such expert, however, has had the courage to tackle the challenge alone. In *A Reasonable Defense,* (Washington, The Brookings Institution, 1986), Professor William W. Kaufmann compares alternative U.S. force structures against major combat scenarios. The foreword by Brookings president MacLaury summarizes Kaufmann's finding that "if U.S. forces could be coherently designed to address major U.S. vulnerabilities, they would not only outperform the currently programmed force, but would also save at least $200 billion in outlays between fiscal 1986 and fiscal 1990." (p. viii).

home, might respond with genuine mutuality will be explored later in this paper. There have, however, been some encouraging signs of progress—on intermediate range missiles for example—in the period since the abortive Reykjavik summit.

One must conclude, then, that the United States faces major, growing gaps between likely available resources for defense and the military requirements to be met.[6] The problem is postponable for only a short time; and ignoring it will not make it go away. There is, to paraphrase Henry Kissinger, a "necessity for choice"; and any inability in the American polity to face and make such choices has grave implications for the country's future. At the very least, many of the expenditures made or earmarked for defense may be wasted because the United States will be doing a great many things badly, with inadequate support training and spares, etc., instead of doing fewer top priority security tasks well.

III. NATO EUROPE

Without in any way diminishing the overall importance of Canada to the alliance, that country's military contribution to the defense of Europe is relatively small and it has been reduced over the years. Italy, Iberia, and the defense forces of countries on the northern and southern flanks, while vital to the security of these regions, are less relevant to the center. This section, therefore, will concentrate primarily on Germany, France and the United Kingdom, along with the Benelux countries as a group.[7]

Both Britain and France have experienced, on a smaller scale, the superpowers' dilemma of how to maintain adequate conventional strength while modernizing and increasing the survivability of their strategic nuclear components. The choices made have ultimately favored the latter, at the expense of the former.

West Germany has pursued a restrictive monetary and fiscal policy,

---

[6]Articles in the defense-oriented press have implied from time to time that even the spending *goals* of the Administration are inadequate to meet the actual requirements of its stated strategic objectives, a question which cannot be evaluated here; but if true, then the mismatch between funding and strategy becomes even more serious. For example, L. Korb and S. Paggett estimate the five-year shortfall at about 25 percent, or $500 billion against the nearly $2 trillion estimated for 1986–1990 in the February 1985 five-year Defense Plan, based on planned annual Pentagon requests of about $300 billion per year—which may be more than Congress will actually appropriate (*Defense News,* March 16, 1987). The Washington *Post* reports that a "Pentagon briefing on the shortfall for all services puts the total between $500 billion and $750 billion." (November 19, 1986, page A1)

[7]In 1985, according to NATO data, the United States contributed nearly 75 percent of the total US$358 billion defense spending by alliance members. Britain contributed 6.2 percent, France 5.4 percent, and Germany 5.3 percent. All the others together only add up to 7.7 percent of the total.

and evidently plans to continue this course, despite pleas from her allies, notably the United States, to shift to a more accommodative, lower-tax, growth-oriented approach in order to stimulate international trade. Thus real growth in the Federal Republic should average about 2.5 percent per annum for the next several years, and while defense will consume some 20 percent of total Federal spending, real annual growth in defense expenditure is likely to increase only by about one half of one percent, far below that of the economy as a whole. The German government's 1985 White Paper on defense states clearly that no substantial increases in defense are in sight, although an average expenditure of over 3 percent of GDP should continue. In addition, Germany is facing demographic problems which will, over time, shrink the available manpower pool for compulsory military service to a marginal level.

Britain is plagued with high and rising unemployment, despite substantially lowered inflation and a return to respectable real growth of about 2.5 percent. The Thatcher government's medium-term financial plan, with its tight fiscal and monetary policies, may generate tensions between defense programs and civilian public expenditures programs, especially as the sharp drop in world oil prices cuts into government revenues from North Sea oil. Following a few years of significant increases, mainly for nuclear modernization and the eventual replacement of Polaris submarine missiles, Britain's defense spending is likely to level off at or below inflation rates, i.e., with little or no real increases in the near term.

France is trying to adjust to an unprecedented "cohabitation" between a socialist President and a conservative Prime Minister and government. The resulting strains will intensify as the next national elections approach in 1988. Both parties have been staunch in maintaining and improving France's independent nuclear deterrent, albeit at the expense of some other military programs; and France will likely continue to allocate about 4 percent of its GDP to a defense posture which, while increasingly coordinated with NATO, is not integrated with it. As elsewhere in Europe, unemployment remains a significant problem, even with 2-3 percent real growth rates in the economy.[8]

Despite periodic crises as coalition governments are shuffled, both Belgium and the Netherlands have been able to allocate close to a 3 percent average of GDP for defense, even during disappointing

---

[8]A national service requirement is traditional in most nations on the continent. The writer has tested informed opinion in several European countries about the possibility of supplementing the career and conscripted forces with a volunteer force designed to utilize the large pools of unemployed manpower by providing salary incentives for longer tours of service. These could be paid for, in part, by transferring equivalent resources from social welfare agencies to defense ministries. Despite some apparent advantages in utilizing the unemployed for national defense functions, the concept has been coolly received, to say the least, and often simply dismissed as impractical.

economic performances. But the competition for resources for social welfare programs, especially those aimed at industrial restructuring and unemployment, will continue to limit defense expenditures to modest real annual increases at best.

Overall, NATO Europe's defense expenditures in constant prices have remained essentially flat over the years 1970-85, rising only slightly since the late seventies. In current dollars (converted at current exchange rates)[9], they have shown a slight downward trend since peaking in 1980.[10] The best one can say is that, absent some sharp upturn in threat perceptions, NATO Europe will barely hold its own, while the practically available resources will remain insufficient for highly ambitious conventional force improvement programs, let alone high-tech weaponry for some of the newer strategic concepts such as deep interdiction, air-land battle, and follow-on forces, or for strategic missile defense beyond limited R&D participation in SDI. This not-too-optimistic overview, reached independently by the writer in the course of economic surveys of Western Europe, is also confirmed by the International Institute for Strategic Studies reference to "the looming difficulties which will face NATO as its efforts to accelerate conventional defense improvements collide head-on with stringent resource constraints."[11]

Certainly, there is no realistic prospect that Europe will fill the gap implied by the preceding analysis of the U.S. requirements versus resources. This fact may be increasingly relevant if the U.S. balance of payments deficit remains intractably high, possibly forcing curtailment of U.S. government foreign exchange expenditures for various purposes, including NATO defense. The effect would be a rerun of the problems experienced by the United States and NATO in the late sixties.

Finally European opinion will remain vulnerable to Soviet "peace" initiatives, especially if they appear to offer some real substance which might lower defense burdens and relieve some of Europe's internal political tensions. However, as outlined in a forthcoming Atlantic Council study, there are other approaches to burden-sharing in a broader alliance context that ought to be explored.[12]

It would seem, then, that NATO as a whole faces the same dilemma of how to use limited resources more effectively in the defense, against a backdrop of a continuing Warsaw Pact conventional superiority, nuclear parity, and escalating costs of "smart" and other military technologies.

---

[9]This situation partially reflects the strength of the dollar against most foreign currencies until recently.

[10]Source: NATO Press Release, December 1985.

[11]The International Institute for Strategic Studies *Strategic Survey, 1985-86* (London: 1986), p. 92.

[12]See "Comprehensive Security: Balancing National Contributions to Western Prosperity" by Leonard L. Sullivan Jr. and Jack A. LeCuyer (Washington: University Press of America, 1987).

Something therefore may have to give in the central region of NATO, whether it be planned resort to tactical nuclear weapons at an earlier than desirable stage of conflict; greater reliance on resources and mobilization potential at the expense of readiness; or the use of heavier screening forces backed up by concentrations of mobile counterattack formations and defined strong points. This would have to take place at the expense of the "forward defense" which is politically vital to the West Germans or bold new efforts would be needed in such areas as mutual force reductions and anti-surprise attack measures with the East.

Failing any of the alternatives, the alliance leaders may have to take draconian steps to *force* economies of scale by improving the division of labor in defense procurement, intensifying standardization and interoperability, and constructing a better two-way procurement street across the Atlantic. Difficult as such steps may be politically, savings or effectiveness increases of up to 25 percent have been postulated by some experts.

Again, painful choices would be involved, and the instincts of NATO's civilian and military bureaucracies would be to maintain the flexible response strategy in effect for twenty years, despite a diminishing "thin blue line", making improvements at the margin when possible and in procurement when forced to do so. The point, of course, is that the U.S. and its allies must try to seek common solutions to shared problems, rather than unilateral ones.

IV. THE SOVIET UNION AND WARSAW PACT[13]

In March 1986 the CIA and DIA together submitted to the Joint Economic Committee of Congress a comprehensive report on "The Soviet Economy under a New Leader." Much has been written about that leader, General Secretary Mikhail Gorbachev, including the rapidity with which he has consolidated power, the concessions he may have made or will have to make to various power centers and factions, his assertiveness in establishing his agenda, with domestic economic reform at the top, during the 27th Party Congress and subsequently, and his supposed flexibility in dealing with the West. Less has been said, however, about the state of and prospects for the Soviet economy.

Gorbachev inherited an economy that was largely stagnant, with productivity declining as both investment and growth in the labor force tapered off. Energy and materials inputs reflected rising costs and the 1981-85 five year plan (FYP) was well below targets. One of the factors, other than general sluggishness, corruption and inefficiency, was

---

[13]Although this section draws heavily upon the analysis of "Soviet Economic Constraints on Defense to Year 2000" by John Hardt, which is incorporated into this paper as an appendix, the evaluations and comments are those of the writer.

the direct and indirect costs of the massive military buildup. That effort increased from roughly 12 percent of GNP in the seventies to about 16 percent in the early eighties. Moreover, the recent annual growth rate of that buildup has outstripped the growth of the economy, which averaged under 3 percent for the FYP just ended, in effect robbing the nonmilitary sector of vital inputs, although there is a complementarity between the military and civilian industrial complexes which must be taken into account.[14]

One must add to these factors the dramatic decline in world oil prices, especially when priced in cheaper dollars, which may lead to a $5-7 billion loss in hard currency in 1986, as well as the $2.8 billion estimated costs of the Chernobyl nuclear accident. It is clear as Gorbachev starts his effort to reform and modernize the Soviet economy that he faces an uphill struggle and is unlikely to achieve his ambitious goals.[15] His objectives envisage GNP growth of 3.5 percent a year for 1986-90, 5 percent from 1991-2000, with the agricultural target at 3 percent and industrial output at 4.5 percent, an increase of 150 percent in productivity by 2000, higher oil and gas production, and large order of magnitude increases in both the quantity and quality of consumer goods. Few Western observers believe such goals are attainable, at least without "unleashing" the economy in ways that could be dangerous ideologically and politically.

Dr. Hardt's analysis of the Gorbachev dilemma (Appendix) postulates three alternative scenarios:

(1) The projection of past trends, with defense allocation characterized as incremental, ideological, and institutional;

(2) defense buildup in response to perceived foreign threats or opportunities, with defense allocations essentially unconstrained by civilian needs; and

(3) A pragmatic approach, with reduced defense burdens and a reassessment of the world environment, strategy, forces and budgets. This would involve the triad of elements in the triangular analogy outlined in Section I.

It would appear to be in the West's interest to respond to current Soviet arms control initiatives in ways that would encourage the third scenario. If the Soviets choose to face the hard choices, as Dr. Hardt points out, they will be faced less in the fiscal-budgetary terms which are the driving constraints in the West than in the difficult and costly allocation of specific physical resources and plant capacity, particularly machinery and procurement, manpower, and the ingredients of scientific development. Qualified R&D personnel will be in short supply,

---

[14]See IISS, *Military Balance, 1985-86,* pp. 17-18. This source, however, also underscores the many unresolved methodological problems in assessing Soviet military expenditures.

[15]See Appendix for details.

as will computer-literate workers and the owners of other high-tech skills. Moreover, the Soviet demographic problem is growing. Most population increases are occurring in the non-Slavic and Central Asian regions to the point that the Great Russians may already be a minority in "Russia."

More detailed analysis can be found in the Appendix. It implies, however, that the West may have available both a carrot and a stick. To choose the latter, in which case the West would observe no arms control constraints and proceed to maximize its technological advantages, such as SDI and new subnuclear military potentials, would probably propel Gorbachev toward the second, or buildup scenario. He would then be forced to abandon his goals for the civilian economy, except for its spinoff benefits from military modernization. But this course would also intensify the West's own dilemma of resources versus requirements. In such contests, totalitarian states have an inherent advantage over democracies when it comes to enforced belt-tightening, even though the latter, as wealthier countries, may have more slack to take up. The political consequences of a renewed cold war and essentially unconstrained arms buildup on the chances for stable security by the year 2000 are also formidable, for a high threat perception and response by one side will almost inevitably produce a counter-response by the other.

The carrot on the other hand, could offer a lower threat perception, make possible clear constraints (if verifiable) on defense and especially strategic, deployments, and hence bring about the shorter economic hypotenuse suggested in Section I. This prospective easing of their guns vs. butter dilemma would encourage the Soviet leadership towards Scenario 3, the "pragmatic reassessment," which could prove mutually reinforcing in terms of East-West relations, and a favorable vector toward stable and mutual security as the century winds down.[16]

In purely military-economic terms, the Soviet Union's Warsaw Pact allies contribute less than 10 percent to the total Pact expenditures of approximately US$275 billion.[17] This contrasts with the more than 25 percent provided by the U.S. NATO allies. Nevertheless, their manpower, economic potential, and geographic location are of great strategic and political importance to the U.S.S.R. Because of the high degree of Pact military integration and to a lesser extent, economic integration under CMEA, we need not discuss the six non-Soviet Pact members individually, after noting that their national interests vary. (In MBFR negotiations, for example, East Germany hewed closely to

---

[16]For more details of this scenario—and its alternatives, see the writer's article on "Strategic Stability and Mutual Security in the Year 2000, Getting There From Here" in the U.N.'s *Disarmament* magazine (forthcoming) in a report on a U.N. meeting of experts in Erice, Italy, April 1986.

[17]As estimated and converted in the *IISS, Military Balance, 1985-86,* cited.

the Soviet line; Poland made known its own interests in achieving a reduction of the superpower (read Soviet) deployments in Europe and easing both the manpower and economic burdens of defense; and Rumania played its customary maverick role.)

For this discussion we can assume that the future options of the other Warsaw Pact countries are tied to those outlined above for the Soviet Union. But they display even greater tendencies to seek butter over guns in their economic tradeoffs, for with spotty exceptions, the CMEA economic performance in recent years has been plagued by economic reversals and debt problems. Thus the Soviet Union can expect even less help from its Warsaw Pact allies which, as the Appendix points out, are a net cost to Moscow in both military and economic terms, than can the United States from its NATO allies. In neither case, however, can the superpower concerned look to its alliance system for significant relief from its own resource squeeze.

V. CONCLUSIONS

A medium-to-low threat perception on both sides coupled with medium-to-low economic growth rates, could reinforce other incentives toward arms control and even limited disarmament. But initially

TABLE III
PROGRAM COSTS

FY 1986

(Billions of dollars of budget authority)

Program

Strategic forces	29.9
General purpose forces	132.1
Intelligence and communications	27.9
Airlift and sealift	8.0
National Guard and Reserve	16.9
Research and development	30.4
Central supply and maintenance	26.5
Training, medical and other general personnel activities	35.6
Administration and associated activities	5.9
Support of other nations	0.5
Total budget authority	313.7

Source: *Budget of the U.S. Government, FY 1986* and estimates of William W. Kaufmann in *A Reasonable Defense* (Washington: The Brookings Institution, 1986), Table 2.7. Kaufmann estimates total direct and indirect "strategic nuclear retaliation" costs at $51.5 billion, theater nuclear retaliation at $3.2 billion, and conventional defense of NATO Europe, excluding the Atlantic, as $107.2 billion, *Ibid.,* Table 2-6.

there will not likely be significant savings, since nuclear forces are a relatively small part of the whole. For the United States, at least, achieving substantial budgetary savings would require cancellation of entire weapons programs, closing of installations, and large-scale reductions of personnel—which, however, could be accomplished on the military side by greater emphasis on reserves. There is always a high initial cost for such measures, which only pay for themselves over time. Some rough indications of current budget breakdowns by mission are contained in Table III.

It should be emphasized, however, that potential economic savings of whatever magnitude are not enough of a magnet to draw either superpower away from a course it considers essential for its major national security objectives. And their mutual relations will be characterized for the foreseeable future as a mixture of competitive and cooperative elements.

Even though it is unlikely that there will be a substantial detente dividend in an economic sense, the stresses and strains of coping with a growing divergence between defense requirements and resources on both sides, as a minimum, may create incentives to reduce the pressure by easing off on the requirements side, improving the climate for the third scenario for the USSR in Section IV and making way for a parallel reassessment for the United States and for NATO. Arms control negotiators are, by necessity negotiating about each other's intentions as well as capabilities.

Under any but the worst scenario, however, structural change will probably have to come to the Pentagon over time. The real squeeze, one hopes, however, would come only after renewed arms control progress is on course and verifiable. As President Reagan stated in his February 26, 1986 address to the nation, perceptions of U.S. weakness or lack of will in defense can only weaken Soviet incentives for arms control concessions. The need for effective dialogue between East and West is thus apparent.

On the other hand, a high threat perception by either side would generally produce a reciprocal response by the other, leading to renewed tensions and higher defense requirements. The Soviet Union would find it easier to cope politically with such a development than would democracies, especially under low-growth assumptions. For the United States, this situation could mean a significant rise in the overall tax burden, unless we also postulate a long-term high growth scenario, which is without precedent in this country.

Burden-sharing may again become an issue within the alliance unless the U.S., European, and Japanese assessments of the threat are more nearly parallel than they have been traditionally. It is a common assumption that real threats to the peace are more likely to arise in the Third World than in Europe. Unless the other industrialized countries feel themselves directly at risk, this attitude could become divisive, endangering the cohesion of the alliance and impeding its approach to common problems of resource allocation.

As we look ahead to the year 2000, it appears that both East and West are likely to face an increasingly painful ends and means dilemma which is parallel in some respects, and asymmetrical in others. If each side sees the other's problem in a zero-sum game context as a weakness to be exploited, then little can be expected beyond continued mutual insecurity at mounting costs and consequences to the economies of all concerned. But if each side is prepared to look at its strained "economic hypotenuse" in positive-sum terms, then perhaps improved mutual security may be obtainable at lower costs—and even more important, with lower risks of military conflict and escalation to thermonuclear disaster.

This is the crux of the issue facing both leaders. Some of President Reagan's advisers are urging that this is precisely the time to maximize the armaments squeeze on the Soviet Union, hoping thereby to intensify its economic crisis and force major concessions. The writer believes this misjudges the Soviet character, which has always responded negatively to perceptions of external pressure, and underestimates their ability to sustain a garrison state if necessary. Additional viewpoints by Soviet specialists are noted in the Appendix.

Conversely, advisors in Moscow undoubtedly point to the West's economic constraints as reasons why they should not pay any substantial price, in arms controls or other concessions, for the more tranquil external environment Gorbachev has said he needs in order to concentrate on domestic problems. This, too, seems to the writer to be a misjudgment of the Western resolve.

Nevertheless, by the end of the decade, the United States is probably going to have to choose between the difficult options outlined in Section II, specifically No. 5: major defense restructuring, which would be better done in conjunction with major arms control measures, not as ends in themselves, but as the other side of the overall security coin. And here, the Soviet dilemma is quite parallel, as suggested by new signs of greater civilian control over military spending and deployments, as in the Far East and Afghanistan.

The possibility of an East-West superpower summit meeting within the next six months offers the chance to explore and test whether a real window of opportunity for improved East-West relations is there to be opened, or whether it is only an illusion created by the so-called "Americanists" who now hold key positions in the Soviet foreign policy establishment, in order to affect western public opinion.

With both Secretary Gorbachev and President Reagan self-confident and relatively secure in the leadership of their respective constituencies, the time seems ripe for a real dialogue, with all of the cards on the table, about future East-West relations and arms control possibilities. Some general and positive guidelines from the top, for example about SDI limitations and strategic offensive cuts, would then enable the negotiators for both sides to seek real progress in their various fora.

Appendix to Chapter VIII

SOVIET ECONOMIC CONSTRAINTS ON DEFENSE TO YEAR 2000

*John P. Hardt**

DEFENSE ECONOMICS IN FLUX

The Soviet Union, like the United States, appears to be at a point of potential change in the priority and process for economic allocations to defense. While Gorbachev's focus on the revitalization and reform of the economy as the central task of the leadership for the rest of the century suggests that changes in methods of planning and management may occur throughout the economy, including defense support, the outcomes remain uncertain. In this context, we may see one of several different scenarios developing with respect to both the way economic decisions are made in the defense sector and the kind of decisions that result.

(1) The first scenario consists of a projection of the past trends established under Brezhnev. In this case, a defense buildup may be supported in areas of competition with the United States and in areas of perceived opportunity even though requirements for improved economic performance could have a dampening effect on defense budgets. This *Past Projection Scenario* also would seem to find the Soviet defense establishment continuing to dictate the progress of new programs within the policy framework of the defense philosophy of the past, i.e., responding to new technological developments in the West and servicing global commitments, while retaining capabilities for the defense of the homeland. Under this scenario, defense allocation decisionmaking might be described as incremental, ideological and institutional.

*Personal views of the author, not necessarily those of the Congressional Research Service, the United States Congress or any United States government agency

Under Brezhnev, military allocations were constrained by economic performance, but increased sufficiently to support a substantial military buildup, the policy basis of which was both ideological and pragmatically political. Constrained by civil needs and performance, defense allocations were *incremental;* although influenced by pragmatic, Great Power politics, the policy framework was dominated by *ideological* and *institutional* criteria. The Soviet Union may continue to increase its military expenditures in this way. With slowing overall growth, defense growth (measured in dollars) is estimated to have remained at a two percent rate from 1974-1985—half the rate of the previous decade. (Measured in rubles and assuming increasing cost of procurement, the slowdown would be somewhat less severe.) Even with slower overall growth in the economy, according to United States intelligence estimates the share of GNP allocated to defense increased from 13-14 percent of Soviet GNP in the early 1970s to 15-17 percent by the early 1980s; in dollar equivalents defense was $146.2 billion in 1985. In this period, the qualitative inputs to the military balance from Soviet military procurement, manpower and R & D were sufficient to assure attainment of bipolar parity.

(2) Perceptions of threats or foreign opportunities may dictate an increase in the growth of allocations to defense. A breakdown in arms negotiations and a decision to confront the United States, NATO, and other Western countries more aggressively might lead to an increase at least to the trend lines of the pre-1974 period that is, 4.5 percent growth per annum. In this *Defense Buildup Scenario,* decision-making would be largely unconstrained by needs and performance of the civilian economy and would be largely ideologically and institutionally driven.

If the Soviet leadership decides to allocate more to defense in response to perceived opportunities or threats and if the economy grows as planned, the Soviets might be able and willing to devote twice the increase of resources to defense without materially changing the defense share of total output. The defense procurement rate of the early Brezhnev period (1968-74) of 4-4.5 percent might return or be exceeded. However, assuming economic growth and constrained defense allocations are closely related, a high defense budget would probably have to be pursued at the expense of civilian programs and stepped-up performance. A resumed buildup of manpower, as occurred during the late Khrushchev period for manning the China border and replacing Czech forces in the Warsaw Pact, might not fully return but the pressure to reduce military manpower might be resisted. Military research and development would likely be increased, but how effective it would be in meeting the new technological challenges may be open to question.

(3) A modified, restructured and lower defense claim on the economy might be an outgrowth of Gorbachev's new strategy.

A greater emphasis on regional over global threat assessments, greater attention to the economic and political value of the trade-offs to defense, and an increased Party involvement in military policy and defense planning could together lead to a *Reduced Defense Burden, Pragmatic Scenario*. Such a scenario would be closer to the more pragmatic, politically oriented process of U.S. defense planning and more likely to produce a reduced economic burden. If some further restraint on defense were to derive from Gorbachev's priority to domestic investment and consumption and a perception of an environment conducive to arms negotiations, the defense share would likely fall.

The late 1980s and 1990s may be a period of change in the trend and level of growth of resources for defense in both the Soviet Union and the United States. Economic and political modernization, revitalization and reform are the central ingredients of the strategy of Gorbachev coming out of his first Party Congress—the 27th Congress of the CPSU in February-March 1986. With the possibility of restraints on defense budget growth deriving from budgetary constraints and the possibility of a process of arms control negotiations relating to bilateral Summits, the United States may share a prospective down-turn in defense priority and a reform in the administration of defense, at least in procurement.

Soviet change under the spirit of the Gorbachev strategy of the 27th Party Congress would move away from the past resource policy of *incremental* growth—an increasing share of absolute and relative goods and services devoted to defense; *ideological* threat assessment—balancing a global view of Moscow-centered Communism with a more pragmatic Great Power and regional perspective; *institutionalization* in defense planning and programming that relies less on the decisions generated by the military-industrial complex and rather more on the broader political view of the top Party. The ideological component would be less in enforcing a Suslov-Brezhnev type doctrine with the CMEA-Warsaw Pact and more in flexibility in dealing with Communist parties abroad as similar to other parties in non-Socialist countries.

The 'commanding heights' approach of politicalization takes power for policy and planning up from the Ministerial and regional party levels to the 'super' Ministries and Politburo and Secretariat of the Central Committee with skilled staff at the Secretariat level providing the administrative muscle for increased top Party control. Applied to the military bureaucracy, this would, by analogy, shift the policy decision-making and key information support and implementation up to the level of the Party Secretariat.

Let us explore these three scenarios in the context of the defense decision-making process with emphasis on the third: a scenario with constrained defense spending and restructured defense decision-making that moves toward the more pragmatic, politicized American model. Such a scenario may be considered most consistent with Gorbachev's rhetoric and his requirements: it would respond to the incremental burden of rising military costs, address the special requirements of space-age research and development, and support Gorbachev's commitment to improved economic performance.

I. TRIAD OF DECISON MAKING: GORBACHEV'S MOVEMENT TOWARD A REDUCED DEFENSE, PRAGMATIC MODEL.

Mikhail Gorbachev seems to be interested in changes in the triad of defense decision-making: a reassessment of the world environment or a revised threat assessment; a reevaluation of military programs and security strategies; and a consideration of military programs and budgets in the context of economic constraints or burden assessments. It remains a question, however, in just what sequence these changes may be considered, and whether the institutional imperatives of the defense establishment rather than threat or environment assessment still drive military programs.

But just as the leadership in the United States seems constrained by budgetary limitations that restrict military and domestic programs, the Soviet leadership may feel the burdens of budgetary limitations as the competitive claims of investment and consumption restrict their defense allocations (Gramm-Rudman in the USA; Gorbachev-Ryzhkov in the USSR). The budgetary constraints may in turn lead to reevaluation of the other aspects of decision-making.

A. International Environment Estimate (Threat Assessment)

The assessments of the international security environment by the Party leadership and defense institutions are becoming global assessments of requirements based more on a pragmatic Great Power role rather than on ideological considerations as in the past. The appointment of Anatoly Dobrynin to the Secretariat of the Party, assuming the position occupied for years by Boris Ponomarev, presents some evidence of this shift from ideology toward pragmatism by focusing more foreign policy expertise and clout in the Party Secretariat. Power in foreign and security policy (arms negotiations) has shifted toward the Secretariat. Although the regional and global assessments that result may still be inimical to U.S. interests, they may nevertheless be more pragmatic. These threat assessments may thus be likened in Gorbachev's calculus to some political cost-effectiveness scale that would provide a basis for negotiation and for the limitation of military claims on resources.

B. Requirements Planning and Programming

Military programs and security strategies that may have been driven in the past by bureaucratic pressure (from the Defense Council and the Ministry of Defense complex) may now be coming more under top leadership control. Moreover, the psychology of past defense orientation and post war experience may be giving way to a new generation's assessment based more on pragmatic Great Power politics.

Such trends in defense planning might be advanced if the Soviet leadership applies the same principle of economic reform to the defense economy that is being adopted in agriculture. In this case, it might centralize key policy analysis and decision-making for the defense establishment at top Party and government levels and decentralize management decisions. A national security unit created in the Party (such as the Economic Department in the Secretariat of the Central Committee) could take on a role similar to that of the National Security Council in the United States with the Party Secretariat unit developing its own staff. A Party Politburo member such as Lev Zaikov, who currently holds the defense industry portfolio in the Politburo, might be Gorbachev's designated civilian security adviser, with the Defense Council taking on a role like that of the Joint Chiefs of Staff and with the new Party Secretariat security unit staff providing support for Zaikov. On the government side, the creation of a National Security Committee (such as Gosagroprom for agriculture) could provide Gorbachev and Ryzhkov a unit above the Ministry of Defense Industries that could coordinate and oversee both defense and civilian management.

C. Economic Constraints and Defense Burden

New strains could be placed on defense spending under the pressures of Gorbachev's economic prescriptions: (1) his emphasis on energizing the economy and using the best cadres for civilian production enterprises; (2) the intensification of industry and agriculture requiring larger shares of growth for investment and consumption; (3) improvement in the scientific and research establishment to compete in the technological-information revolution. In each case, the deferral of military claims, an increase in the openness of the military production and research establishment, and the sharing of high quality military assets may be required to bring about improved economic performance.

The Gorbachev Five-Year (1986-1990) and Fifteen-Year Plans (1986-2000) call for higher growth, improved capital efficiency, labor productivity and quality of output for which a dynamic and productive research and development environment is essential. The formula for reaching these economic goals, necessary for the political and military claimants alike, involves short term military sacrifices and change. Such changes could be necessary to attain an improved civilian technological-economic base that will allow for long-term civilian and military competitiveness (this could be called the larger thrust of SDI).

II. GORBACHEV'S TRADEOFFS: GUNS OR GROWTH

Even more than budgetary pressures, limited physical resources and capacity may severely constrain growth of Soviet military allocations. Soviet leadership is not constrained by its state budget but by physical resource limitations. Moreover, the aggregate levels are not the burden specific physical resource limitations present the tradeoff problems. The hard choices are to be found especially in procurement, manpower, and research and development:

Procurement—The incremental priority requirements of machinery for fulfilling Gorbachev's Five and Fifteen Year Plans of modernization squeeze incremental military procurement demands.

Manpower—The reduction in the available draft-age manpower cohort and the increasingly non-Slavic character of this cohort will make it difficult to maintain current military manpower levels without denying increments to the civilian labor force and without enhancement of the education of the cadre; there will be more competition for the limited number who are educated.

R&D—Future military and civilian needs in the age of SDI require opening, diversion or amalgamation of the priority military R&D establishment with the backward and less productive civilian scientific establishment.

A. Military-Civilian Tradeoffs: Procurement

To the extent the Soviets have difficulty finding the resources to simultaneously meet Gorbachev's industrial modernization goals and satisfy military requirements in the near term, a central problem of choice will arise in the machinery sector which traditionally has allocated a large portion of its output to the military.[1]

As noted by U.S. intelligence assessments, the increased demands for resources needed for these programs will be centered around several areas:

• *Factory Capacity.* Implicit in Gorbachev's call for increased output of advanced machinery is the competition—in the absence of rapid plant expansion—for modern workspace at production facilities. In this connection, robots, computer-numerically-controlled machine tools, computer-aided design systems, flexible manufacturing systems, and other highly automated manufacturing systems are important for the production of both advanced manufacturing equipment needed for boosting industrial productivity and for producing sophisticated weapon systems.

---

[1]"The Soviet Economy Under a New Leader," a paper prepared jointly by the Central Intelligence Agency and the Defense Intelligence Agency submitted to the Subcommittee on Economic Resources, Competitiveness, and Security Economics of the Joint Economic Committee, U.S. Congress, March 19, 1986, 43 pages.

• *Basic Materials.* Chemicals and metals are used in producing both weapons and advanced machinery. The ferrous metals ministry, for example, has failed to meet its targets for many types of steel in recent years.

• *Intermediate Products.* Engineering plastics, advanced composite materials, electronic components, and microprocessors are currently in high demand in the defense industry and, as modernization proceeds, will be needed increasingly by civil industry as well. These products, however, are in short supply.

• *Labor.* Both the defense industry and modern civil industry require highly skilled workers, particularly computer technicians and software engineers.

The near-term competition for factory floorspace and investment goods has been mitigated by the substantial expansion and upgrading of defense-industrial plants over the past decade. Comprehensive programs to modernize many weapons production facilities began in the early 1970s. Efforts to modernize defense industry accelerated in the late 1970s, and we believe a large portion of the best domestically produced machinery was delivered to defense industry during this period. In addition, the defense sector was helped by a surge in clandestine and open acquisition of Western manufacturing equipment.[2]

In the short-run—into the early 1990s—competition for additional investment goods for new capacity will not, they argue, be critical, as the joint CIA-DIA assessment sees the investment crunch coming in the 1990s:

As a result of this investment in defense industry, almost all of the production capacity required to support Soviet force modernization over the next six years or so is already in place. Our calculations suggest that virtually no additional investment in the plant and equipment is needed to manufacture the military hardware that we believe will be in production in 1986-88 and that most of the capacity required to turn out the military equipment projected to be in production in the early 1990s is already available. Moreover, weapons development and industrial construction indicate that investment in defense industries will continue at a high level, adding new capacity with greater capabilities. Thus, military production would not be constrained in the near term by a reallocation of new fixed investment in favor of civilian machinery and other priority sectors.

Although the Soviets have the production capacity to maintain or even increase the current level of weapons production, competition for labor and material inputs used in the production process could force some trade-offs at the margin between military and civilian production. The nature of this competition is shown in Figure 1 which summarizes our judgments on (a) the degree of

----

[2]*Ibid.,* p. 21.

USSR: Military-Civil Competition for Resources *

Resource	Need in Civilian MBMW Sector for Modernization	Availability Outside of MBMW Sector	Transferability from Military to Civilian MBMW	Comment
Materials				
Basic/Raw:				
Energy	Medium	High	High	
Intermediate:				
Chemical feed stock	High	Medium	Med-High	
Engineering fibers	High	Low-Med	High	In very short supply in both sectors.
Micro-electronics	High	Low	High	
Specialty steel	Med-High	High	Med-High	
Aluminum	Med-High	High	High	
Titanium	Medium	Medium	Medium	
Construction materials	Medium	High	High	
Intermediate Products				
Conventional:				
Electric motors	Med-High	Low	Med-High	
Diesel engines	Med-High	Low	Med-High	
Advanced:				
Engineering plastics	High	Low-Med	High	
Micro-processors	High	Low-Med	High	
Composites	Medium	Low-Med	Medium	
Micro-electronic components	High	Low	Medium	In short supply.
Manpower				
Skilled:				
Computer programers	High	Low-Med	High	Shortage exists throughout economy.
Electronics technicians	High	Low-Med	High	
Software engineers	High	Low-Med	High	
Researchers	Med-High	Med-High	Medium	
Machinists	Medium	Low-Med	High	
Industrial engineers	Medium	Low-Med	High	
Unskilled:				
Laborers	Low-Med	High	High	

need for the particular resource in civilian machinery, (b) its availability in non-machinery sectors of the economy, and (c) how easy it would be to shift the resource from military defense industry to civilian machinery.

High-quality steel and energy, for example, will be in great demand to manufacture machines needed for both industrial modernization and weapons production. The high targets the Soviets have set for machinery production will place tremendous demands on the ferrous metals branch. This industry, however, has been doing poorly in recent years and apparently will receive little, if any, increase in investment during the 1986-90 FYP. Although there is likely to be some growth in the energy sector, the energy situation may be tight.

Others see the defense claims affecting economic performance in the current 1986-1990 Plan differently in terms of the timing of the difficult choices. Dr. Jan Vanous notes, "we found that the amount of machinery available for investment and defense use combined will not be adequate, at least in 1986, under any reasonable scenario to satisfy both domestic investment and defense needs. Moreover, *except in the case when the growth of domestic defense machinery production is slashed to 4 percent per year during 1986-90,* which is an extremely slow growth rate by historical standards—*the Soviets do not stand a reasonable chance of freeing enough machinery for investment purposes to achieve their ambitious investment and capital modernization target.*"[3]

B. Military-Civilian Tradeoffs: Manpower

Quantitatively hard choices will have to be made among allotments for the civilian labor force, the university student cadre and the military. The difficult decisions on qualitative allocations involve regional, ethnic, and educational limitations on quality and reliability of current draft age cohorts.

During the 1980s, the 'second echo of World War II,' is preventing the Soviet leadership from maintaining the military manpower level, while increasing the civilian labor force. (Table 1). As indicated by Dr. Murray Feshbach's analysis of the Soviet census, the U.S.S.R. will not be able to keep up military force levels and expand the labor force at the same time until the 1990s. Thus, the short-term competition for human resources could be even more intense than for investment and material resources. Extensive underemployment exists in the Soviet economy, and Gorbachev may hope that he can support his modernization program by mobilizing currently underemployed engineers

---

[3]Jan Vanous and Bryan Roberts, 'Time to Choose between Tanks and Tractors: Why Gorbachev Must Come to the Negotiating Table or Face a Collapse of His Ambitious Modernization Program,' *Plan Econ,* Inc., Volume II, June 27, 1986. [original underlined].

TABLE 1—ESTIMATES AND PROJECTIONS OF THE NUMBER OF 18-YEAR OLD MALES IN THE U.S.S.R., R.S.F.S.R.,* CENTRAL ASIA, KAZAKHSTAN, AND TRANSCAUCASUS, 1970-2000**
(In thousands, except percent)

Year	U.S.S.R.	R.S.F.S.R.	Central Asia, Kazakhstan and Trans-caucasus	Central Asia and Kazakhstan	Central Asia	Central Kazakh-stan	Trans-caucasus	R.S.F.S.R. (As a percent of U.S.S.R.)	Central Asia, Kazakhstan and Trans-caucasus (As a percent of U.S.S.R.)	Central Asia and Kazakhstan (As a percent of U.S.S.R.)	C. Asia Kazakhstan and Trans-caucasus as a percent of R.S.F.S.R.
1970	2,229	1,258	411	301	171	130	110	56.4	18.4	13.5	32.7
1971	2,247	1,264	430	312	185	127	118	56.7	19.1	13.9	34.0
1972	2,174	1,226	424	312	185	127	112	56.4	19.5	14.4	34.6
1973	2,410	1,327	485	354	213	141	131	55.1	20.1	14.7	36.5
1974	2,469	1,345	534	392	244	148	142	54.5	21.6	15.9	39.7
1975	2,465	1,301	556	408	257	151	148	52.8	22.6	16.6	42.7
1976	2,526	1,327	577	425	265	160	152	52.5	22.8	16.8	43.5
1977	2,593	1,335	608	447	280	167	161	51.5	23.4	17.2	45.5
1978	2,619	1,330	630	461	287	174	169	50.8	24.1	17.6	47.4
1979	2,674	1,354	663	492	312	180	171	50.6	24.8	18.4	49.0
1980	2,601	1,296	670	497	315	182	173	49.8	25.8	19.1	51.7
1981	2,484	1,206	663	494	316	178	169	48.6	26.7	19.9	55.0
1982	2,383	1,132	661	491	321	170	170	47.4	27.7	20.6	58.4
1983	2,236	1,030	652	485	325	160	167	46.1	29.2	21.7	63.3
1984	2,111	979	620	465	306	159	155	46.4	29.4	22.0	63.3
1985	2,102	962	618	466	310	156	152	45.8	29.4	22.2	64.2
1986	2,024	906	606	462	310	152	144	44.8	29.9	22.8	66.9
1987	2,016	886	623	474	329	149	145	43.9	30.9	23.6	70.3
1988	2,007	895	612	481	325	148	138	44.6	30.5	23.7	68.4
1989	2,056	913	626	481	333	148	145	44.4	30.4	23.4	68.6
1990	2,128	949	650	505	352	153	145	44.6	30.5	23.7	68.5
1991	2,143	969	641	502	348	154	139	45.2	29.9	23.4	66.2
1992	2,132	961	657	516	361	155	141	45.1	30.8	24.2	68.4
1993	2,204	1,000	680	538	375	163	142	45.4	30.9	24.4	68.0
1994	2,234	1,013	695	551	386	165	144	45.3	31.1	24.7	68.6
1995	2,286	1,032	723	573	402	171	150	45.1	31.6	25.1	70.1
1996	2,336	1,054	743	588	414	174	155	45.1	31.9	25.2	70.5
1997	2,389	1,076	766	606	428	178	160	45.0	32.1	25.4	71.2
1998	2,441	1,095	789	624	441	183	165	44.9	32.3	25.6	72.1
1999	2,488	1,111	814	643	456	187	171	44.7	32.7	25.8	73.3
2000	2,529	1,121	837	661	470	191	176	44.3	33.1	26.1	74.7

Source: Unpublished estimates and projections prepared by the Foreign Demographic Analysis Division, U.S. Bureau of the Census, in March 1977.

*Russian Soviet Federated Socialist Republic

**Murray Feshbach, "Prospects for Outmigration in Central Asia and Kazakhstan in the Next Decade," Soviet Economy in A Time of Change, GPO: Washington, D.C. Joint Economic Committee, Volume 1 1979 p. 701.

and labor. But shortages persist in the U.S.S.R. in several skill areas (as indicated in Figure 1). Critical to both defense and modernization, for example, are systems analysts, computer programmers and selected types of engineers and skilled machinists. Thus, the most likely immediate source of additional specialists for the civilian machine building metal working industry is a reallocation of the employees already working in the machinery sector through increased labor productivity.

Soviet additions to the military will be predominantly non-Slavic, especially youth from Central Asia and Kazakhstan. This change in the draft age labor force pool adds a qualitative factor to the quantitative shortage. Rural Central Asians tend to be less skilled and educated, and many have limited Russian language facility.

C. Military-Civilian Tradeoffs: R&D

In the past, military R&D has received priority over civilian programs. Well funded and staffed, with supplementary inputs to its core military programs gained from effective foreign intelligence, the military R&D program has provided a basis for keeping up, closing the technical gaps in many traditional military areas, and moving ahead in some. In the 1990s, military and civilian technological needs alike will be met only if the Soviet scientific establishment can join the technical information revolution of the West. The research base required for the U.S. Strategic Defense Initiative (SDI) is an important factor in determining the range of likely needs for efficient and effective military and civilian establishments. The demands of new weapons development, the shift to an intensive economy and the greater emphasis on innovation, point to the need for reform in the Soviet approach to defense allocations. The continued decoupling of defense and civilian sectors of the economy deprives the total system of a stronger advanced technological base and reduces prospects for overall productivity increases.

The U.S. SDI program is organized in five specific research areas. These consist of Kinetic Energy Weapons Technologies (KEW); Directed Energy Weapons Technologies (DEW); Systems Analysis and Battle Management (SA/BM); Surveillance, Acquisition, Tracking and Kill Assessment (SATKA); and Survivability, Lethality and Key Technologies (SLKT). The scope of technologies embedded in the SDI symbolizes the enormous difficulties inherent in preparing the Soviet military for the next century if the reforms in research and development now under consideration by Gorbachev are not implemented.[4]

Condoleeza Rice of Stanford University writes:

There are those in the Soviet military who are arguing that it is really in the area of new technologies, microelectronics, particle

---

[4]The discussion of SDI is essentially from communication with Barry Breindel, Manager, Research and Defense, Washington Operations, Aerojet Telesystems Co.

beam weapons, and artificial intelligence that there is a challenge from the West. These people may be willing to forego short-term acquisition in favor of research, development, and investment in militarily promising technologies. Their time horizon might not be the same as that of those who wish to invest in basic research and to divert funds from military research, but it could bring about a temporary bargain between those who seek investment in technology for civilian purposes and those who seek the same for military use. In the short-term, this could lead to a less intensive purchase of hardware and investment in future technologies. Then, should promised reform of the economy bring an end to the period of economic stringency, the Soviet military would be well prepared to acquire forces for the battlefield of the twenty-first century.[5]

The technologies under development to support the U.S. SDI are creating a pool of innovative concepts which will have potential applicability to the U.S. defense industry in strong interaction with the civilian sector. For example, Battle Management Command, Control and Communications requires the development of computer hardware and software on an unprecedented scale. KEW systems require research on microelectronic controls, advanced infrared and radar sensors, compact chemical propulsion devices, and electro-magnetic launchers which could lead to advanced anti-tactical weapons and propulsion systems. DEW creates a focal point for laser research, particle beam concepts, and large space structures. Systems analysis involves studies of large space transportation systems paving the way for space exploration in the 21st century. Finally, SDI countermeasure studies are evaluating the vulnerability of defense systems to possible offensive responses which could drive improvements in technologies such as nuclear radiation hardened electronic means to counter a Soviet maneuvering missile threat.

The scale of the U.S. SDI effort will probably incline the Soviets to restructure their efforts in the reform of research and development planning. The dual character of SDI technology may require Gorbachev to incorporate technological reforms for both civilian and military needs. For example, investment in computer technology has a military and civilian commonality. Institutional pressure may build to force greater cooperation between research institutes and the scientific enterprises, serving both the civilian and military sectors.

It is widely assumed in the West that the Soviet Union can only adequately compete in the technological information revolution if it opens its advanced military and civilian research establishments to the effective scientific communication systems successful in the West. Open-

---

[5]Condolezza Rice, 'The Development of Soviet Military Power,' *The Gorbachev Era,* Edited by A. Dallin and C. Rice, Stanford Alumni Association, Stanford, California, 1986, p. 137.

ness with a relevant scientific community is a requisite for a dynamic, technologically successful R&D establishment. Foreign imports must be effectively assimilated in a system of incentives and rewards for a successful innovation system to work. To the military, such an amalgamation of its research within the civilian establishment and immediate priority toward developing a new, more dynamic system would require the deferral of traditional, short-term military claims on their R&D establishment and a long-term sharing of the scientific results. A leading factor in this new revolution is the civilian economy. Logically, the military cannot satisfactorily meet its needs from its own privileged, R&D monopoly; how many in the military hold this view is not known. Furthermore, the requirement of openness to foreign research makes the reliance on espionage less effective. Use of KGB middlemen in an era of space age research is likely to be less effective and inefficient. The opening of the scientific establishment to provide results for the entire scientific community also runs directly counter to the strongly held penchant for secrecy in the Soviet system.

It is easy to say that the military and KGB—the powerful institutions in the Soviet system—will not allow openness of their scientific research and R&D establishment and broadening of priorities for civilian-military research. But if they do not, they will probably lose ground, falling farther behind the United States, Japan and other industrial countries in critical areas. Gorbachev seems to understand this problem of 'neo-backwardness.' Still, he may not appreciate the full political and economic cost of the tradeoffs in institutional and resource priority changes, or the resistance of the traditional military support institutions to change.

III. GORBACHEV'S POLITICAL TRADEOFFS: COST OF EMPIRE AND GREAT POWER STATUS

A. Cost of Empire and Alliances

The Soviet Union provides support to its allies and clients through military and economic transfers. The value of military deliveries has been increasing as indicated in Table 2. To the extent these are not sales of state of the art military equipment for hard currency or 'hard' goods (oil), but rather are military aid of less modern equipment or non-marketable, 'soft' goods, the resource burden may be modest; the political risk may be the major factor. Still, Gorbachev at the Party Congress seemed to be leading Angola, Cuba, and Ethiopia to expect less support. Certainly Soviet leaders have been telling their East European allies that they plan to reduce what the Soviets perceive as a subsidy. How they follow through on limiting aid in hard goods will determine the incremental economic burden of their global role.

The Soviet Union also provides economic as well as military aid to the same countries to assist them in pursuing goals of common interest. Oil exports on barter terms and soft currency accounts provide some

TABLE 2.
USSR: ESTIMATED VALUE OF MILITARY DELIVERIES, 1974-85
(billion U.S. dollars)

Recipient	1974-79	1980-85	1974-85
Six Warsaw Pact countries	8.7	9.8	18.5
Syria	4.5	10.3	14.8
Iraq	6.0	8.2	14.2
Libya	5.4	5.8	11.2
Vietnam	2.1	4.9	7.0
India	2.0	4.8	6.8
Algeria	1.6	3.6	5.2
Cuba	1.3	3.9	5.2
Ethiopia	1.5	2.6	4.1
Angola	0.7	2.8	3.5
60 other countries	7.7	11.3	19.0
Total	41.5	68.0	109.5

Source: "Soviet Economy Under A New Leader" CIA-DIA Statement, March 19, 1986.

measure of the cost. Various estimates of the implied subsidy of these transfers center on the supply of oil for reduced hard currency (dollar) imports compared to what may be obtainable by sale of oil in the world market. There are varying estimates of the volume of the net transfer but unless increased it may be a tolerable burden. The question for Gorbachev for the future may be whether the resource costs of these alliances provide sufficient benefits in usable political terms.

Soviet relations with East Europe have been by far their most important in political-military terms and the most costly. The Soviet total and relative East European contributions to Warsaw Pact and hard goods trade make policy changes in this region most important. The Soviet Union might like to have its East European allies take on a larger burden of the Warsaw Pact costs, increase their delivery of high quality machinery and consumer goods to the Soviet Union and hold down their imports of oil and gas, but it seems very unlikely that these wishes will all come true. Moreover, East Europeans have always favored the claims of domestic investment and consumption on scarce quality resources over fulfillment of Soviet perceived economic needs for the Warsaw Pact. Soviets also favor revival of East European growth for resultant favorable trade and political stability. As a result, the least attainable of Soviet hopes among these competing claims would be an increase in East Europe's military burden sharing.

B. Cost-Benefit Outlook for Confrontation or Comity

The policy of Gorbachev's predecessors since 1975, especially Brezhnev, has been to opt for military augmentation and confrontation in regional issues rather than economic cooperation and comity. This policy is best illustrated in the northern flanks of the Soviet Eurasian policy: North Asia and Scandinavia. In North Asia the policy of military buildup has been costly. Whether the benefits have been proportional is open to question. Shared development of Soviet East Siberia and the Far East would certainly be facilitated under a policy of comity, e.g. with Japan. Likewise, in North Europe the buildup of defense in the Kola peninsula and elsewhere has been expensive; the benefits may not have been commensurate. Negotiation of conflicting claims and joint development of oil in the Barents Sea would seem to be a benefit of a policy of comity with Norway.

In this past policy of Eurasian defense buildup and confrontation the greatest economic costs have been the foregone benefits of joint development of Soviet resources.

IV. NEGOTIABLE ISSUES

From the assessment of Gorbachev's tradeoffs as he may see them, some improvement in benefits and reduction of resource costs or burden seems possible in three areas of the Great Power agenda:

Strategic Arms Reductions: Mutual need for stability and reduced likelihood of strategic weapons use or reduced perceptions of external threat could generate a basis of agreement, especially if tied to constraints on SDI.

Conventional military forces in Europe and Asia: Mutual need to reduce instability and economic burden through reduction of current order of battle buildup to maintain control in East Europe.

Global Policy Understandings: Acceptance of some implicit codes of conduct, e.g., mutually acceptable levels of support to insurgencies, common opposition to international terrorism.

Whether and under what circumstances the Soviet leadership feels economic pressure to reduce the defense burden is a matter of conjecture. Some Western specialists would argue with Scenario One or Two that allocations to defense are not likely to be constrained. Others accept a version of Scenario Three (reduced defense, pragmatic scenario), that it is currently imperative for Soviet leadership to reduce the defense burden. Jan Vanous and Bryan Roberts, for example, feel that the Soviet General Secretary's view should be that now is the time for negotiations in order to avoid 'collapse' of his ambitious economic modernization program:

> It is apparent that the Soviets will not unilaterally sacrifice what they perceive to be an adequate defense capability in order to improve the performance of the economy. They will try to come to the negotiating table and, in all probability, offer the United States unprecedented concessions for economic reasons outlined below. If they cannot secure a 'satisfactory' arms deal, they will follow the U.S. lead and mount a counter-SDI program, even though this may well push the Soviet economy perilously close to an unprecedented economic crisis.[6]

---

[6]Vanous and Roberts, *op. cit.,* pp. 1-2.

Appendix I

THE POLICY OF
THE SOVIET UNION
TOWARD THE UNITED STATES*

Pavel Podlesny

The Soviet Union, guided by the principle of peaceful coexistence between states with different social systems, has been and is implementing a policy line of continuing normal relations with the United States, striving to channel these relations in the direction of a stable and positive development. The USSR and the United States being sovereign states, there are no contradictions between them which would doom them to inevitable confrontation, and all the more so, to war—there are no territorial or other disputes, no financial or any other claims. The Soviet Union sees nothing which would lead to conflicts between the two countries—be it in the U.S. Constitution, or in the American system of government, or in the U.S. Criminal Code, or in the U.S. emigration laws—irrespective of whether it likes them *per se*, or not. The USSR strives to establish normal relations with the United States, which would develop on the basis of mutual respect for sovereignty,

*Late in their deliberations, members of the Atlantic Council's Working Groups on "U.S. Policy Towards the Soviet Union: A Long-Term Western Perspective, 1978-2000," and on "Defending Peace and Freedom: Strategic Stability Towards the Year 2000," held discussions in Moscow with a Soviet delegation composed of representatives from the Ministries of Defense and Foreign Affairs, the International Department of the Central Committee, and two institutes from the Soviet Academy or Sciences, namely, the USA-Canada Institute and the Institute of World Economy and International Relations (IMEMO). The differences of perspectives between the sides remained too great to be subsumed into the Policy Paper itself. However, it seemed appropriate to have the Soviet side speak for itself on these important issues. We include in this volume, therefore, one of the papers prepared for this purpose by a member of the Soviet delegation. It appears unedited in any way, in the translation prepared by the Soviets in anticipation of the discussions held in May 1986 in Moscow. A second paper "On Strategic Stability" is being published in the Atlantic Council companion volume *Defending Peace and Freedom: Toward Strategic Stability in the Year 2000*, also published by the University Press of America.

territorial integrity, recognition of the principle of equality of the two sides, and non-interference into each other's internal affairs. This policy line of the USSR has recently been reaffirmed at the XXVII Congress of the Communist Party of the Soviet Union. It follows from the experience accumulated during the period of detente in the 1970s that an improvement of Soviet-American relations and mutually advantageous cooperation between the two countries is both possible and practically feasible.

Special responsibility for the preservation of peace, consolidation of international security and limitation of the arms race belongs to the Soviet Union and the United States because of their military, economic, scientific and technological potential as well as the international prestige of these two great powers. Relations between the two countries profoundly affect world politics as a whole. Both the USSR and the United States have at their disposal all the necessary means and resources for solving urgent problems facing mankind.

On the other hand, a conflict between these two powers may result in mankind's total annihilation. Objectively, because of these factors, the task of normalizing and improving relations with the United States becomes one of the most important tasks in Soviet foreign policy priorities. This does not mean, however, that all other factors of world politics play a strictly subordinate role. The Soviet Union has never looked and is not looking at the world in the light of Soviet-American relations alone. In the view of the Soviet side, all states can and must take part in a search for realistic solutions of acute and urgent problems.

The USSR has fundamental differences of view with the United States, a country belonging to a different social system, in as far as the world social perspective is concerned. These differences are of an objective character, which is derived from the differences in the nature itself of the two social systems—socialism and capitalism—and they create between the two countries, representing two major and most powerful societies in their respective social systems, an atmosphere of competition and rivalry for fuller satisfaction of material and spiritual needs of man, for a society based on the principles of social justice. Within this context it must be added that confrontation between capitalism and socialism should develop only and exclusively in the form of peaceful competition and peaceful rivalry. As General Secretary of the CCCPSU M.S. Gorbachev noted during his press conference at Geneva on November 21, 1985, "differences between our countries will remain. The same can be said about rivalry. But everything must be done not to let it go over the permitted levels, and lead to a military confrontation. Each of the two social systems must prove its advantages by way of example."

The foreign policy of the USSR does not threaten the security of any state, including the United States, and is not aimed at undermining the regime existing in any state. Its main task is to create such international conditions which would ensure the security of the USSR and its allies and would be conducive to creating favorable conditions for the construction and improvement of socialist society in those countries which have chosen the socialist path of development. The USSR resolutely opposes the "export of revolution," but at the same time it denounces all attempts aimed at the "export of counter-revolution." The USSR stands for the right of each people to choose freely its way of life, its friends and allies, and has no intentions whatsoever to artificially influence this choice. Forcible establishment of socialism in the world is not and cannot be a foreign policy objective of the USSR, because development of a new system in any country can proceed in a natural way only, stemming from the socio-economic and political conditions which exist in that country.

The interconnection and interdependence between the USSR and the United States in the world of today have reached such levels that the two countries, the Soviet and the American people, have absolutely no alternative to peaceful coexistence. The basis for such coexistence is provided by the fact that the two countries have interests which coincide, the most important of such interests being prevention of a nuclear war and cessation of the arms race. It is becoming obvious at the present stage of development that neither this problem, nor any other urgent and acute problem of today, can be solved under the conditions of confrontation, without combining the efforts of the entire world community of nations and, first of all, the efforts of the two major and most powerful states in the world—the Soviet Union and the United States.

A serious problem has arisen for the Soviet Union in its relations with the United States, in that there are influential forces in the U.S. which have persistently refused to recognize the so-called "legitimacy" of the socialist regime in the USSR and which seek to subvert and undermine it. These forces have always exerted considerable influence on the U.S. foreign policy by pushing it toward confrontation and the exacerbation of tensions in Soviet-American relations. U.S. policies during the first half of the 1980s have given many vivid manifestations of the intolerance of the above-mentioned forces to a different social system, of their stubborn wish that it be "destroyed," that "communism should be left on the ash-heap of history." We can understand all this only as a threat to the security of the USSR and its allies. Some circles within the American leadership and the U.S. Congress, which are close to the military-industrial complex, have made military force the main level of their policy, using which they want to exert pressure on the Soviet Union and other socialist countries. A steady build-up and improvement of the U.S. military and strategic potential coupled with the appearance of fresh doctrines and plans of its use, including the use against the Soviet Union, is viewed by us as actions increasing the threat of a nuclear war.

A nuclear war between the USSR and the United States would lead to complete annihilation of both sides and to a catastrophe for mankind as a whole. A nuclear war cannot be won and it must never be allowed to happen. The gist, the main essence of Soviet-American relations, is seen by the Soviet side to be in the prevention of a nuclear war, in the limitation and reduction of armaments.

In the military and strategic sphere the Soviet Union strives to assure for itself a reliable defense potential, to be able to deter, by its nuclear power, a possible aggression, to demonstrate the futility of all attempts aimed at achieving, through an accelerated arms race, military and strategic superiority over the USSR.

At the same time the USSR proceeds further from stating the fact that the present level in the balanced nuclear potentials of the two countries is much too high. So far this level has given equal insecurity to both of them. Continuation of the nuclear arms race will inevitably increase this danger and may even bring it to such a point when even nuclear parity would cease to be a factor of military and political deterrence.

The Soviet Union is prepared, jointly with the United States and its allies, to reduce the strategic balance to the level of reasonable sufficiency, including the elimination of nuclear and of other types of weapons of mass destruction. It is in a radical reduction of the military arsenals that the Soviet Union sees the way out of the deadlock of "nuclear deterrence." The USSR is also prepared to accept the intermediate variants—to reduce by 50 percent the nuclear weapons capable of reaching the territories of the USSR and the United States. The Soviet Union has repeatedly stated that there is no type of weapons which it would not agree, on a mutual basis, to reduce.

The nature of modern weapons is such that no state can hope to be able to protect itself by military-technological means, including by setting up a defense system, even the most powerful one. Moreover, such attempts can only give the arms race a new push, extending it to other spheres. This is why the Soviet Union is categorically against the American plans of deploying a large-scale anti-missile defense system with space-based echelons, i.e. the plans linked to militarization of outer space. The USSR has every reason to believe that the purpose in this case is, using this system in conjunction with the capabilities of pre-emptive strike against the Soviet forces of retaliation, to make unpunished nuclear aggression really possible, to give the United States unilateral military and strategic advantages.

As was noted at the XXVII Congress of the CPSU, the USSR claims no greater security for itself, nor will it accept a lesser security. It does not work out its policies wishing to damage the national interests of the United States. Security can only be mutual in the context of Soviet-American relations. Soviet leadership, as was repeatedly stated, would not wish the strategic balance to be changed in its favor, because such a development would increase suspicion of the other side and, therefore, instability of the situation as a whole.

If the United Staes tries to overtake the USSR in building up and improving their weapons systems, or in some other way to achieve military and strategic superiority, the Soviet Union will respond to such actions by taking appropriate measures which would create commensurate threats to the security of the United States. Such a response may not necessarily be symmetric, taking into consideration the state-of-the-art of nuclear potentials and the nature of weapons systems. For example, as Soviet leaders have warned, the Soviet Union, if SDI is implemented, will undoubtedly find a convincing response, and it will find it not necessarily in outer space. But this course will not be a result of the Soviet Union's free choice—it will be imposed upon it, and the Soviet side has been active in opposing it.

The Soviet Union is always open to a political dialogue and negotiations, which would lead to just, mutually advantageous and verifiable practical steps in the field of disarmament. It is the Soviet Union's intention to continue taking an active stand in this question, putting forward new initiatives and showing its good will by unilateral actions, as in the case of the Soviet moratorium on nuclear testing.

The Soviet side attributes great significance to the international aspects of Soviet-American relations, so as to exclude a military confrontation between the USSR and the United States in various regions of the world.

There are many dangers in the situation in Europe where NATO and the Warsaw Treaty Organization, the military alliances headed by the two countries, are in direct confrontation, and where enormous concentrations of the armed forces and armaments have been accumulated. Historically, the task of upholding peace on the continent is one of the highest priority in the foreign policy of the USSR. The Soviet Union is actively fighting for the establishment of a reliable system of collective security under the conditions of eliminating all types of weapons of mass destruction and reducing the conventional armed forces and armaments to the level of reasonable sufficiency. Numerous Soviet initiatives addressed to NATO countries and, more specifically, to the United States are aimed exactly in this direction—including the Soviet proposal on eliminating Soviet and American medium-range missiles deployed in the region, as well as on an equitable and gradual reduction of the armed forces and armaments throughout the entire continent—from the Atlantic Ocean to the Urals Mountains.

Following its policy line of strengthening the security in Europe, the USSR does not aim at driving a wedge in the relations between the United States and its European allies.

Insofar as the Soviet Union's attitude to the policy of the United States in other parts of the world is concerned, the USSR recognizes that the United States as a great power has legitimate interests in the world arena (and the USSR has a right to expect that legitimate Soviet interests should similarly be recognized). The Soviet Union, however, rejects American claims on any exclusive rights arising from the existence of such interests, all the more so if they amount to the use of military force.

The Soviet Union views the socio-political upheavals that are occurring in the world arena, particularly in the zone of the developing countries, as a legitimate and unavoidable process. The United States, for its part, strives to freeze the social *status quo* and, moreover, to eliminate progressive regimes, including by use of military force, as is being done in Nicaragua, Angola and in other countries. In doing so, Washington is whipping up tensions in its relations with the Soviet Union, linking, without any justification, the social changes that occur, with USSR policies. In the view of the Soviet side, what is necessary is to observe rigorously the principle of non-interference into the internal affairs of other countries and to respect the right of peoples to choose freely their way of life, their friends and allies.

The problem of settling regional conflicts makes it necessary that a certain level of mutual understanding be reached between the USSR and the United States. The Soviet Union attributes considerable significance to consultations between the USSR and the United States on regional issues, resolutely comes out for a peaceful settlement of the existing conflict situations and prevention of possible conflict situations in the future. In the view of the USSR an important means of reaching this objective is an obligation of non-use of force in international relations. The USSR puts forward initiatives to reduce the probability of armed conflicts between the two countries, including declaration of nuclear-free zones, limitation of naval military activities in the Mediterranean, the Baltic Sea, the Indian Ocean, in other regions of the world, as well as strengthening of confidence building measures. Both sides at their Summit Meeting in Geneva in November 1985, agreed to study the question of setting up, jointly with the United States, a center for the prevention of nuclear conflicts.

The general climate of Soviet-American relations to a considerable degree depends on the solution of these questions. These relations cannot develop independently of the behavior of the United States in the international arena, and of the world situation resulting from it.

In its bilateral relations with the United States the Soviet Union's policy line is toward their normalization and improvement on the basis of mutual respect and complete equality of sides without any discrimination. It welcomes a development and extension of mutually beneficial trade with the United States, as well as an improvement of cooperation in other areas, viewing such cooperation first of all from the political viewpoint as a factor which stabilizes the relations between the two countries. The Soviet Union comes out for the development and extension of various ties and contacts between the two countries within the framework of separate ministries and agencies, as well as between the legislative organs of the USSR and the United States. No lesser importance is attributed by the USSR to contacts between public organizations in both countries—in such areas as tourism, sports, and trade union activities. The USSR is prepared in a humane and positive spirit to solve the questions of family reunification, marriages and other problems relating to the humanitarian sphere of Soviet-American relations.

The Soviet Union formulates its policy toward the United States strictly on the basis of reciprocity. The USSR believes that extension and deepening of relations between the Soviet Union and the United States is being held up by the American side, which persists in its attempts to interfere in the internal affairs of the USSR, establishes discriminatory restrictions of all kinds and applies economic and other "sanctions" as a means for exerting political pressure.

Taking into account all the above-mentioned considerations, it should be stressed that the aim of the policy of the Soviet Union toward the United States is to reach such a form of coexistence with that country, which would make it possible to eliminate the threat of a nuclear war and to make the competition between the two countries develop peacefully and in such forms which would damage neither the state interests of these two countries, nor those of third countries. Such a development, in its turn, would make it possible for both sides to cut down non-productive expenditures and to use the funds saved in this way for improving the well-being of nations, to strengthen international security, to create the necessary conditions for restructuring the system of international relations on a genuinely democratic basis, which would enable each sovereign nation to choose freely its way of life, the path of its social development, its friends and allies, to combine the efforts of the entire international community in solving acute global problems.

The Soviet Union is resolutely in favor of smooth and civilized relations with the United States, so that differences of views, opinions and ideology should not hinder good-neighborliness and cooperation. The world has come to a new frontier, when concern for the security of other countries has become no less important than concern for one's own security. It is from this standpoint that the Soviet Union views the improvement of its relations with the United States and expects a similar approach on the part of American leadership.

Appendix II

ADDITIONAL COMMENTS
AND DISSENTS BY MEMBERS
OF THE WORKING GROUP

DISSENT, by Barry Blechman

I can endorse enthusiastically the overall content and tone of the policy paper, and also the vast majority of its recommendations. I differ sharply with its analysis and findings concerning the modernization of U.S. strategic forces, however, in two respects:

1. *Modernizing Land-Based Offensive Forces:*

A prospective problem of ICBM vulnerability was recognized within the U.S. government in the early 1960s, and discussed publicly by then-Secretary of Defense Melvin Laird as early as 1969. The fact that four presidents and six secretaries of defense have been unable to solve this problem over a period of nearly twenty years is no coincidence, nor does it reflect incompetence on the part of the executive branch, mendacity on the part of Congress, fatal flaws in arms control, or the evil intentions of the Soviet Union. Rather, the persistence of this problem reflects certain inalterable technological trends, as well as geographic, sociological, and political constraints on American strategic choices. Instead of continuing to ignore these real, and apparently impervious, constraints, as would be the case if the study group's recommendations were implemented, it is long past time for the country to turn to alternative means of achieving the purposes of its strategic offensive forces.

There are certain unique characteristics of ICBMs that cannot be abandoned. These characteristics pertain primarily to the ICBM force capabilities to execute discrete and precise strikes, flexibly and reliably. The United States should retain a substantial number of ICBMs in its force posture for these purposes; a portion of the existing Minuteman

IIIs and the 50 already authorized MXs can fill this need well into the next decade, probably through the century. At some point they will have to be replaced, and a mobile ICBM with one or two warheads is probably the best way to go about it.

This proposed force of land-based missiles would be intended to provide certain limited options to the United States in the event of extraordinary situations—involving either the Soviet Union or third nations. It would not, however, be intended to play a role in deterring a large-scale attack on this country or our allies, nor to survive such an attack. That should be made clear, publicly and explicitly. For the survivable retaliatory capabilities necessary to deter such attacks, the United States can depend solely on its stategic submarines and bombers, and the planned size of those forces should be increased explicitly to compensate for the declared subtraction of ICBM capabilities. Additions to the SLBM force probably should involve the placement of Trident II missiles on a less expensive type of submarine than the *Ohio*-class so as to increase the number of potential aimpoints, but detailed studies are required to determine the most efficient means of ensuring the required number of survivable warheads to compensate for reductions in survivable land-based missile warheads.

By moving toward this modified Triad over the remainder of this century, the United States would both retain the special capabilities of ICBMs for those roles in which, realistically, they might be required—and yet also finally be rid of the weakness in our retaliatory capabilities which has bedevilled four administrations.

2. Exploring Strategic Defenses: *

I agree with the study group that "a vigorous research program on anti-ballistic missile technologies is needed". The final draft of the policy paper does not, however, mention the need to carry out that research in such a way that our enthusiasm for the long-term promise of strategic defense does not force the nation to incur too great a price in the near term. Specifically:

a) Our research should be carried out within the confines of the ABM Treaty. Termination of that treaty's restrictions within the near to mid term can benefit only the Soviet Union, which is in a far better position to deploy strategic missile defenses based on existing ground-based technologies, than the United States is to deploy either space-based or ground-based defenses. To protect the treaty, it is necessary in negotiations with the Soviet Union to clarify current ambiguities or disagreements about the types of research and radar deployments which are permitted by the treaty at present, as a matter of the greatest urgency.

---

*Robert Bowie wishes to associate himself with this section of Barry Blechman's dissent.

b) Our determination to pursue research on Ballistic Missile Defense (BMD) technologies should not be permitted to forestall U.S.–USSR agreement on deep reductions in strategic offensive forces. Restrictions on offensive forces would be a helpful adjunct to any defensive system. Moreover, those BMD technologies with the greatest promise would not be ready for full-scale development until the next century. A commitment to sustain the ABM Treaty, clarified as described above, for a substantial period of time, would not preclude a deliberate and efficient research program into BMD technologies, and could be a very helpful means of securing deep cuts in offensive forces.

c) Finally, in view of the tight constraints on defense spending likely to be maintained over the next five years, it is imperative that ABM research not be permitted to crowd out research on other important defense needs. Moreover, research cannot be driven by political agendas, at least not efficiently. If the nation is neither to waste a great deal of money nor deprive itself of the scientific talent and other resources necessary to solve other pressing problems in defense and civilian technologies, BMD research should be pursued on a far more deliberate schedule than is currently envisioned by the administration.

DISSENT, by Helmut Sonnenfeldt

I believe that certain portions of this paper tend to overestimate the extent to which the desire "to avoid a nuclear holocaust" constitutes a basis for mutually beneficial initiatives and agreements between the United States and the USSR. In the past, at any rate, this undoubted desire, on both sides, does not appear to have greatly advanced significant arms control agreements. While it presumably contributed to caution at moments of crisis, it has not produced substantial cooperative arrangements to reduce the incidence and severity of crises. Containment of crises seems to have been largely the result of risk assessments and unilateral decisions on both sides.

Perhaps this pattern will change, but real alteration needs to be demonstrated.

Against this background, I believe the paper may give excessive weight to the role arms control, as hitherto achievable, can play in reducing risks of confrontation and conflict. Most of the crises that involved U.S.-Soviet confrontations and risks of direct conflict have occured in conditions when the strategic forces of the two sides were smaller in number and less sophisticated than they are today or will be in future.

At the same time, the paper, in my view, gives inadequate emphasis to dangers stemming from conflict situations around the world in which the interests of the two superpowers are or may become engaged. Many of these situations are affected by recent, as distinct from historically-asserted, Soviet ambitions for influence and presence and, in particular, by the injection of Soviet and Soviet-supplied military forces. As noted, agreed resolutions of such clashes are difficult to achieve. Continued efforts and dialogue toward this end are necessary. But for many years to come, the danger of U.S.-Soviet conflict is likely to stem at least as much from clashes of interest and ambition as it is from shifts, in one direction or other, in the military programs of the two sides. I believe the paper should have given greater weight to this aspect of the U.S.-Soviet relationship and made arms control a less central focus.

DISSENT, by Leonard Sullivan, Jr.

I find the policy paper's emphasis on the details of strategic force modernization to be excessive and unbalanced. The West's emphasis on maintaining substantial, well-modernized, and fully sustainable conventional forces—including naval forces—must also be increased.

There is room for argument about which Western nations should provide what share of the West's conventional force capabilities; whether the distribution of active and reserve forces might be shifted to somewhat lower peacetime costs; and whether we might depend more on the West's enormous industrial mobilization potential. But in any event, the West must remain collectively willing to deter the use of massive Soviet conventional land, air, and naval forces either for aggression, or, as may be far more likely, for purposes of intimidation.

Unlike the nuclear balance, however, the conventional balance will continue to be achieved only through full consideration of allied contributions—on both sides. Furthermore, the deterrence of Western intimidation depends on factors of confidence well beyond the perceived military balance. Hence the overall correlation of Western strengths is fundamental to U.S.-Soviet relations.

While the chances of Soviet-backed military attacks into Western Europe or South Korea may be relatively—if not vanishingly—slight, the chances of accidental encounters between superpower conventional forces during pursuit of lesser but conflicting objectives in the Third World cannot be overlooked. The need to assure the prompt and rational defusing of such unintentional confrontations is as important at the lower end of the conflict spectrum as it is at the nuclear level.

Finally the West cannot afford to grant a unilateral edge to the Soviet Union in defensive or offensive military capabilities for chemical or biological warfare. In fact, some of these weapons are probably potentially at least as devastating to the future of the civilized world as nuclear weapons.

In all of these areas, the ability to achieve an assured "balance" in military capabilities is virtually impossible due to the extraordinary range of uncertainties in any such estimates. Such uncertainties can only be alleviated by reducing the total size of the forces, their state of readiness, and the willingness of their national leaders to lash out with them. These considerations all belong within the domain of arms control.